SYLLOGE OF COINS OF THE BRITISH ISLES

64

SYLLOGE OF COINS OF THE BRITISH ISLES

A British Academy Research Project

The British Sylloge project was first promoted in the early 1950s by Christopher Blunt and other members of the British and Royal Numismatic Societies. An informal committee was formed under the chairmanship of Sir Frank Stenton, who in 1956 secured its admission as a Committee of the British Academy. The first volume, on Anglo-Saxon coins in the Fitzwilliam Museum, Cambridge, was published by the British Academy in 1958.

The aim of the series is to publish detailed and fully illustrated catalogues of coins of the British Isles in British and foreign collections. The volumes range in scope from Ancient British coins to seventeenth-century tokens, with most detailed coverage of the Anglo-Saxon coinage. The collections recorded include those in more than two hundred national, university and provincial museums in Britain and Ireland and of museums in Scandinavia, Germany, Poland, Latvia, Estonia, Russia and the United States of America.

A full listing of the series is printed at the end of this volume. The SCBI Database can be consulted on the Internet via www.britac.ac.uk/arp or www.medievalcoins.org.

SYLLOGE OF COINS OF THE BRITISH ISLES

64

GROSVENOR MUSEUM, CHESTER

Part II
Anglo-Saxon Coins and Post-Conquest Coins to 1180

BY
HUGH PAGAN

Published for THE BRITISH ACADEMY
by OXFORD UNIVERSITY PRESS
and SPINK & SON LIMITED
2012

Oxford University Press, Great Clarendon Street, Oxford OX2 6DP
Oxford New York
Auckland Cape Town Dar es Salaam Hong Kong Karachi
Kuala Lumpur Madrid Melbourne Mexico City
Nairobi New Delhi Shanghai Taipei Toronto

With offices in
Argentina Austria Brazil Chile Czech Republic France
Greece Guatemala Hungary Italy Japan Poland Portugal
Singapore South Korea Switzerland Thailand Turkey
Ukraine Vietnam

Published in the United States
By Oxford University Press Inc., New York

First published 2012

British Library Cataloguing in Publication Data
Data available

Library of Congress Cataloging in Publication Data
Data available

Typeset by New Leaf Design, Scarborough, North Yorkshire
Printed in Great Britain on acid-free paper by
Henry Ling Limited, at the Dorset Press, Dorchester DT1 1HD

ISBN 978–0–19–726502–4

The publication of this volume has been assisted by a generous grant from the Stenton Fund.

CONTENTS

LIST OF TABLES

PREFACE

THE present volume has had a long genesis. Following the publication of Elizabeth Pirie's initial volume in the SCBI series devoted to the holdings of the Grosvenor Museum, Chester in 1964, it was at first envisaged that she would prepare its sequel, but her duties as Keeper of Archaeology at Leeds City Museum, and the distance between Leeds and Chester, made it impracticable for her to do so.

In 1976 Nicholas Moore, Curator of the Grosvenor Museum, prepared the first draft of a typescript list of those Anglo-Saxon, Norman and early Plantagenet coins in the Grosvenor Museum that had not been published in the earlier SCBI volume. In October 1976, Christopher Blunt reported to the Sylloge Committee on his discussions with Mr Moore, and Chester II was adopted as a 'project in hand'. Preparatory work on this continued, the basic listing being completed in 1978, but Mr Moore's other curatorial responsibilities would soon prevent him from progressing the volume. In September 1982, the Committee gladly accepted Dr A. J. P. Campbell's offer to assist with the volume, even though as a practising GP and a JP the amount of time he could devote to it was limited. Through the 1980s and 1990s he greatly assisted in reorganising the collection, in taking polaroid photographs of part of the collection himself, and in facilitating the photography of the coins for this volume by Dr Kristin Bornholdt Collins (to whom thanks are due).

Following the departure of Mr Moore from the Museum in 1990, the Sylloge Committee invited the present writer in 1992 to take up the task of preparing a publishable text. By this time the classification of the coinages struck in the names of Anglo-Saxon rulers between the death of Ælfred of Wessex (871–99) and the coinage reform carried out towards the end of the reign of Edgar (959–75) had been put on a new footing by the publication of Blunt, Stewart and Lyon's *Coinage in Tenth-Century England*, and it was immediately apparent that a wholly new listing of the coins struck within this period, which comprise over three quarters of the coins falling within the ambit of the present volume, would be necessary.

The Sylloge Committee and the present writer would however like to record their very considerable gratitude to Nicholas Moore for his work on the collection in the late 1970s and for his preliminary listing of the material. It is convenient to note here that the present writer has had to rely exclusively on Moore's typescript list for information on the provenances of a group of Anglo-Saxon and Norman coins given to the Grosvenor Museum in 1963 by Mrs Willoughby Gardner, Dr Willoughby Gardner's widow, for which no other explicit evidence could be located in the Grosvenor Museum's archive.

The Sylloge Committee and the present writer would also like to express their gratitude to Dr A. J. P. Campbell, who has been consistently generous with advice, practical help and hospitality during much of the long period which it has taken for this volume to come to fruition.

The present writer would also like to record his personal obligations to Dan Robinson, lately Keeper of Archaeology at the Grosvenor Museum, who was at all times helpful, both when invigilating the present writer on visits to the collection and in providing requisite information from the Museum's accession registers and files. Thanks are also due to Dr Martin Allen and Dr Tim Crafter for their respective help in identifying coins of Henry I and of the Cross and Crosslets type of Henry II, and to Dr William Day for the identification of coin no. 809.

Dr Stewart Lyon was kind enough to photograph a small number of additional coins that only came to light at a late stage in the volume's compilation. Andy Woods was responsible for cutting out and mounting the photographs, which were then scanned by Dr Jonathan Jarrett to be mounted electronically as plates. Thanks are due to them all, and also to Dr Rory Naismith and Andy Woods for their hard work in getting the text of the present volume into its final pre-publication state.

April 2011 HUGH PAGAN

INTRODUCTION

In 1964 the British Academy published as the fifth volume in the *SCBI* series a volume edited by the late Elizabeth Pirie, FSA, cataloguing 464 coins of the Chester mint then in the possession of the Grosvenor Museum (*SCBI 5*, *Grosvenor Museum, Chester, Part 1, The Willoughby Gardner collection of coins with the Chester mint-signature*). The great majority of these coins derived from an outstanding specialist collection of coins struck at Chester formed over a long period of time by Willoughby Gardner, DSc, FSA (1860–1953), a colonial broker in Liverpool who had retired from business early in life to devote himself to archaeology and entomology. This collection, amounting to 652 coins in all, had been purchased for the Grosvenor Museum by public subscription in 1952, shortly before Dr Gardner's death.

As Pirie explained in her introduction, an editorial decision was taken that *SCBI 5* should contain only those coins in the Grosvenor Museum's collection, whether from Willoughby Gardner's collection or from other sources, that carried an identifiable Chester mint-signature. The result was that the volume omitted a significant number of coins from the Willoughby Gardner collection that were attributable to the Chester mint by type, by style or by their carrying the names of moneyers plainly associable with Chester. This was especially unfortunate in that during the 65 years which preceded Edgar's coinage reform in the early 970s, a period in which coinage operations at Chester made a very significant contribution to the volume of coin circulating in the British Isles as a whole, the Chester mint-signature only appeared on coins struck at Chester during part of the reign of Æthelstan and for a brief period in the reign of Edgar. *SCBI 5* thus contained no Chester-struck coins at all dating from the reigns of Edward the Elder, Edmund, Eadred and Eadwig, and only a handful of the numerous Chester-struck coins produced in Edgar's reign prior to the reform of the coinage.

It can however be seen in retrospect that the decision to omit from *SCBI 5* those Chester-struck coins that do not carry mint-signatures was prudent to the extent that numismatists' understanding of the coinage of tenth-century England up to the time of Edgar's reform was then only partial. Authoritative attributions of coins without mint-signatures to particular mints were not, indeed, generally possible until the study of tenth-century English coinage was transformed by the appearance in 1989 of *Coinage in Tenth-Century England* (*CTCE*), the authoritative monograph by Blunt, Stewart and Lyon which both set out the evidence on which mint attributions can now be based and established the nomenclature for types and styles which has been followed in the text of the catalogue part of this volume.

The present volume thus contains three broad groupings of coins that were omitted from the volume of 1964. The first of these are the 246 coins from the Willoughby Gardner collection that were excluded from the volume of 1964, either because although Chester-struck they did not carry Chester mint-signatures or because they were not coins of the Chester mint.

It is proper to note that Gardner had been a pioneer in identifying and acquiring Chester-struck coins of mid-tenth-century date without mint-signatures, and it was thus a distinct injustice that his achievement on this front was not explicitly recognised in the introduction to the volume of 1964. He had, however, also acquired a certain number of coins which were not of the Chester mint, his errors in these cases often being attributable to an incorrect assumption on his part that coins carrying the name of a moneyer associable with Chester were likely to have been struck by the Chester moneyer of that name rather than by a moneyer of the same name operating elsewhere. It is thus that the portion of Gardner's collection catalogued in the present volume includes numerous coins of Edgar's Horizontal Trefoil and Circumscription Cross types by the York moneyer Durand, who can now be seen to have been a different individual from the contemporary Chester moneyer of the same name.

The second grouping comprises 89 coins of this period given to the Grosvenor Museum in 1963 by Mrs Gardner, Willoughby Gardner's widow. This was a residual portion of her husband's collection, excluded from the transaction of 1952 because the coins were not of the Chester mint or were considered at the time to be duplicates. As it was too late for a gift of coins made to the Grosvenor Museum in 1963 to be included in *SCBI 5*, the result is that the present volume includes a number of coins with Chester mint-signatures from the Willoughby Gardner collection that are additional to those catalogued in *SCBI 5*; most are die-duplicates of those that feature in that volume, but there are a few which are not.

The third and largest grouping is made up of coins not of the Chester mint or without Chester mint-signatures that derive from three substantial coin hoards of the second half of the tenth century found in Chester in the nineteenth and twentieth centuries. These are the Chester (1950) hoard, deposited *c.* 965; the Chester (1857) hoard, deposited *c.* 970; and the Chester (1914) hoard, deposited *c.* 980. From among the coins that reached the Grosvenor Museum before 1964 from these three hoards, only eight coins from the Chester (1950) hoard and three from the Chester (1914) hoard carried Chester mint-signatures and were included in *SCBI 5*, and in consequence nearly all the coins concerned fall to be published in the present volume. The content of each of these hoards is listed in detail on pp. 17–32.

The Grosvenor Museum had also acquired by gift or purchase prior to 1964 a small number of other Anglo-Saxon and Norman coins from other sources. Most of these are coins of the Chester mint carrying Chester mint-signatures and which were therefore published in *SCBI 5*, but the rest are published for the first time in the present volume.

Post-1964 acquisitions by the Grosvenor Museum include four important coins from the Chester (1862) hoard, deposited *c.* 917, lost from view between its discovery and the mid-1960s; additional parcels from the Chester (1857) hoard and the Chester (1950) hoard; eight coins of the Quatrefoil type of Cnut from the Bryn Mælgwyn, Conwy hoard, found 1979, deposited *c.* 1025; a hoard of 11 coins of Edgar found at Ford Farm, Hargrave, Cheshire, in 1997, deposited *c.* 972; and a hoard of six coins of the Two Stars type of William I found at Tiverton, Cheshire, in 2000, deposited *c.* 1075 or a little later.

COINAGE AT CHESTER TO EDGAR'S REFORM

For much of the ninth century Canterbury, London, Rochester and an as yet unlocated town in East Anglia (Ipswich?) were the only places south of the Humber where coin was struck. After the disruption caused by the invading Viking armies in the late 860s and early 870s, coin production in the area that remained under English control seems initially to have taken place at Canterbury and London only, but Alfred's Cross and Lozenge type may have been struck elsewhere as well, and during the 880s and 890s coins were certainly struck at Winchester, Oxford, Gloucester and Exeter, and perhaps at some other of the larger towns in Southern England and the West Midlands.

Towards the end of the reign of Alfred (871–99) a West Midlands variety of Alfred's Horizontal type is identifiable. This was struck by five moneyers, Buga, Cuthberht, Dudig, Eadwald and Wynberht, who were still active in the reign of Alfred's successor, Edward the Elder (899–924). In Edward's reign all these moneyers are known from non-portrait coins of similar type and style to those struck in the last years of Alfred, while all except Wynberht are also known for coins of Bust Diademed type, known to have been struck early in Edward's reign from the occurrence of examples of it in the Cuerdale hoard, deposited *c.* 905.

At this date in Edward's reign it is not possible to separate these moneyers into groups who might have been working at different places in the West Midlands, although a die-link indicates that Buga and Dudig shared a workshop. The position is different in the next phase of the coinage, probably extending from shortly before 910 to a date close to the death of Æthelflæd, Lady of the Mercians, in 918. During this period the coinage struck in the West Midlands is distinguishable from that struck in the rest of England by the fact that the reverses of the coins carry a range of pictorial designs: a tower (or reliquary?), stems, fronds, rosettes, a flower, a bird, a church and a representation of the Hand of Providence. Coins with Tower designs exist of six moneyers (Cuthberht, Eadmund, Eadwald, Irfara, Walter and Wulfsige), while coins with the Hand of Providence design exist of a different six moneyers (Alhstan, Athulf, Deormod, Eadred, Fugel and Gunne), and it has been suggested by Stewart Lyon, that the first group of moneyers has 'a Chester flavour' and the second group of moneyers 'a Shrewsbury flavour';[1] these suggestions are based on the reappearance of some of the moneyers' names on later coins more

[1] In *CTCE*, pp. 51–2.

certainly associable with Chester or Shrewsbury. Lyon goes on to suggest that the moneyers Brece, Buga (or Boiga), Osulf, Wighard and Wulfgar, known for other pictorial types, 'also have a Chester flavour'.

Chester is described in the *Anglo-Saxon Chronicle*'s annal for 893 as a deserted city, but the same annal shows that it was capable of being put into a state of defence, and it is reasonable to suppose that it was not long before it developed into the thriving port and urban community which it was to become in the tenth century. All Chester's inhabitants would have benefited from the security engendered by the surviving walls of the Roman town, particularly after 907 when an entry in the *Anglo-Saxon Chronicle* records that Chester was 'rebuilt' (the reference presumably being to a general refurbishment of its existing defences), and it is no surprise that a number of moneyers should have been operating there by the middle of Edward's reign and should have been responsible for the production of a substantial proportion of the coins of these pictorial types.

During the final years of Edward's reign, after Æthelflæd's death, the coinage struck in the West Midlands reverted to being of Horizontal type. Lyon has suggested that two groupings of coins of this nature were struck at Chester: the first struck on broad flans by the moneyers Brece, Eadmund, Osbearn, Sigeferth, Walter and Wulfgar; and the second struck on slightly smaller flans by the moneyers Abba, Beorard, Brece, Tiot, Wulfgar and Wulfstan.[2] Here he is on strong ground, for the coins in each grouping have a stylistic uniformity, and of the moneyers in his second grouping Abba, Beorard, Tiot, Wulfgar and Wulfstan recur as the moneyers of coins of Æthelstan with Chester mint-signatures. A further grouping struck on flans slightly smaller still comprises coins of the moneyers Abba, Brece, Mægenfreth, Snel, Waleman and Walter, and this too is likely to be of Chester manufacture (Snel recurs as a moneyer of coins of Æthelstan with the Chester mint-signature).

The evidence of the 'Vatican' hoard, deposited *c.* 930, shows that for some years after Edward the Elder's death in 924 at Farndon-on-Dee, not far up river from Chester, coins of Horizontal type continued to be struck under Æthelstan (924–39) and were the only coins of Æthelstan produced at this time in the West Midlands and in much of the rest of his kingdom. Coins of this type of a style associable with Chester are known of the moneyers Abba, Ælfwine, Beorard, Eadmund, Osulf, Paul, Snel(e), Tidger, Tiot, Winard and Wulfgar, and perhaps also of the moneyer Eadulf (on the basis of a reverse die of Horizontal type muled with an obverse die of Circumscription Cross type).

This Horizontal type seems to have given way before the end of the 920s to a coinage of Circumscription design, in which the obverse inscription on the coins customarily terminates with Æthelstan's newly assumed regnal title *rex totius Britanniae*,

[2] *Ibid.*

typically in the form REX TOT BRIT or similar, and the reverse inscription comprises a moneyer's name followed by the name of the town in which the moneyer was based, typically in a form such as +DEORVLF M-O LEGE CFI. The earliest coins of this design struck at Chester appear to have been of the Circumscription Cross type, with a cross as the central feature of both sides of the coin, but at a later date in the reign coins struck at Chester, Hereford, Shrewsbury, Stafford and at a mint VERI (Warwick?) begin to carry a rosette instead of a cross as the central feature of one or both of their dies. The introduction of rosettes as part of the design was evidently intended to differentiate coins struck in this region from coins struck elsewhere in the Midlands or in England south of the Thames, and it was to remain a distinguishing feature of coins struck at Chester and at neighbouring towns right down to Edgar's reform.

Mint-signed Chester coins of Circumscription Cross type are known of at least 22 moneyers: Abba, Ælfwine, Beorard, Boigalet, Cnapa (or Cnath), Deorulf, Eadmund, Eadulf, (E)frard, Mældomen, Mærten, Oslac, Osulf, Paul, Rægenulf, Sa(e)lce, Sigferth, Snel(e), Tidger (or Tidgar), Wiard, Wulfgar and Wulfstan. Of these Abba, Ælfwine, Cnapa, Oslac, Paul and Wiard, as well as Tiot (previously recorded as a probable Chester moneyer under Edward the Elder), are known for coins struck from a Circumscription Cross obverse die and a Circumscription Rosette reverse die; while Ælfwine, Eadmund, Wiard and Wulfstan are known for coins struck from a Circumscription Rosette obverse die and a Circumscription Cross reverse die. The number of surviving coins struck from combinations of Circumscription Cross and Circumscription Rosette dies is sufficiently large to have caused Blunt to conclude that 'they should not be regarded as mules in the ordinary sense', but rather as evidence that the issue of Circumscription Cross coins and Circumscription Rosette coins overlapped,[3] and that seems to be a correct view.

Mint-signed Chester coins with the Circumscription Rosette design on both obverse and reverse exist of the following 18 moneyers: Ælfwine, Beorard, Boiga, Boigalet, Cnapa (or Cnath), Deorulf, Eadmund, Frard, Mældomen, Megred, Oslac, Osulf, Paul, Snel(e), Tidger, Tiot, Wulfgar and Wulfstan.

When the totality of these Circumscription coins are taken together they show that throughout the last decade of Æthelstan's reign Chester must consistently have housed a larger number of moneyers than any other English town or city. Allowance must be made for the fact that coinage production was differently organized at York, where the moneyer Regnald seems to have established a personal monopoly at this time and may have been responsible for the production of much the same quantity of coin as all the Chester moneyers put together, but a comparison with more readily comparable coinage operations at London, Winchester and elsewhere suggests

[3] Blunt 1974, p. 48.

that Chester may have surpassed other English mints of the period not merely in the number of moneyers working there but also in output. Blunt thought that the activity of the Chester mint in Æthelstan's reign might reflect the availability of bullion from silver mines in North Wales, but although this is a tempting hypothesis, it has yet to be shown that any significant amount of silver emerged from mining in North Wales, and an increase in coining activity at Chester probably has more to do with the town's developing role in trade across the Irish Sea.

What these coins additionally provide is a body of indubitable evidence for the names of Chester moneyers and for the stylistic character of Chester-produced coins that is of material assistance in attributing to Chester coins without mint-signatures struck in the reign of Edmund (939–46), Æthelstan's younger brother and successor. It is apparent that on Æthelstan's death in 939 the production of coins of Circumscription design was discontinued and that moneyers throughout Southern and Midland England began to strike coins of Horizontal type in the name of the new king. At Chester the very earliest coins of the reign may have been of the Horizontal Trefoil 1 (HT1) type, in which three pellets arranged in a triangle appear above and below the lines of the reverse inscription; this type is evidenced by two coins of the moneyer Eroth and half a dozen surviving coins of the moneyer Paul, all of obvious Chester style.The HT1 type must however have been almost immediately superseded at Chester by the Horizontal Rosette 1 (HR1) type, in which a rosette of pellets appears above and below the lines of the reverse inscription, and all subsequent coins struck at Chester down to the early 970s carry rosettes as a primary feature of their reverse type.

As in Æthelstan's reign, the intention of incorporating rosettes as a design feature on the coins was evidently to distinguish coins struck at mints in the North-West Midlands from coins struck elsewhere, but as Edmund's coins do not carry mint-signatures, it is not an entirely straightforward task to distinguish Chester-struck coins of Edmund of HR1 type from coins of HR1 type struck at other mints in the region.The present writer has discussed the issues involved,[4] and has been able to associate with Chester coins of HR1 type by as many as 25 moneyers: Ælfwald, Ælfwine, Boiga, Cnapa, Dorulf, Eadmund, Eadstan, Eroth, Frard, Mældomen(e), Mærten, Megred, Oslac, Osulf, Oswine, Paul, Regnulf, Teothred, Theodulf, Thurmod, Wihtelm, Wilaf, Wilsig, Wulfgar and Wulfstan. Coins by two further moneyers, Burnwald and Wisstan, also appear to have been struck from dies of Chester style, but as only one coin of each moneyer has so far been traced, the association of these moneyers with Chester must for the present remain uncertain.

It can be seen that even though not all of these moneyers may have been operating at the same time, 15 of them (Ælfwine, Boiga, Cnapa, Dorulf, Eadmund, Frard,

[4] Pagan 1995.

Mældomen(e), Mærten, Megred, Oslac, Osulf, Paul, Regnulf, Wulfgar and Wulfstan) had previously worked under Æthelstan, and may consequently be presumed to have been working together for Edmund in the early years of his reign. It is reasonable to suppose that the number of Chester moneyers in Edmund's reign remained substantial throughout.

Coins of HR1 type of Chester style in the name of Edmund's brother and successor Eadred (946–55) are known of three moneyers, Thurmod, Wilsig and Wulfstan. The majority of Eadred's Chester coins are not, however, of this type but of a new design, the HR2 type, in which the lines of the reverse inscription are divided not by three crosses, as on Chester coins of Eadmund's reign, but by annulet-cross-annulet, the annulets replacing the crosses at left and right. The only known HR1 coin for Eadred's reign of the moneyer Wilsig (*SCBI 9*, 376) is in fact a mule struck from an Eadred obverse die and a reverse die previously used to strike a coin of Edmund (Fitzwilliam Museum, ex Blunt), and the extant coins of Thurmod and Wulfstan of Chester style which combine Eadred obverses with HR1 reverses are struck in each case from one obverse die per moneyer only, and are not likely to constitute a substantive HR1 issue for Eadred.

Fortunately for the numismatist, coins of HR2 type for Eadred appear to have been struck at Chester only, and despite the absence of a mint name on the coins there is no difficulty at this time in distinguishing Chester-struck coins from coins struck at other mints in the West Midlands or at Derby, where coins of HR1 type had been struck since Edmund's recovery of the town from Viking rule in 942. In the years that followed, the HR1 type was not again struck at Chester, but continued to be struck in quantity at Derby well into the reign of Edgar (959–75). Additionally, coins of similar stylistic character to those produced at Derby are recorded from Eadred's reign onwards for moneyers who do not seem to have been based in Derby itself, and it looks likely that coins of HR1 type and of various scarcer related HR types were produced at other East Midland towns in a swathe of territory extending south from Derby.

Coins of HR2 type are known of the following 19 moneyers: Ælfsig(e), D(e)orulf, Duran, Eadmund, Eoferard, Eoroth (or Æroth), Frard, Frothric, Gilles (or Gillys), Mærten, Siferth, Sunu, Teothred, Theodulf, Thurmod, Werstan, Wilaf, Wilsig and Wulfstan. Gil(l)ys is additionally known from a round halfpenny of HR2 type, and Ælfstan, Dorulf, Eadmund, Frothric, Gilles and Theodulf are also known for coins of minor HR2 sub-varieties. Of these moneyers, Eadmund (if the same individual) and Wulfstan had been Chester moneyers since the reign of Edward the Elder, while eight or nine were still moneyers of Edgar at the beginning of the 970s (Ælfsige, Deorulf (if the same individual as Deorlaf), Duran, Eadmund, Eoroth, Frothric, Gillis, Martin and Thurmod). It is apparent from this that there was considerable continuity from reign to reign in the personnel responsible for coin production at Chester, but it is also worth noting that surviving coins of the moneyers Frothric and Thurmod of Eadred's HR2 type are rather more common than those of this type by other moneyers, which might suggest that these two moneyers were responsible for a larger proportion than their colleagues of the total volume of coin struck at Chester in this period.

The moneyer Gillys, known for Chester-struck coins of Eadred and of Edgar, is also the moneyer of the single extant coin of the Welsh king Hywel Dda (*c.* 904–49/50) (*SCBI 34*, 719). Gillys's coin for Hywel Dda is struck from dies engraved a little more elegantly than was customary at Chester at this date, with three pellets in a trefoil arrangement at the end of the obverse inscription, two crosses and another group of three pellets incorporated in the two-line inscription on the reverse, and a letter S in the reverse field. As Gillys has not so far been recorded as a moneyer for Edmund, the coin ought on general principles to date from between Eadred's accession in 946 and Hywel Dda's death, but as it is of HR1 type rather than of HR2 type, it may be that the coin was struck a little before 946 and that it is only by accident that no contemporary coin by Gillys in Edmund's name has so far turned up.

In the next reign, that of Eadwig (955–9), Eadred's nephew, the HR2 type is represented by five surviving coins only, two of which, struck from the same reverse die but differing obverse dies, are of the moneyer Eadmund, and the others are unique examples of the moneyers Efrard, Sunu and Thurmod. Of these the coin of the moneyer Sunu, published in the present volume, is certainly an Eadwig HR3/Eadred HR2 mule, re-using a reverse die used to strike a true HR2 coin of Eadred, and this may also prove to be the case with the rest. At all events, it is clear that as in Eadred's reign a decision was quickly taken that moneyers at Chester should strike coins of a new two-line design, the HR3 type, in which the annulet-cross-annulet arrangement dividing the two lines of the reverse inscription is adapted to include a letter on either side of the cross, the letters chosen being customarily N and E or other letters which, when taken together with the letters MO in the bottom line of the inscription, provide an abbreviated form of the word moneyer in Latin.

All extant HR3 coins of Eadwig are attributable to Chester, and the moneyers involved are the following: Ælfsie, D(e)orulf, Eadmund, Eoferard, Eoroth, Æthelstan, Frard, Frothric (or Freotheric), Thurmod, Werstan and Wilsig. Coinage at Chester in this reign seems to have been on a less extensive scale than in previous reigns, and it appears that this may not simply be because the reign was shorter, for the number of dies employed to strike the extant coins was certainly small and there is more evidence than in previous reigns for the same obverse dies being used by more than one moneyer. One particular obverse die is used with four reverse dies each carrying the name of a different moneyer (Eoroth, Freotheric, Thurmod and Werstan), and other obverse dies are found in combination with reverse dies of two or three different moneyers. It is pertinent here that Eadwig lost power in Mercia to his younger brother Edgar in 957, halfway through his reign, and although there is no positive evidence that coins were struck at Chester in Edgar's name until after

Eadwig's death in 959, there may well have been no particular zeal among Chester moneyers for commissioning new obverse dies in Eadwig's name or for striking coins in Eadwig's name at all after 957.

In their *CTCE*, Blunt, Stewart and Lyon record two die-duplicate coins of Eadwig by the Chester moneyer Ælfsige as being of Circumscription Cross/Circumscription Rosette type, but in an appended comment they recognize that these are in fact mules struck from an HR3 obverse die of Eadwig, utilised in Eadwig's reign by the moneyer Frard, and a Circumscription Rosette reverse die produced for Ælfsige in Edgar's reign.[5]

Once again the design of the coins struck at Chester was to change when coins began to be struck there in the name of the new king Edgar, whether this actually occurred in 959 or as early as 957. On this occasion the new coins were of Circumscription design, and although Chester-struck coins are known both of Circumscription Cross type and of Circumscription Rosette type, it is probable that the coins of Circumscription Rosette type, which are the more numerous, were the initial issue of the reign (the evidence of the mules just cited points in that direction). Chester moneyers known for coins of Circumscription Rosette type are Ælfsige, Aldewine, Eadmund, Eoferard (or Eaferard), Eoroth, Freotheric, Gilys, Siferth, Thurmod, Werstan and Wilsig.

As hardly any of the Chester coins of this Circumscription Rosette type carry mint-signatures, and the type was also struck by moneyers operating at Derby, Stafford and Tamworth, there is room for debate about the mint attribution of some of the coins of one additional moneyer, Deorulf. Deorulf's production in this type includes coins carrying a Tamworth mint-signature and coins of similar style which (although without mint-signatures) were presumably struck at Tamworth as well, but also includes coins without mint-signatures struck from dies of Chester style. As Deorulf is a well-recorded moneyer of coins of Chester style in earlier types, it is reasonable to assume that the Chester-style dies in the present type represent continuing production by him at Chester, whether or not he is to be identified as the same individual who strikes in this type at Tamworth. Further coins without mint-signatures by the moneyers Daniel, Elfstan, Frothald and Hildulf are not of obvious Chester style and may perhaps have been struck at Shrewsbury. Another not dissimilar coin without a mint-signature by the moneyer Siulf may have been struck at Stafford, where the moneyer reappears in Edgar's reform type, but here the argument is complicated by the fact that Siulf is also recorded for a coin of Edgar's HR3 type with the apparent mint-signature **NE** (discussed below, p. 12).

Circumscription Cross coins with Chester mint-signatures (and with the letter **S** in the obverse field) are known of the moneyers Ælfsi(g), Freotheric and Thurmod, and coins of similar style without mint-signatures are known of the moneyers

[5] *CTCE*, p. 185.

Ælsig, Eoroth and Freotheric. Eoroth is also known from two die-duplicate coins struck from a Circumscription Rosette obverse and a Circumscription Cross reverse die, while Freotheric is known from a slightly larger number of coins struck from Circumscription Cross obverse dies and Circumscription Rosette reverse dies.

If the coins of Circumscription Cross type represent a substantive issue, it can only have been of the briefest duration, for the surviving coins of the type are both uncommon and struck from a very limited number of dies.

The Chester-struck coins of Edgar's reign in the Chester (1950) hoard, deposited *c.* 965, comprised 18 coins of Circumscription Rosette type, eight coins of Circumscription Cross type, one coin struck from a Circumscription Rosette obverse die and a Circumscription Cross reverse die, and 11 coins of HR2 type (the design with annulet-cross-annulet dividing the reverse inscription, last struck at Chester at the beginning of Eadwig's reign). It is clear from this that at some date towards the end of the first half of the 960s a decision was taken that the Two-line design in its HR2 form should be reintroduced. Although the coins of the type in the Chester (1950) hoard are struck by only seven moneyers, a total of 21 moneyers are known for the type as a whole: Ælfred, Ælfsig, Æthelm, Aldewine, Alhmund, Deorulf, Eadmund, Ealfsige (if a different individual from Ælfsig), Eoroth, Freotheric (or Frothric), Gillis (or Gillys), Gunar, Hrodulf, Leofstan, Martin (or Mertin), Othelriht, Siferth, Teothred, Teothuc, Thurmod and Werstan.

All the coins of the moneyers involved are of Chester style, and it is clear that all the dies for the type were produced by a Chester-based die-cutter. The coins do not, however, carry mint-signatures, and it seems likely that the moneyers Gunar and Othelriht, new names at Chester, are to be identified as the Derby moneyers Gunar and Othelric, still operating in Derby but temporarily in receipt of Chester-cut dies.

This reduces the number of likely Chester moneyers in the type to around 20, but 20 is still a substantial number, and many of the moneyers involved, particularly Ælfred, Ælfsig, Freotheric/Frothric and Thurmod, are known from numerous specimens surviving today. A good many of these derive from the Chester (1857) hoard, deposited *c.* 970, in which coins of this type were particularly well represented, but coins of the type also occur in contemporary hoards from Scotland, Ireland and Man, and it is apparent that Chester moneyers were again making a significant contribution to the volume of coin in circulation (although it should at the same time be noted that HR2 coins of Edgar are often of visibly lower silver content than coins of earlier types).

The Chester (1857) hoard contained just one coin, by the Chester moneyer Thurmod, of a new version of the HR3 type, similar to the HR3 type struck in Eadwig's reign but differentiated by the fact that the letters inserted on either side of the cross in the centre of the reverse stand for one or other of the three or possibly four mint towns where coins of this nature were struck. Thus, HR3 coins of Edgar with the letters LE in this position are by Chester moneyers, coins with the letters DE are by Derby moneyers, and coins with the letters TE are by Tamworth moneyers (despite the fact that, as Stewart Lyon has observed,[6] TE is not a plausible abbreviation for Tamworth's town name in Old English). A fourth mint in the type may perhaps be evidenced by rare surviving coins of the moneyers Ælfred and Siulf, on which the letters NE appear in the same position; these letters may simply be the final two letters of the word MONE (as on coins of this type struck under Eadwig), in which case Siulf may well be associable with Stafford, where an individual of the same name was a moneyer after Edgar's reform, but if the N of NE is the first letter of a mint town beginning with N, one possibility is that these moneyers were based in Newark-on-Trent, which although a long way from Chester is not far from Derby.[7]

HR3 coins carrying the Chester mint-signature LE are known of the following 19 moneyers: Ælfsig, Ælfstan, Aldewine, Boia, Deorlaf, Duran, Eadmund, Eoroth, Ethelm, Flodger, Frothric, Gillis (or Gillys), Leofstan, Mælsuthan, Martin (or Mertin), Monna, Teothuc, Thurmod and Wulgar. As many of the surviving Chester-struck HR3 coins have turned up in hoards in Scotland, Ireland and Man, it was the view of the late Michael Dolley that the type was struck as something akin to a nineteenth- or twentieth-century 'trade dollar', for specific use in trade with Ireland. This was never a very plausible hypothesis, and the discovery of a recent hoard from Ford Farm, Hargrave, Cheshire,[8] composed entirely of coins of this type, has underlined the fact that the reason why HR3 coins of Edgar have hardly occurred in hoards from England is simply chronological. The reality is that the type only began to be struck around 970, and the absence of it from the Chester (1950) hoard is due to the fact that this hoard was deposited well before the issue of the type commenced, while the occurrence of only one coin of the type in the Chester (1857) hoard is because the Chester (1857) hoard was deposited very early in the type's period of production. No other relevant hoards from England except that from Ford Farm have yet come to light. They are also scarce among single-finds, in part because they would not have been in circulation long before being demonetised in Edgar's coinage reform.

The history of coining operations at Chester from Edgar's reform of the coinage onwards falls outside the proper scope of the present remarks, but the coins from the Willoughby Gardner collection catalogued by Elizabeth Pirie in *SCBI 5* provide the student with a firm evidential foundation for an understanding of the subsequent history of the mint. Here it is enough to record that no more than five moneyers have so far been identified as working at Chester in the initial years after

[6] *Pers comm.*
[7] *Pers. comm.* Dr A. J. P. Campbell.
[8] See p. 30 below.

the reform (Ælfstan, Boiga, Deorlaf, Mælsuthan and Thurmod),[9] from which it might be concluded that at Chester at least the reform extended beyond reform of the physical character of the coinage into a cut-back in the number of individual moneyers responsible for its manufacture.

TABLE 1

Chester moneyers c. 910–46 (attributed and, in bold, with mint-signatures)

EDWARD THE ELDER			*ÆTHELSTAN*			*EDMUND*
Pictorial	*Horizontal*	*Horizontal CC*	*CR/CC*	*CC/CR*	*CR*	*HR1*
Boiga/Boga					**Boiga**	Boiga
Brece	Brece					
Cuthberht						
Eadmund	Eadmund	Eadmund	**Eadmund**	**Eadmund**	**Eadmund**	Eadmund
Eadwald						
Irfara						
Osulf		Osulf	**Osulf**	**Osulf**	Osulf	
Walter	Walter					
Wighard						
Wulfgar	Wulfgar	Wulfgar	**Wulfgar**		**Wulfgar**	Wulfgar
Wulfsige						
	Abba	Abba	**Abba**	**Abba**		
	Beorard	Beorard	**Beorard**	**Beorard**		
	Mægenferth					
	Osbearn					
	Sigeferth		**Sigeferth**			
	Snel	Snel	**Snel**		**Snel**	
	Tiot	Tiot		**Tiot**	**Tiot**	
	Waleman					
	Wulfstan		**Wulfstan**	**Wulfstan**	**Wulfstan**	Wulfstan
		Ælfwine	**Ælfwine**	**Ælfwine**	**Ælfwine**	Ælfwine
		Eadulf?	**Eadulf**			
		Paul	**Paul**	**Paul**	**Paul**	Paul
		Tidgar	**Tidgar**		**Tidgar**	
		Winard				
			Boigalet		**Boigalet**	
			Cnapa	**Cnapa**	**Cnapa**	Cnapa
			Deorulf		**Deorulf**	Dorulf
			(E)frard		**Frard**	Frard
			Mældomen		**Mældomen**	Mældomen
			Mærten			Mærten
			Oslac	**Oslac**	**Oslac**	Oslac

[9] Jonsson 1987, pp. 128–30.

TABLE 1

Continued

EDWARD THE ELDER			*ÆTHELSTAN*			*EDMUND*
Pictorial	*Horizontal*	*Horizontal CC*	*CR/CC*	*CC/CR*	*CR*	*HR1*
			Rægenulf			
			Sa(e)lce			
			Wiard	**Wiard**		
					Megred	Megred
						Ælfwald
						Eadstan
						Eroth
						Oswine
						Teothred
						Theodulf
						Thurmod
						Wihtelm
						Wilaf
						Wilsig
						Burnwald?
						Wisstan?

Note: The moneyers Paul and Eroth are known additionally for Chester-style coins of Eadmund of HT1 type.

TABLE 2

Chester moneyers 946–mid-970s (attributed and, in bold, with mint-signatures)

EADRED	*EADWIG*		*EDGAR*			
HR2	*HR3*	*CR*	*CC*	*HR2*	*HR3*	*Reform*
Ælfsig(e)	Ælfsie	Ælfsige	**Ælfsi(g)**	Ælfsig	**Ælfsig**	
D(e)orulf	D(e)orulf	Deorulf		Deorulf	**Deorlaf**	**Deorlaf**
Duran			**Duran**			
Eadmund	Eadmund	**Eadmund**		Eadmund	**Eadmund**	
Eoferard	Eoferard	Eoferard				
Eoroth	Eoroth	Eoroth	Eoroth	Eoroth	**Eoroth**	
Frard						
Frothric	Forthric	Freotheric	**Freotheric**	Frothric	**Frothric**	
Gilles		Gilys		Gillis	**Gillis**	
Mærten				Martin	**Martin**	
Siferth		Siferth		Siferth		
Sunu						
Teothred				Teothred		
Thurmod	Thurmod	**Thurmod**	**Thurmod**	Thurmod	**Thurmod**	**Thurmod**
Werstan	Werstan	Werstan		Werstan		

TABLE 2

Continued

EADRED	*EADWIG*		*EDGAR*			
HR2	*HR3*	*CR*	*CC*	*HR2*	*HR3*	*Reform*
Wilsig	Wilsig	Wilsig				
Wulfstan						
	Ethelstan					
		Aldewine		Aldewine	**Aldewine**	
				Ælfred		
				Æthelm	**Ethelm**	
				Alhmund		
				Ealfsige		
				Hrodulf		
				Leofstan	**Leofstan**	
				Teothuc	**Teothuc**	
					Ælfstan	**Ælfstan**
					Boia	**Boia**
					Flodger	
					Mælsuthan	**Mælsuthan**
					Monna	
					Wulgar	

Note: In addition there exist HR1 coins of Eadred by the moneyers Thurmod, Wilsig and Wulfstan (the coin of Wilsig struck from a HR1 reverse already used in Eadmund's reign); HR2 coins of Eadwig by the moneyers Eadmund, Efrard, Sunu and Thurmod (the coin of Sunu struck from a HR2 reverse already used in Eadred's reign); and a coin of the moneyer Ælfsige struck from a HR3 obverse die of Eadwig and a reverse die of Edgar's reign of Circumscription Rosette type. There also exist coins of the moneyer Eoroth for Edgar struck from a Circumscription Rosette obverse and a Circumscription Cross reverse, and coins of the moneyer Freotheric of the same reign struck from Circumscription Cross obverses and Circumscription Rosette reverses. Gunar and Othelriht, known from HR2 coins of Edgar of Chester style, are omitted from the table as they appear to have been moneyers working at Derby.

ANGLO-SAXON AND NORMAN COIN HOARDS FROM CHESTER AND ITS VICINITY

Six Anglo-Saxon and Norman hoards found in Chester or its vicinity contained coins that are represented in the Grosvenor Museum's collection. These warrant fuller discussion here.

1. CHESTER (1862) HOARD

Deposited c. 917 — *c.* 40 pennies? (18 recorded)

Viking kingdoms 8:
- St Edmund memorial coinage 1
- St Peter (Swordless) coinage 7

Edward the Elder 7

Contemporary imitations of Edward the Elder 3

References. Peacock 1862; Hughes 1864; Thompson 1956, no. 83; BP no. 99.

On 4 March 1862 a group of workmen excavating for a new vestibule outside the west end of St John's Church, Chester, discovered a little heap of coins at a depth of some 16 feet below the modern surface. There may in all have been around 40 coins, but some were broken or purloined, and the local antiquary Thomas Hughes, who read a paper on the hoard to a meeting of the Chester Architectural, Archaeological and Historic Society on 20 May 1862, reported that 'not more than 20 at the utmost' could be traced. Descriptions and illustrations of 17 of these accompanied Hughes's subsequent note on the hoard in the Society's Journal.[1]

Of these, six were coins of Edward the Elder; three were contemporary imitations (one carrying Edward's name on its obverse, two with meaningless inscriptions on both sides); one was a specimen of the St Edmund coinage struck in East Anglia at the end of the ninth century and in the early tenth century, this specimen being of a variety struck from *c.* 905 onwards; and the remaining seven were coins struck under Viking rule at York after *c.* 905, all in the name of St Peter.

It had been the intention that the coins should be presented to the Grosvenor Museum, but this never happened, and they vanished from sight until 1966, when

[1] Hughes 1864.

the bulk of them were acquired from a London coin dealer by the late Cdr Richard Paston Mack (1901–74). By then only 14 of the 17 coins published by Hughes remained, but the overall number of coins acquired by Mack was 15, for the parcel included one further coin of Edward the Elder, Tower type, moneyer Wulfsige, not recorded by Hughes. Mack republished the hoard shortly afterwards,[2] and the coins also featured in *SCBI 20*.

At auction sales of Mack's collection following his death, the Grosvenor Museum was able to purchase the coins numbered **22, 31**, **75** and **77** in the present volume.

Blackburn and Pagan have dated the hoard's deposit to *c.* 917.[3] Blunt, Stewart and Lyon have argued that the hoard was deposited no earlier than *c.* 915, while inclining to the view that it might have been deposited as late as 918.[4]

2. *CHESTER (1950) HOARD*

Deposited c. 965 546+ coins

Viking Kingdom of York 5:
- Anlaf Guthfrisson 2
- Anlaf Sihtricsson 2
- Eric Bloodaxe 1

Kingdom of Wessex 14:
- Alfred 1: Horizontal type
- Edward the Elder 13: Horizontal types

Kingdom of England
- Æthelstan 55:
  - Horizontal types 23
  - Circumscription types 26
  - Circumscription-Bust Crowned mule 1
  - Bust Crowned types 5
- Edmund 67:
  - Horizontal types 63
  - Circumscription types 1
  - Bust Crowned types 3
- Eadred 147:
  - Horizontal types 132
  - Bust Crowned types 14
  - Floral type 1

[2] Mack 1967.
[3] Blackburn and Pagan 1986, no. 99.
[4] *CTCE*, pp. 40–1

Eadwig-Eadred mule 1: Horizontal type
Eadwig 109:
- Horizontal types 102
- Circumscription types 3
- Floral type 2
- Ornamental types 2

Eadwig-Edgar mule 1: Horizontal type
Edgar 142:
- Horizontal types 63
- Circumscription types 55
- Bust Crowned types 23
- Floral type 1

Uncertain ruler 2: Horizontal types
Carolingian rulers 3

References: Blunt and Dolley 1954; Thompson 1956, no. 86; BP no. 144.

This hoard of tenth-century Anglo-Saxon coins, ingots and hacksilver, contained in a small domestic cooking pot of the period, was discovered on 29 November 1950 by workmen relaying an electrical cable on the west side of Castle Esplanade, Chester. In their ensuing publication of the coins from the hoard, Blunt and Dolley noted that 'the greater part of the hoard was recovered, though it is known a few coins were destroyed and a few more were not accounted for'.[5] Happily, one of the coins not reported to the authorities at the time was shown at the Grosvenor Museum in October 1975, and further enquiries led to a treasure trove inquest in November 1976 at which 15 previously unrecorded coins and five silver ingots from the hoard were declared treasure trove. These were purchased for the Grosvenor Museum, and their discovery raised the number of coins and fragments of coins associable with the hoard to 546.

Of the coins published by Blunt and Dolley, 213, acquired by the British Museum, have since been listed and illustrated by Archibald and Blunt in *SCBI 34*. The British Museum also acquired from the hoard two coins of Edward the Elder, which have as yet to be published in an *SCBI* volume. Of the remaining 309 coins published by Blunt and Dolley (all acquired by the Grosvenor Museum), five coins of Æthelstan and four coins of Edgar, each carrying a Chester mint-signature, were published by Elizabeth Pirie in *SCBI 5*.

The present volume publishes the rest of the Anglo-Saxon coins recorded by Blunt and Dolley; two additional coins likely to be from the hoard which may have been

[5] Blunt and Dolley 1954, p. 125.

omitted from Blunt and Dolley's list as a result of casual error;[6] a number of fragments, mostly very small, of which Blunt and Dolley were aware but did not list individually; and the 15 coins declared treasure trove in 1976, although the details of 10 of these have had to be taken from a typescript list prepared at the time of the inquest, as it has not proved possible to locate the coins concerned in the Museum's collection today.

Blunt and Dolley's publication of the hoard was exemplary for its date, listing the coins' exact legends and recording their die-axes and weights in grains, but many of the coins represented in the hoard carried moneyers' names only, without accompanying mint-signatures, and subsequent advances in our understanding of the coinage of this period now permit the following more informative tabulation of its content. Coins identified by numbers in bold are coins published in the catalogue part of the present volume, while coins identified by numbers preceded with the prefixes *SCBI 5* and *SCBI 34* are coins published in those *SCBI* volumes.

The date of deposit of the hoard can be put at *c.* 965, for it contains no coins of Edgar's HR3 type, struck by numerous moneyers at Chester (and also by moneyers at Derby, Tamworth and an apparent mint 'NE') in the last years before Edgar's reform of the coinage. A date in the mid 960s is indirectly confirmed by the absence from the hoard of any examples of an extensive coinage of Circumscription Cross type struck towards the end of the pre-reform period by the York moneyers Durand, Fastolf and Herolf, as well as by the fact that the hoard contained coins by only seven of some 20 moneyers who were active at Chester during the span of Edgar's HR2 type.

The Edgar element in the hoard has been the subject of detailed discussion by Kenneth Jonsson.[7]

Among the Carolingian coins, coin **809** attributed by Blunt and Dolley to Berenger I as emperor (915–24), has now been identified by Dr William Day as a coin of Berengar II and Adalbert, Kings of Italy (950–61).

As has recently been pointed out by James Graham-Campbell,[8] the only formal publication of the ingots and associated hacksilver from the hoard remains the brief description of them within Graham Webster's initial report on the hoard's discovery and content.[9] Kruse and Tait have however published XRF analyses of 62 out of 98 ingots or ingot fragments from the hoard as part of a broader study of silver ingots from the Viking Age.[10]

The container was the subject of a note by G. C. Dunning appended to Webster's original report.[11]

[6] The suggestion that they may derive from the hoard was first made by Archibald 1967.
[7] Jonsson 1987, pp. 39–41.
[8] Graham-Campbell 2001, p. 52.
[9] Webster 1953.
[10] Kruse and Tait 1992.
[11] Webster 1953, pp. 31–2.

TABLE 3

Contents of the Chester (1950) hoard
(BD refers to Blunt and Dolley 1950)

VIKINGS OF NORTHUMBRIA	
ANLAF GUTHFRITHSSON 2	
Circumscription Cross (Derby), no moneyer's name, **23** (BD 518)	1
Raven/Cross (York), Athelferth, **24** (BD 517)	1
ANLAF SIHTRICSSON 2	
Triquetra/Standard (York), Farman, **25** (BD 516)	1
Cross Moline/Cross (?) (York), Radulf, **26** (BD –)	1
ERIC BLOODAXE 1	
Sword/Cross (York), Radulf, **27** (BD –)	1
KINGDOM OF WESSEX	
ALFRED 1	
Horizontal Pellet, Canterbury, Diarwald, **28** (BD 1)	1
EDWARD THE ELDER 13	
Horizontal Trefoil (HT1), London style, Beahstan, **32** (BD 3)	1
Horizontal Trefoil (HT1), Winchester style, Æthered, **45** (BD –); [ ]ed, **51** (BD 7); [ ]bold, **52** (BD 358)	3
Horizontal Pellet (HP1), Winchester style, Æthered, **56** (BD 2); Biornred, BM (BD 4); Eadstan, BM (BD 5); Wulfred, **73** (BD 6)	4
Horizontal (HT1 imitative), East Anglian style, meaningless inscription, **79** (BD 8)	1
Horizontal (fragments of uncertain variety and style), [ ]od, **80** (BD –);]er[, **81** (BD –); uncertain, **82** (BD –); uncertain, **83** (BD 361)	4
KINGDOM OF ENGLAND	
ÆTHELSTAN 55	
Horizontal Trefoil (HT1), Chester style, Abba, **88** (BD 9); Beorard, *SCBI 34*, 10 (BD 12); Eadmund, **90** (BD 15)	3
Horizontal Trefoil (HT1), Southern and Midlands styles, Ælfwine, *SCBI 34*, 5 (BD 10); Berhelm, *SCBI 34*, 11 (BD 13); Eadmund, **99** (BD 16); Ethelsige, *SCBI 34*, 6 (BD 11); Frithestan, *SCBI 34*, 20 (BD 17); Iohann, **101** (BD 19); Mannia, *SCBI 34*, 24 (BD 20); Mathelbrht (or Brhtmathel), *SCBI 34*, 25 (BD 21); Wealdhelm, **102** (BD 24)	9
Horizontal Trefoil (HT1), North and Central East Midlands style (NE1), Burtvoclf, *SCBI 34*, 207 (BD 26); Clacl, **103** (BD 14); Godfred, *SCBI 34*, 216 (BD 18); Oda, **104** (BD 22); Stefanus, **106** (BD 23); Winele, **108** (BD 25); uncertain, **109** (BD 27)	7
Horizontal (fragments of uncertain variety and style), **128** (BD 28), **129** (BD –), **130** (BD –), **131** (BD 29)	4
Circumscription Cross, Chester, Abba, *SCBI 5*, 4 (BD 35); Chester, Eadulf, *SCBI 34*, 55 (BD 37); Chester, Oslac, *SCBI 34*, 58 (BD 38); Chester, Oslfe, *SCBI 34*, 60 (BD 39); Chester, Wulfstan, *SCBI 5*, 36 (BD 40); Oxford,	

KINGDOM OF ENGLAND (*cont.*)

Ingelri, **115** (BD –); Shaftesbury, Æthelwi(ne), *SCBI 34*, 94 (BD 42); Shrewsbury, Berhthelm, **116** (BD 43); Shrewsbury, Eofermand, *SCBI 34*, 97 (BD 44); Shrewsbury, Frotger, *SCBI 34*, 98 (BD 45); Southampton, Eadgild, *SCBI 34*, 99 (BD 41); York, Regnald, **117**, **118**, **119**, **120** (BD 51, 50, 48, 49) 15
Circumscription Cross (variant), Chester, Cenapa, **121** (BD –) 1
Circumscription Cross/Bust Crowned (mule), Winchester, Rægenulf, *SCBI 34*, 121 (BD 47) 1
Circumscription Cross/Circumscription Rosette, Chester, Abba, *SCBI 5*, 47 (BD 53); Chester, Wiard, *SCBI 34*, 180 (BD 54) 2
Circumscription Rosette, Chester, Eadmund, *SCBI 5*, 16 (BD 52), **122** (BD –) 2
Circumscription (variety uncertain), London, uncertain, **123** (BD –); uncertain fragments, **132**, **133** (BD –) 3
Bust Crowned, Canterbury, Torthelm, *SCBI 34*, 124 (BD 30); Norwich, Manticen, **124** (BD 31); Norwich, Secgge, *SCBI 34*, 148 (BD 32); 'Smrie', Eadbald, *SCBI 34*, 152 (BD 33a); York, Ethelerd, *SCBI 34*, 164 (BD 33) 5
Circumscription Cross (imitative), 'Winchester', Eadstan, *SCBI 34*, 274 (BD 46); meaningless inscription, **127** (BD 36), *SCBI 34*, 267 (BD 34) 3

EDMUND 67

Horizontal Trefoil (HT1), Southern and Midlands styles, Ælfstan, **138**, **139** (BD 58, 59); Ælfwald, **141** (BD 63); Æthelgar, *SCBI 34*, 285 (BD 64); Birhtsige, *SCBI 34*, 295 (BD 66); Birneard, **143**, **144**, **145** (BD 67, 68, 69); Burnwald, **146**, **147** (BD 71, 73); Heremod, **148**, **149** (BD 85, 84); Herewig, **150** (BD 86); Ivan, *SCBI 34*, 313, *SCBI 34*, 314 (BD 89, 90); Lifinc, *SCBI 34*, 318 (BD 92); Osefrth/Osfred, *SCBI 34*, 323, *SCBI 34*, 324 (BD 97, 98); Rægenold, *SCBI 34*, 331 (BD 103); Rægenulf, **152** (BD 102); Siedeman, **154** (BD 104); Sigeferth, *SCBI 34*, 336 (BD 106); Stfan, *SCBI 34*, 337 (BD 108); Tælia, *SCBI 34*, 338 (BD 109); Wigeard, **155** (BD 110) 25
Horizontal Trefoil (HT1), York style, Ingelgar, **157**, **158** (BD 88, 87) 2
Horizontal Pellet (HP1), Southern style, Byrneard, **160** (BD 70); Eadred, **161** (BD 80); Eardulf, **162** (BD 83) 3
Horizontal Pellet (HP2), Southern style, Ælfhun, *SCBI 34*, 356 (BD 56); Pehtred, *SCBI 34*, 357 (BD 111) 2
Horizontal Cross, Southern and Midlands styles, Diarweld, *SCBI 34*, 358 (BD 76); Elfric, **163** (BD 57) 2
Horizontal Rosette (HR1), Chester style, Ælfwald, **164**, **165** (BD 61, 62); Burnwald, *SCBI 34*, 411 (BD 72); Dorulf, **170**, **172**, **175** (BD 77, 79, 78); Elfstan, *SCBI 34*, 426 (BD 60); Mældomene, **185** (BD 93); Maerten, **190**, **191** (BD 95, 96); Osulf, *SCBI 34*, 439 (BD 99); Wulfstan, **203** (BD 113) 12
Horizontal Rosette (HR1), Derby style, Demence, **208** (BD 75); Othelric, **209**, *SCBI 34*, 440, *SCBI 34*, 441 (BD 101, 100, 114); Sigar, **210** (BD 105); Sigwold, **211** (BD 107); Wulfgar, **212** (BD 112) 7
Horizontal Rosette (HR1), Central Mercia styles, Athelulf, **213** (BD 65; Cenberht, *SCBI 34*, 412 (BD 74), **214** (BD –); Eadstan, **215**, **216** (BD 81, 82) 5
Horizontal Rosette (HR1 var.a), Derby, Afra, **220** (BD –) 1
Horizontal Rosette (HR1 imitative), meaningless inscription, *SCBI 34*, 461 (BD 94) 1
Rosette/Horizontal Rosette (HR1), unlocated West Midlands style, Amund, **217** (BD 117) 1

KINGDOM OF ENGLAND (*cont.*)

Rosette/Horizontal Rosette (HR4), unlocated West Midlands style, Amund, *SCBI 34*, 469 (BD 116); Elfsan, *SCBI 34*, 470 (BD 115) 2
Circumscription Cross (imitative), 'Chester', Baro, *SCBI 34*, 472 (BD 118) 1
Bust Crowned, Norwich, Giongbald, *SCBI 34*, 476 (BD 120); Norwich, Hrodgar, *SCBI 34*, 478 (BD 119); Bruinic, *SCBI 34*, 480 (BD 121) 3

EADRED 147

Horizontal Trefoil (HT1), Derby style, Theodmær, **221** (BD 225) 1
Horizontal Trefoil, Northern East Midlands style, Hunred, **222**, **223**, **224**, **225**, **226** (BD 190, 192, 193, 194, 191); Theodmær, **228** (BD –), *SCBI 34*, 584 (BD 226) 7
Horizontal Trefoil (HT1), Southern and unlocated Midlands styles, Canterbury, Ælfric, *SCBI 34*, 493 (BD 122); Athelmund, **229**, **230** (BD 127, 128); Baldwin, **231**, **232** (BD 139, 140); Beahred, **233**, *SCBI 34*, 503 (BD 142, 141); Bernehe, **234** (BD 145); Biorhtulf, **235**, *SCBI 34*, 508 (BD 147, 146); Byhrtred, *SCBI 34*, 510 (BD 143); Cilien, *SCBI 34*, 512 (BD 154); Crisotin, *SCBI 34*, 514 (BD 155); Dellel, *SCBI 34*, 515 (BD 156); Deoereh, *SCBI 34*, 516 (BD 157); Dun, *SCBI 34*, 517 (BD 159); Eferbrd, *SCBI 34*, 519 (BD 162); Gislehelm, 236 (BD 176); Grim, 237 (BD 180); Heremod, **238**, **239**, **240**, **241**, *SCBI 34*, 525 (BD 182, 183, 184, 185, 186); Leofhelm, **242**, **243**, *SCBI 34*, 530 (BD 197, 196, 195); Osefd, **246** (BD 204); Oswine, *SCBI 34*, 536 (BD 209); Otic, **247** (BD 214); Thurferth, *SCBI 34*, 540 (BD 227); Wulfhelm, *SCBI 34*, 544 (BD 240) 31
Horizontal Trefoil (HT1), York style, Heriger, **249** (BD 187) 1
Horizontal Pellet (HP1), Southern style, Leofwine, *SCBI 34*, 550 (BD 199) 1
Horizontal Cross Trefoil, Southern style, Osulf, **250** (BD 208) 1
Horizontal Trefoil Cross, Southern style, Osulf, *SCBI 34*, 551 (BD 207) 1
Horizontal Trefoil (HT1), Central East Midlands style (NE1), Liofstan, *SCBI 34*, 560 (BD 198); Manna, **251** (BD 203); Osmund, *SCBI 34*, 561 (BD 206); Wilebert, **252** (BD –) 4
Horizontal Rosette (HR1), Chester style, Thurmod, **254** (BD 228) 1
Horizontal Rosette (HR1), Derby and Central Mercia styles, Ælfwine, *SCBI 34*, 590 (BD 126); Æthered, *SCBI 34*, 594 (BD 130); Agtard, **257**, **258**, **259**, **260** (BD 131, 134, 133, 132); Amund, **313**, *SCBI 34*, 598 (BD 135, 136); Baldc/Baldric, **314**, **315** (BD 137, 138); Bernard, **261** (BD 144); Boga/Boiga, **262**, **265**, **266**, **271**, **272** (BD 149, 148, 151, 150, 152); Cenberht, **316** (BD 153); Dudid, **317** (BD 158); Elfric, *SCBI 34*, 612 (BD 123); Ethelulf, **274** (BD 129); Frethic, **276**, **277**, **278**, **279**, **280**, **281** (BD 163, 164, 165, 166, –, 167); Gislemer, **282**, **283** (BD 177, 178); Grim, **284**, **285** (BD 181, 179); Hildulf, **318**, *SCBI 34*, 618 (BD 188, 189); Londberht, *SCBI 34*, 620 (BD 200); Man, **286** (BD 202); Oslac, *SCBI 34*, 635 (BD 205); Othelric, **289**, **290**, **291**, **292**, **293** (BD 210, 212, 213, 211, –); Redwine, **294** (BD 215); Regther, **295**, **296**, **297** (BD 217, 218, 216); Scurve, *SCBI 34*, 633 (BD 219); Sfear, **298** (BD 222); Sigar, **299**, **300**, **301** (BD 221,223, 224); Ugelberd, *SCBI 34*, 638 (BD 232); Wergerd, *SCBI 34*, 639 (BD 233); Wulfgar/Wulgar, **306**, **308**, **309**, **310** (BD 237, 239, 238, 236); Wulfstan, *SCBI 34*, 644 (BD 242) 56
Horizontal Rosette (HR2), Chester style, Ælsie/Ælfsige, **319**, **320** (BD 124, 125); Derolf, **322** (BD 520); Eadmun(d), **325** (BD 161); Frard, **333** (BD –); Frothric, **335**, **336**, **337**, **338** (BD 173, 170, 171, 172); Gilys, *SCBI 34*, 657, *SCBI 34*, 669 (halfpenny) (BD 175, 260); Mærten, *SCBI 34*, 659 (BD 201);

KINGDOM OF ENGLAND (*cont.*)

Siferth, *SCBI 34*, 660 (BD 220); Thurmod, **347**, **348**, **349** (BD 229, 230, 231); Werstan, **356** (BD 234); Wilaf, **357** (BD 235); Wulstan, **359** (BD 241) 19

Horizontal Rosette (HR2 var), Chester style, Frothric, **364**, **365** (BD 168, 169); Gilles, *SCBI 34*, 672 (BD 174) 3

Horizontal Rosette (variety), unlocated Midlands style, Eadmund, *SCBI 34*, 675 (BD 160) 1

Horizontal Rosette (HR1 imitative), meaningless inscription, *SCBI 34*, 677 (BD 243) 1

Rosette/Horizontal Cross (HC4), Central Mercia style, Æthered, **367** (BD –) 1

Rosette/Horizontal Rosette (HR1), Central Mercia style, Manin, *SCBI 34*, 679 (BD 244); Manne, **369**, **370** (BD 245, 246) 3

Floral, unlocated Midlands style, Hildulf, *SCBI 34*, 685 (halfpenny) (BD 261) 1

Bust Crowned, Athelverth, *SCBI 34*, 695 (BD 247); Brainic, *SCBI 34*, 696 (BD 248); Copman, *SCBI 34*, 700 (BD 249); Manna, **371**, **372** (BD 251, 250); Norbert, *SCBI 34*, 708 (BD 252); Nothel, *SCBI 34*, 709 (BD 253); Osulf, *SCBI 34*, 710 (BD 254); Sarvvrd, **373** (BD 255); Walter, *SCBI 34*, 715 (BD 256); Wilebert, **374**, **375** (BD 257, 258); Wine, *SCBI 34*, 718, (BD 259); uncertain, **376** (BD –) 14

EADWIG 109

Horizontal Trefoil (HT1), Southern and Midlands styles, Ælfsige, *SCBI 34*, 720 (BD 303); Æthelsige, *SCBI 34*, 721 (BD 306); Biorhtulf, *SCBI 34*, 722 (BD 312); Brothar, **377**, **378** (BD 315, 316); Byrnferth, **379**, *SCBI 34*, 725 (BD 311, 310); Cillm, *SCBI 34*, 726 (BD 317); Clac, **380**, **381**, *SCBI 34*, 727 (BD 320, 319, 318); Cytel, **382** (BD 321); Eadulf, **383**, *SCBI 34*, 729 (BD 325, 324); Eneg[ ], *SCBI 34*, 730 (BD 327); Frodgar, *SCBI 34*, 732 (BD 329); Grmh (Grim ?), **385**, *SCBI 34*, 735 (BD 330, 331); Heremod, **386**, **387** (BD 332, 333); Leofhelm, **388**, **389**, **390**, *SCBI 34*, 737 (BD 342, 344, –, 343); Mann, **391**, **392** (BD 347, 346); Oswald, *SCBI 34*, 742 (BD 349); Sigeferth, *SCBI 34*, 743 (BD 351); Winenon, **393** (BD 353); Wulfmær, *SCBI 34*, 737 (BD 354); Wulfric, *SCBI 34*, 747 (BD 355); Wulfstan, *SCBI 34*, 748 (BD 356) 32

Horizontal Trefoil (HT1), York style, Æsculf, **394** (BD 305); Heriger, **395**, **396**, **397**, **398**, **399**, **400** (BD 334, 335, 336, 337, 338, 339) 7

Horizontal Trefoil (HT1), Central East Midlands style (NE I), Æthelstan, *SCBI 34*, 766 (BD 307); Eaenulf, 403 (BD 326); Ivnm, *SCBI 34*, 761 (BD 341); Manna, *SCBI 34*, 762 (BD 348) 4

Horizontal Trefoil (HT1), Lincoln style (NE IV), Levich, **404** (BD 345) 1

Horizontal Trefoil Cross (HTC1), Southern or Midlands style, Wulfstan, **401** (BD 357) 1

Horizontal Pellet (HP1), Southern or Midlands style, [ ]red, **402** (BD 359) 1

Horizontal Trefoil (HT3), Bath, Biorhtulf, *SCBI 34*, 794 (BD 262); Bedford, Ælfshe, *SCBI 34*, 795 (BD 263); Bedford, Baldwine, **405**, **406**, **407** (BD 265, 266, 264); Bedford, Boiga, **408** (BD 267); Bedford, Frodgar, **409**, *SCBI 34*, 798 (BD 268, 269); Bedford, Grim, **410**, **411**, **412**, **413**, **414** (BD 270, 271, 272, 273, 274); Bedford, Herewig, **415**, **416** (BD 275, 276); Bedford, Leofstain, **417** (BD 277); 'Newe' (Newport Pagnell ?), Cilm, *SCBI 34*, 813, *SCBI 34*, 814 (BD 278, 279); 'Newe' (Newport Pagnell ?), Clac, **423**, **424** (BD 280, 281); Northampton, Baldric, *SCBI 34*, 804 (BD 282); Northampton, Wærin, **418**, **419**, *SCBI 34*, 808 (BD 287, 286, 285); Northampton (or Huntingdon ?), Wineman, **420**, *SCBI 34*, 809 (BD 289, 288); Oxford, Wynhelm, *SCBI 34*,

KINGDOM OF ENGLAND (*cont.*)

816 (BD 290); Southampton, Eadgild, *SCBI 34*, 805 (BD 283); Southampton, Mangod, **421** (BD 284) 29

Horizontal Rosette (HR1), Derby and Central Mercia styles, Æthelulf, *SCBI 34*, 825 (BD 308); Agtard, **425** (BD 309); Boiga, **426**, **427** (BD 313, 314); Demence, *SCBI 34*, 821 (BD 322); Elfstan, *SCBI 34*, 823 (BD 304); Frethic, **428** (BD 328); Hildulf, *SCBI 34*, 827 (BD 340); Regther, *SCBI 34*, 824 (BD 350) 8

Horizontal Rosette (HR2), unlocated Midlands style, Eadmund (*SCBI 34*, 828 (BD 323) 1

Horizontal Rosette (HR3), Chester style, Ælfsie, **430** (BD 291); Deorulf, **431** (BD 292); Eadmund, **433** (BD 293); Eoferad, **434**, **435** (BD 294, 295); Eoroth, *SCBI 34*, 836 (BD 296); Frard, **438** (BD 297); Freotheric, **439**, **440**, *SCBI 34*, 838 (BD 300, 299, 298); Wilsig, **441**, *SCBI 34*, 844 (BD 301, 302) 10

Horizontal Rosette (HR5), Central Mercia style, Eferulf/Iferulf, *SCBI 34*, 847, *SCBI 34*, 848 (BD 362, 363); Manin, **442**, *SCBI 34*, 850 (BD 365, 364); Ucelberd, *SCBI 34*, 851 (BD 366) 5

Horizontal Rosette, uncertain variety,]e[, **443** (BD 360) 1

Circumscription Cross, Barnstaple, Byrhtsieg, *SCBI 34*, 852 (BD 368); Totnes, Wynstan, *SCBI 34*, 853 (BD 369); Æthelgar, *SCBI 34*, 854 (BD 371) 3

Floral, Southern style (?), Æthelsige, *SCBI 34*, 856 (BD 373); Eadwine, *SCBI 34*, 857 (halfpenny) (BD 374) 2

Ornamental (var.c), unlocated Midlands style, Oswald, **444** (BD 367) 1

Ornamental (var.d), Southern style (?), Æthelsige, **445** (BD 372) 1

EADWIG-EADRED mule 1

Eadwig, *Horizontal Rosette* (HR3)/Eadred, *Horizontal Rosette* (HR2), Chester style, Sunu, **446** (BD 352) 1

EADWIG-EDGAR mule 1

Eadwig, *Horizontal Rosette* (HR3)/Edgar, *Circumscription Rosette* (CR), Chester style, Ælfsige, **448** (BD 370) 1

EDGAR 138

Horizontal Trefoil (HT1), Southern or Midlands styles, Ælfsige, *SCBI 34*, 874 (BD 381); Broder/Brothar, *SCBI 34*, 897, 898 (BD 387, 388); Grim, **449**, *SCBI 34*, 921, SCBI 34, 922 (BD 402, 403, 404) 6

Horizontal Trefoil (HT1), Lincoln style (NE V), Adelaver, **451**, *SCBI 34*, 862 (BD 375, 376); Bernulf, *SCBI 34*, 894 (BD 385); Eanulf, **455** (BD 393); Farthein, **458** (BD 397); Hacuf, **460** (BD 405); Harcer, **461** (BD –); Ingolf, **462**, **463** (BD 421, 422); Isenberht, **464** (BD 423); Ive, **465**, **466**, **467** (BD 424, 425, 426); Manai/Manan, **468**, **469** (BD 431, 430); Manolet, **470**, **471** (BD 428, 429) 17

Horizontal Trefoil (HT1), York style, Æsculf, **472** (BD 382); Durand, **488** (BD 390); Heriger, **489**, **490**, **491**, **492**, **493**, **494**, **495**, **496**, **497**, **498**, **499**, **500**, **501**, **502** (BD 406, 407, 408, 409, 410, 411, 412, 413, 414, 415, 416, 418, 419, 417) 17

Horizontal Trefoil (HT1), Central East Midlands style (NE1), Umbein, **503** (BD 420) 1

KINGDOM OF ENGLAND (*cont.*)

Horizontal Cross (HC1), Southern style, Byrnferth *SCBI 34*, 988 (BD 384) 1

Horizontal Rosette (HR1), Derby style, Æthelulf, *SCBI 34*, 1008 (BD 383); Ælfred, *SCBI 34*, 1009 (BD 379); Boiga, *SCBI 34*, 1011 (BD 386); Demence, **507** (BD 389); Frethic, **511**, **512** (BD 398, 399); Leofstan, *SCBI 34*, 1022 (BD 427); Sigar, **515** (BD 432) 8

Horizontal Rosette (HR2), Chester style, Ælfred, **517**, **518** (BD 377, 378); Ælfsig/Ælfsige, **523**, **525** (BD –, 380); Eadmun/Eadmund, **541**, *SCBI 34*, 1193 (BD 391, 392); Eoroth, **546**, **547**, *SCBI 34*, 1198 (BD 394, 396, 395); Freothric/Frothric, **553**, **558** (BD 400, 401); Thurmod, **576** (BD 433); Werstan, *SCBI 34*, 1200 (BD 434) 13

Circumscription Cross, Southern style, Oxford, Wulfsan, *SCBI 34*, 1078 (BD 455); Shaftesbury, Leofstan, *SCBI 34*, 1079 (BD 456); uncertain mint (Oxford ?), Wulsta(n), **608** (BD 521) 3

Circumscription Cross, South-Western style, Exeter, Ead Ælfstan, *SCBI 34*, 1086 (BD 459); uncertain mint ('Hn'), Brrehtferth, *SCBI 34*, 1088 (BD 452) 2

Circumscription Cross, Chester, Ælfsi/Ælfsig, *SCBI 34*, 1102, *SCBI 34*, 1103 (BD 435, 442); Chester, Freotheric, *SCBI 5*, 74, *SCBI 34*, 1104 (BD 437, 436); Chester, Thurmod, *SCBI 5*, 75, *SCBI 5*, 76, *SCBI 5*, 77, *SCBI 34*, 1105 (BD 438, 439, 441, 440); Derby, Boia, *SCBI 34*, 1100 (BD 443); Northampton, Thurferth, *SCBI 34*, 1095 (BD 454); 'Weardburh', *SCBI 34*, 1099 (BD 458); Eoferard, *SCBI 34*, 1091 (BD 460); Leofhelm, *SCBI 34*, 1088 (BD 446); Oswald, *SCBI 34*, 1094 (BD 485) 14

Circumscription Cross, imitative, meaningless inscription, *SCBI 34*, 1233 (Blunt.Dolley 55); "Refmferth", *SCBI 34*, 1234 (BD 466) 2

Circumscription Rosette, Chester style, Ælfsie/Ælfsige, **625**, **626**, **627** (BD 468, 467, –); Boia, *SCBI 34*, 1052 (BD 453); Deorulf, **628**, *SCBI 34*, 1054 (BD 474, 475); Eadmund, **631** (BD 476); Eoferard, *SCBI 34*, 1057, 1058 (BD 477, 461); Freotheiric/Freotherci, **633**, *SCBI 34*, 1060 (BD 481, 480); Gilys, *SCBI 34*, 1062 (BD 482); Siferth, **636**, *SCBI 34*, 1064, *SCBI 34*, 1065 (BD 465, 464, 486); Thurmod, **643**, **644** (BD 488, 489) 17

Circumscription Rosette, Derby and Central Mercia styles, Derby, (Boig)a (?), *SCBI 34*, 1039 (BD 451); Derby, Iole, **622**, *SCBI 34*, 1041 (BD 445, 444); Derby, Man, *SCBI 34*, 1042 (BD 447); Derby, Osulf, **623**, *SCBI 34*, 1043 (BD 448, 449); Derby, Othelric, *SCBI 34*, 1044 (BD 450); Tamworth, Deorulf, **624** (BD 457); Amund, *SCBI 34*, 1051 (BD 471); Daniel, *SCBI 34*, 1053 (BD 472); Deorulf, **646** (BD 473); Elfstan, **648**, **649** (BD 469, 470); Eofermund, **650**, *SCBI 34*, 1059 (BD 463, 462); Frothald, **651** (BD 479); Hildulf, **652**, *SCBI 34*, 1063 (BD 483, 484); Siulfl, **653** (BD 519) 16

Circumscription Rosette/Circumscription Cross mule, Chester style, Eoroth, *SCBI 34*, 1069 (BD 478) 1

Bust Crowned, Bath, Biorhtulf, *SCBI 34*, 1146 (BD 490); Bedford, Ælfsig, **654** (BD 491); Exeter (?), Wnebirht, *SCBI 34*, 1149 (BD 492); Hertford, Abenel, *SCBI 34*, 1150 (BD 493); Huntingdon, Prim, **655** (BD 494); London, Æthered, *SCBI 34*, 1155 (BD 495); Totnes, Burhstan, *SCBI 34*, 1159 (BD 496); Ælfsige, *SCBI 34*, 1160 (BD 497); Æthelbrand, **SCBI 34**, 1161 (BD 498); Baldwin, **657**, **658**, **659**, *SCBI 34*, 1162 (BD 501, 502, 499, 500); Byrnferth, *SCBI 34*, 1164 (BD 503); Liofstan, **660**, **661**, *SCBI 34*, 1167 (BD 504, 505, 506); Manne, *SCBI 34*, 1178 (BD 507); Norbert, *SCBI 34*,

KINGDOM OF ENGLAND (*cont.*)

1180 (BD 508); Siferth, **662** (BD 487, 513, these being two fragments of the same coin); Tuholf, *SCBI 34*, 1168 (BD 509); Wulfmær, *SCBI 34*, 1169 (BD 510); Wulstan, **663**, *SCBI 34*, 1170 (BD 511, 512)	22
Bust Crowned (London monogram), no moneyer's name, *SCBI 34*, 1172 (halfpenny) (BD 515)	1
Floral, Midlands style, Oswine, *SCBI 34*, 1035 (halfpenny), (BD 514)	1
UNCERTAIN RULER 2	
Horizontal Trefoil (HT1), Southern or Midlands style, Leofric, **664** (BD 91)	1
Horizontal, uncertain variety (HT1 ?), Southern or Midlands style, Thur[ ], 665 (BD –)	1
CAROLINGIAN 3	
Immobilised type of Melle, mid eleventh century. **807, 808** (BD 522, 523)	2
Berengar II and Adalbert, *Christiana Religio*. **809** (BD 524)	1

3. *CHESTER (1857) HOARD*

Deposited c. 970 — *c.* 80 or more coins (60 recorded)

Kingdom of England
- Eadred 3: Horizontal types
- Eadwig 2: Horizontal types
- Edgar 55:
  - Horizontal types 54
  - Circumscription type 1

References: Peacock 1866; Thompson 1956, no. 84; BP no. 84.

This hoard was found on 5 June 1857 at the rear of 97 Eastgate Row, Chester, at a time when its owner or occupier 'was extending his cellarage northwards'. A contemporary list of coins, 'purchased from the workmen by H. J. B.', is preserved in the Grosvenor Museum.

As originally drawn up, the list recorded in its left-hand column the reverse inscriptions of two coins of Eadred of HR2 type, moneyers Thurmod and Wilaf; one coin of Eadwig of HR3 type, moneyer Æthelstan; 26 coins of Edgar of HR2 type, moneyers Ælfred, Ælfsig (two coins), Aldewine, Alhmund, Deorulf, Eadmund, Eoroth, Frethric (four coins, two reading Frethric and two Frothric), Gilys, Hrodulf, Mertin (two coins), Teothuc, Thurmod (three coins) and Werstan (two coins); and one coin of Edgar of HR3 type, moneyer Thurmod. In its right-hand column it recorded the quantity of coins of each moneyer represented in the parcel concerned. Regrettably, although the list specified the exact number of coins where there were one or two specimens of a particular moneyer, its compiler merely wrote 'several' against the names of eight of the moneyers of Edgar's HR2 type, so the list in itself is not decisive evidence for the number of coins involved.

On 14 August 1857 the compiler of the list added a note of the inscriptions of a further coin of Eadwig of HR3 type, moneyer Dorulf, and at some unspecified date the compiler also added some less carefully written transcriptions of further reverse inscriptions, although the only definite addition to the list of varieties represented is a coin of HR2 type by the moneyer Siferth, probably of Eadred's reign.

It will be noticed that of the coins listed in 1857 that of Eadred, HR2 type, moneyer Wilaf, features in neither of the parcels listed below.

In a letter read to a meeting of the Numismatic Society of London on 19 October 1865,[12] John Peacock, of Hough Green, Chester, gave a report of the discovery in which he gave a list of the names of the moneyers for each reign represented in the hoard. The list is evidently based on that drawn up in 1857, so is of no independent authority, but Peacock provides the additional information that 'the list represents about 70 or 80 coins' and that 'many others found at the same time were ignorantly broken up by the workmen and thrown among the rubbish'. He also records that 'of the coins preserved, about 60 were stolen a few days afterwards, and have never been recovered'; this would indicate that only some 10 to 20 coins remained available for study, but it is likely from the content of the surviving parcels from the hoard that the majority of the stolen coins must have passed into the possession of one or more local antiquaries.

The next evidence for the hoard is that provided by a parcel of 43 coins, 'found … in Eastgate Row in 1857', which was presented to the Grosvenor Museum on 3 April 1941 by Rev. Frederick Arthur Potts, a Church of England clergyman, using as an intermediary his cousin Henry Potts, a partner in the firm of Potts, Martyn & Co, solicitors, 21 King Street, Chester. It is likely that the coins had originally belonged to F. A. Potts's father, Frederick Potts, a Chester resident who had made a substantial collection of antiquities found in Chester. By the first week of June 1941 an accurate manuscript catalogue of the coins had been prepared by Prof. Robert Newstead, FRS (1859–1947), Honorary Curator of the Grosvenor Museum, and this, also preserved in the Museum, remains the primary evidence for the composition of the parcel. A note on the hoard by T. M. Turner, published soon afterwards in the *British Numismatic Journal*,[13] is based directly on information supplied to him by Newstead.

As it happens, only 24 coins out of these 43 can now be traced with certainty in the Grosvenor Museum. The reason for this is not clear, but the condition of all surviving coins from the hoard is poor, and it may be that the missing coins were not thought to be in good enough condition to be incorporated in the Museum's cabinets. In the summary of the parcel in Table 4, coins that appear in the catalogue part of the present volume are identified by numbers in bold, followed by a reference

[12] *NC* n.s. 6 (1866), p. 322.
[13] Turner 1944.

TABLE 4

Parcel of coins from the Chester (1857) hoard presented to the Grosvenor Museum by Rev. F. A. Potts in 1941

EADRED	
Horizontal Rosette (HR2), Chester style, Siferth, **346** (Newstead Eadred 3); Thurmod, – (Newstead Eadred 1, with drawing, 2)	3
EADWIG	
Horizontal Rosette (HR3), Chester style, Ethelstan, – (Newstead Eadwig 1, with drawing)	1
EDGAR	
Horizontal Rosette (HR2), Chester style, Ælfred, **516** (Newstead, Edgar 1); Ælfsig/Ealfsige, **522** (Newstead, Edgar 3), **528** (Newstead, Edgar 15), – (Newstead Edgar 2); Aldewin/Aldewine, **529**, **531**, **532** (Newstead, Edgar 6, 4, 5); Alhmund, **535**, **537** (Newstead, Edgar 8,7); Deorulf, **540** (Newstead, Edgar 19), – (Newstead, Edgar 18, with drawing); Eadmund, **543**, **544** (Newstead, Edgar 16, 17); Eoroth, 551 (Newstead, Edgar 9), – (Newstead, Edgar 10, 11, 12, 13, 14); Frethric/Freothric/Frothric, **554**, **556**, **557**, **560** (Newstead, Edgar 30, 25, 27, 28), – (Newstead, Edgar 24, reading Frethric), – (Newstead, Edgar 26, 29, both reading Frothric); Gilys, **566** (Newstead, Edgar 31 or 32), – (Newstead, Edgar 31 or 32); Hrodulf, – (Newstead, Edgar 33); Mertin, **569**, **570** (Newstead, Edgar 34, 35); Teothuc, **573** (Newstead, Edgar 38); Thurmod, **582** (Newstead, Edgar 20 ?), – (Newstead, Edgar 21, 22, 23); Werstan, **588**, **589** (Newstead, Edgar 36, 37)	38
Circumscription Rosette, Chester style, Thurmod, – (Newstead, Edgar 39, with drawing)	1

to Newstead's catalogue, while other coins are identified by Newstead catalogue references only.

Finally, the Grosvenor Museum possesses a further parcel of 17 coins of the same general character and physical appearance as those given to the Museum in 1941, but without provenance or accompanying documentation (Table 5). The parcel was accessioned to the Museum's collection in 1981, but it is conceivable that the coins had in fact been given to the Museum at some previous point in its history, and that their 1981 accession date is merely the date when their status was officially regularised.

Although some of these are coins that might be equated with coins catalogued by Newstead that are now missing, others of the coins do not feature in Newstead's catalogue and it seems sensible to regard this as a distinct parcel from the hoard. The probability that the hoard was in fact rather larger than scholars have until now supposed gains support from a previously overlooked statement that the hoard was 'immense'.[14]

[14] Hughes and Measom 1880, p. 52. Hughes and Measom supply the additional information that the hoard was found by workmen while excavating for a new building next door to the Church of England Educational Institute.

TABLE 5

Parcel of coins from the Chester (1857) hoard accessioned in 1981

EADWIG	
Horizontal Rosette (HR3), Chester style, Dorulf, **432** 1	1
EDGAR	
Horizontal Trefoil (HT1), Lincoln style (NE V), Adelaver, **453**	1
Horizontal Rosette (HR2), Chester style, Aldewine, **533**; Alhmund, **534**, **536**; Eadmund, **545**; Frothric, **561**, **562**, **563**, **564**; Mertin, **568**; Thurmod, **583**, **584**, **585**, **586**, **587**	14
Horizontal Rosette (HR3), Chester, Thurmod, **600** 1	

The contents of these two parcels are summarised in Table 6. The deposit of the hoard can be assigned to *c.* 970, as it contained at least one coin of Edgar's HR3 type, the last struck at Chester and at neighbouring mints before the reform of the coinage in 973. The presence in the hoard of a coin of the Chester mint of this type by the moneyer Thurmod is separately confirmed by the list compiled in 1857, by Peacock's list of 1866[15] and by the fact that the parcel accessioned in 1981 contains a coin of this moneyer and type.

TABLE 6

Summary of the 1941 and 1981 parcels from the Chester (1857) hoard

EADRED 4	
Horizontal Rosette (HR2), Chester style, Siferth, 1; Thurmod 2; Wilaf, 1	4
EADWIG 2	
Horizontal Rosette (HR3), Chester style, Dorulf, 1; Ethelstan 1	2
EDGAR 55	
Horizontal Trefoil (HT1), Lincoln style (NE V), Adelaver 1	1
Horizontal Rosette (HR2), Chester style, Ælfred 1; Ælfsig/Ealfsige 3; Aldewin/Aldewine 4; Alhmund 4; Deorulf, 2; Eadmund, 3; Eoroth 6; Frethric/Freothric/Frothric 11; Gilys 2; Hrodulf 1; Mertin 3; Teothuc 1; Thurmod 9; Werstan 2	52
Horizontal Rosette (HR3), Chester style, Thurmod 1	1

[15] *NC* n.s. 6 (1866), p. 322.

4. *FORD FARM, HARGRAVE, CHESHIRE, HOARD 1997*

Deposited c. 972 — 11 coins

Kingdom of England

Edgar 11: Horizontal Rosette (HR3) type

References: *Coin Hoards* 1999, no. 41; BP no. 171b.

A hoard of 11 coins of Edgar, all of his HR3 type, was discovered by a metal detectorist on Ford Farm, Hargrave, Cheshire, on 1 September 1997, and was subsequently acquired by Chester Museums Service for the Grosvenor Museum, Chester. Three of the coins are fragments not certainly identifiable as regards mint and moneyer. The content of the hoard can be summarised in Table 7.

TABLE 7

Contents of the Ford Farm hoard.

EDGAR	
Horizontal Rosette (HR3). Chester: Deorlaf 2; Ethelm 1; Thurmod 1. 'NE': Siulf 1. Tamworth: Deorulf 1; Monna 2. Uncertain mint and moneyer: 3	11

The coins from the hoard are nos. **593–5**, **599** and **601–7** in the present volume.

The deposit of the hoard may be assigned to *c.* 972, as it contains no coin of any previous type and no coin of the Reform Small Cross type initiated in *c.* 973.

5. *CHESTER (1914) HOARD*

Deposited c. 980 — 123+ coins

Kingdom of England

- Edgar 24: Reform Small Cross type
  - Canterbury, Derby, Leicester, Lymne, Oxford, Rochester, Southampton, Stamford, Winchester, York
- Edward the Martyr 53: Small Cross type
  - Bedford, Chester, Guildford, Lincoln, London, Lymne, Norwich, Oxford, Rochester, Southampton, Stamford, Tamworth, Wilton, Winchester, York
- Æthelred II 44:
  - Reform Small Cross type 33
    - Bedford, Chester, Derby, Lincoln, Stamford, Tamworth, Totnes, York

First Hand type 12
Chester, London, Shrewsbury, Winchester, York
Uncertain ruler 1: Reform Small Cross type
Stamford

References: Hill 1920; Thompson 1956, no. 85; BP no. 174.

The hoard was found in August 1914, 'during street repairs in Chester, lying about three feet south from the North Wall of the City, opposite the eastern angle of Pemberton's Parlour, Water Tower Street'. This geographical location for the hoard's discovery is taken from G. F. Hill's very competent publication of it.[16] A more recent document in the archives of the Grosvenor Museum indicates that the coins were found 'when laying new gas main in the Rope Walk', but this appears to be merely an alternative description of the same find spot.

Hill provides details of 121 coins, of which 110 were of the Reform Small Cross type (24 in the name of Edgar, 52 in the name of Edward the Martyr, 33 in the name of Æthelred II, and one on which the ruler's name was uncertain) and just 11 were of Æthelred II's subsequent First Hand type.

It is appropriate to note that of the 38 coins recorded by Hill as not having been acquired by the British Museum, 31 are published in the present volume: **666, 667, 668, 669, 670, 671, 672, 673, 674, 677, 678, 679, 680, 681, 682, 683, 684, 685, 686, 687, 688, 689, 690, 691, 692, 693, 694, 696, 697, 698, 699.** All these were entered in the Grosvenor Museum's accession register in November 1955 as part of a larger collection of coins made by the Chester antiquary Edward Davies. Davies's collection also contained three further coins from the hoard, respectively of Edward the Martyr, Reform Small Cross type, Chester mint, moneyer Boigea (Hill no. 32), and two of Æthelred II, First Hand type, Chester mint, moneyers Ælfstan (not listed by Hill) and Leomman (Hill no. 112); these have already been published as *SCBI* 5, 108, 110 and 109.

Of the five coins listed by Hill not then in the British Museum and not now in the Grosvenor Museum, three (his nos. 2, 28 and 76) had not in fact been seen by Hill, who describes them respectively as 'no longer to be traced', 'missing' and 'no longer forthcoming'. That leaves two coins only of those seen by Hill (his nos. 22 and 86) unaccounted for, and Hill's no. 22, a coin of Edgar, Reform Small Cross type, Winchester mint, moneyer Wihtsige, is in fact now in the British Museum.[17] For the record, Hill's nos. 22 and 86 appear from a typescript list in the files of the Grosvenor Museum to have belonged initially to a parcel of 17 coins from the hoard acquired by Alderman W. Vernon, Chester; all the other coins acquired by Vernon

[16] Hill 1920.
[17] Jonsson 1986, p. 48; kindly confirmed by Dr. Gareth Williams.

were accessioned as part of Davies' collection in 1955, but it is likely that some of the coins then accessioned had already been in the Grosvenor Museum's possession for a considerable period of time, for Hill records in his article that Vernon had already presented eight of the coins to the Museum's collection, and the typescript list also indicates that the Museum may have acquired other coins from the hoard long before 1955.

One certain omission from Hill's list, in addition to the coin of Æthelred II's First Hand type mentioned above, is a fragmentary coin in the Grosvenor Museum of Edward the Martyr, Reform Small Cross type, Bedford mint, moneyer Balddig, **675**, which came to the Museum with Edward Davies' collection, and is evidently from the 1914 hoard, in which two other coins of the same type, mint and moneyer were present.

The present catalogue also lists two coins of Reform Small Cross type presented to the Grosvenor Museum by Frank Haswell in 1949, and stated at that time to have been found 'near Chester Cathedral'. They are respectively of Edward the Martyr, Ipswich mint, moneyer Wilebert (**676**), and of Æthelred II, Lincoln mint, moneyer Rodbert (**695**). Both were struck at mints in the geographical area from which the bulk of the coins in the 1914 hoard derive, and are of similar physical appearance to coins from the hoard, and Kenneth Jonsson has therefore suggested that despite their claimed provenance they are strays from the hoard.[18]

Six other probable strays from the hoard have been described by Frank Purvey.[19]

The presence in the hoard of a small number of coins only of Æthelred II's First Hand type suggests that the hoard was deposited no later than the early 980s, and Dolley's suggestion that the deposit of the hoard was connected with a recorded Viking ravaging of Cheshire in 980 is plausible.[20]

6. TIVERTON, CHESHIRE, HOARD 2000 (deposited c. 1075)

Deposited c. 1075 6 coins

Kingdom of England
William I 6: Two Stars type
Canterbury, London, Shrewsbury, Warwick

A hoard of six coins of the Two Stars type of William I was discovered at Tiverton, Cheshire, in June 2000. The hoard was published soon afterwards by Anna Gannon

[18] Jonsson 1987, p. 231.
[19] Purvey 1969.
[20] Dolley and Pirie 1964.

and Gareth Williams.[21] The coins were subsequently acquired by the Cheshire Museums Service for the Grosvenor Museum, and appear as nos. **765–9** and **771** in the present catalogue. They are typically in brittle condition and of below average weight.

Gannon and Williams note that the period of issue of the Two Stars type is conventionally given as 1074–7, and although they are careful to assign no definite date to the deposit of the hoard, a date of *c.* 1075 or a little later would seem plausible.

[21] Gannon and Williams 2001.

COINS WITH OTHER HOARD OR FIND PROVENANCES

BP refers to the numbers in Blackburn and Pagan 1986.

HOARDS

Ballaquayle, Douglas, Isle of Man, 1894 (deposited *c.* 970; BP 143). **288, 384, 596.**

Bournemouth, Hampshire (vicinity), *c.* 1901 (deposited *c.* 1130; BP 407). **783, 786.**

Bryn Mælgwyn, Denbighshire, 1979 (deposited *c.* 1025; BP 208). **720, 721, 722, 723, 724, 725, 726, 731**.

Castle Freke, Rathbarry, Co. Cork, 1799 (deposited *c.* 945; BP 127). **91, 94, 176.**

Cuerdale, Lancashire, 1840 (deposited *c.* 905; BP 87). **805, 806 (?).**

Co. Dublin, 1883 (deposited *c.* 935; BP 117). **34.**

Co. Kilkenny, before 1824 (deposited *c.* 970; BP 170). **526.**

Co. Tipperary, 1843 ? (deposited *c.* 942; BP 125). **76.**

Ireland (stray from unlocated hoard?). **248.**

Killyon Manor, Hill of Down, co. Meath, 1876 (deposited *c.* 955; BP 138). **87, 187, 269, 342, 361**.

London, Westminster Bridge, *c.* 1895 (deposited *c.* 872; BP 68). **17.**

Stryjewo Wielkie, Ciechanow, Poland, *c.* 1970 (deposited after 1044; SCBI 37, pp. 16–17 (no. 29)). Parcel sold Glendining 14 March 1973 as from 'Polish hoard'. **737.**

Tetney, Lincolnshire, 1945 (deposited *c.* 963; BP 141). **481, 482, 483, 484, 485, 486, 487**.

'Vatican', Rome, Italy, *c.* 1928 (deposited *c.* 930; Blunt 1986, pp. 160–1 (no. 2)). Acquired by Willoughby Gardner via Glendining sale 16 May 1929, **49, 55, 65, 72, 100**; via Glendining sale 13 November 1930, **30, 43, 48, 53, 54, 61, 63, 89, 97**.

SINGLE FINDS

Chester, near Amphitheatre (single find, in or before 1955). **270.**

Meols, Cheshire (single finds ?). **703 (?), 804 (?)**. The Meols provenance of the first of these coins cannot readily be substantiated, while the second, if from Meols, may be the only survivor of this period from a collection of coins from Meols formed from 1870 onwards by Charles Potter, a Liverpool businessman, which was purchased by T. S. Gleadowe and presented by Gleadowe to the Grosvenor Museum in May 1899 (Potter's collection of finds from Meols originally contained 12 coins of the Anglo-Saxon and Norman periods, but the remaining coins were already missing from the Grosvenor Museum in 1961). See now Bean 2007.

COLLECTORS, DONORS AND DEALERS

Ailesbury, 5th Marquis of (1842–1911). Sotheby, 29 June 1903 ('Nobleman', the collection presumably accumulated by previous holders of the title). **184**.

Allen, William (*c.* 1808–97). Sotheby, 14 March 1898. **201**.

Bain, Richard Donald (1850–1927). Sotheby, 8 May 1928 ('Collector'). **173, 549, 580**.

Banks, Frederick (1918–76). Purchase, 1965. **741**.

Bascom, George Jonathan (b. 1845). Sotheby, 15 June 1914. **332**.

Bateman, William (1787–1835) and Bateman, Thomas (1821–61). Sotheby, 4 May 1893 ('Bateman Heirlooms'). **202, 429**.

Bearman, Thomas (1846–1921). Collection sold by private treaty to Baldwin. **134 (?)**.

Bliss, Thomas (1849–1914). Sotheby, 22 March 1916. **384, 454**.

Brand, Virgil Michael (1862–1926). Collection widely dispersed by private treaty from 1932 onwards. **302, 638**.

Brice, William (*c.* 1812–1887). Collection sold by private treaty to Hyman Montagu, 1887. **36**

Bridges, George Henry Newington (*c.* 1844–1918). Puttick & Simpson, 12 December 1918 (lots 91–126). **729, 755, 759**.

Briggs, Arthur (1836–1892). Sotheby, 22 March 1893. **193, 287, 331, 355**.

Bruun, Lars Emil (1852–1923). Sotheby, 18 May 1925. **60, 591, 734A**.

Carlyon-Britton, Philip William Poole (1863–1938). Sotheby, 17 November 1913, **35, 40, 64, 84, 94, 256, 302, 303, 323, 345, 362, 368, 474, 574, 613, 638**; Sotheby, 20 November 1916, **74, 95, 134, 180, 184, 248, 263, 268, 288, 326, 477, 504, 508, 521, 548, 567, 571, 612, 656, 789** ; Sotheby, 11 November 1918, **422, 437, 639, 647, 787, 788**. A further portion of the collection was sold through Spink, *NCirc* March–April 1922: **50**. One coin, the only one still to be accompanied by Carlyon-Britton's original ticket, was acquired from him by Willoughby Gardner by exchange: **596**. The following coins are also recorded as having belonged to him: **98, 273, 792, 799**.

'Collector in the North of England'. Glendining, 6 June 1934. **630**.

Copenhagen, Royal Collection. **802** (duplicate sold to Willoughby Gardner).

Cox, Joseph. Sotheby, 6 April 1892. **527**.

Crompton-Roberts, Charles Montague (1865–1931). Collection sold by private treaty to Spink, and offered in *NCirc*, September–October 1920 and November–December 1921 . **19, 36, 38, 46, 71, 188, 189, 193, 202, 287, 331, 355, 641**.

Cuff, James Dodsley (1780–1853). Sotheby, 8 June 1854. **74 (?)**.

Davies, Edward. Antiquary and a donor to the Grosvenor Museum in 1955. **227, 666, 667, 668, 669, 670, 671, 672, 673, 674, 675, 677, 678, 679, 680, 681, 682, 683, 684, 684, 685, 686, 687, 688, 689, 690, 691, 692, 693, 694, 696, 697, 698, 699, 708, 783**.

Dawnay, Hon. Lewis Payan (1846–1910). Sotheby, 1 May 1922. **169, 450**.

Day, George. Unidentified (vendor (?) to Willoughby Gardner, after 1909). **526**.

Drabble, Gilbert Creswick (1875–1939). Glendining, 4 July 1939. **590, 611, 632**.

Duart-Smith, Frederick William (1868–1945). Glendining, 27 November 1945. **169, 752**.

Dudman, John (1846–1913). Sotheby, 15 December 1913. **201, 597**.

Evans, Sir John (1823–1908). Much of collection sold by private treaty to Spink. Most of the coins acquired from it by Willoughby Gardner derive from the listing of coins from the collection in *NCirc*, June 1910 (and some of these are still accompanied by Evans's original tickets). **87, 91, 94, 176, 187, 196, 248, 269, 330, 342, 361, 509**.

Francis, Grant Richardson (1868–1940). Portion of collection sold by private treaty to Spink in 1915 (?). **328 (?), 552 (?)**.

Gantz, Rev. William Lewis (1873–1940). Coins sold by him to Willoughby Gardner by private treaty. **35, 65, 72, 255, 275, 344, 579, 609, 756**.

Gardner, Willoughby (1860–1953). Purchase, 1952; gift, 1963 (by his widow). See introduction.

'Gentleman'. Sotheby, 18 February 1907. **302**.

'Gentleman'. Sotheby, 21 November 1911. **166**.

Gibbs, James (1825–86). Collection purchased by 1891 by Spink (the English and related coins in it had perhaps been collected by his brother Joseph Gibbs). **641**.

Grantley, 5th Baron (1855–1943). Glendining, 27 January 1944, **7**; Glendining, 22 March 1944, **17, 39, 69, 76, 126, 153, 245, 527, 637**. The following coin also belonged to him: **705**.

Harris, Eric James (b.1915). Purchase, 1962. **645**.

Haswell, Frank. Gift, 1949. **676, 695**.

Hazlitt, William Carew (1834–1913). Sotheby, 5 July 1909. **96**.

Heeley, Frank (1891–1964). **803**.

Hirons, A.C. Gift, 1955. **270**.

Howard, Hugh (1675–1738). Sotheby, 20 May 1874 (coins sold by his descendant, 5th Earl of Wicklow). **193, 287**.

Jones, Francis Elmore (1898–1982). Glendining, 12 May 1971. **712, 730, 739, 763**.

Lawrence, Henry (1779–1864). Sotheby, 18 July 1923. **78, 167, 305**.

Lawrence, Laurie Asher (1857–1949). A selection of Anglo-Saxon coins from his first collection were sold by him to 5th Baron Grantley in 1903. **705**.

Lindsay, John (1789–1870). Sotheby, 14 August 1867. **74**.

Lockett, Richard Cyril (1873–1950). Glendining, 4 November 1958. **125**. Two coins from his collection were given by him to Willoughby Gardner. **92, 184**.

Londesborough, 1st Baron (1805–1860). Christie, 4 July 1888 (coins sold as property of his son, 1st Earl of Londesborough). **218**.

Longbottom, Frederick William (1858–1933). Gift, 1899. **734**.

McClean, Frank (1837–1904). Sotheby, 11 June 1906 ('Astronomer'). **35, 40, 64, 429**.

Mack, Cdr Richard Paston (1901–74). Glendining/Spink, 18 November 1975, **22, 31, 77**; Glendining/Spink, 23 March 1977, **75**.

Marsham, Hon. Robert (1834–1914). Sotheby, 19 November 1888. **46**.

Maynard, Rev. John (*c.* 1799–1877). Sotheby, 10 August 1885. **192**.

Montagu, Hyman (*c.* 1845–1895). Sotheby, 18 November 1895. **19, 35, 134, 153, 156, 218, 330, 542, 641**.

Nunn, John Joseph (1835–1896). Sotheby, 27 November 1896. **46**.

O'Hagan, Henry Osborne (1853–1930). Sotheby, 16 December 1908. **542**.

Parsons, Harry Alexander (1876–1952). Sotheby, 28 October 1929. **341, 635, 788**. He also sold coins privately to Willoughby Gardner: **207, 219, 770**. One other coin may derive from his collection: **803 (?)**.

Peace, Maskell William (1834–1892). Sotheby, 15 June 1894. **188**.

Pirie, Elizabeth Jean Elphinstone (1932–2005). **803**.

Potts, Rev. Frederick Arthur. Gift, 1941. See discussion of Chester (1857) hoard above.

Pritchard, William (*c.* 1832–*c.* 1905). Bequest, 1905. **700, 764, 796 (?)**.

Rashleigh, Jonathan (1820–1905). Sotheby, 21 June 1909 (coins sold as property of his son Evelyn William Rashleigh). **74 (?), 125, 526**.

Ready, William Talbot (1857–1914). Sotheby, 15 November 1920 (dealer, but English coins in sale apparently his private collection). **181, 200, 267, 312, 773** (or **774**).

Rebello, David Alves (1741–1796). Collection inherited by his son Isaac Alves Rebello (d. 1803) and subsequently sold to Richard Miles, coin dealer (and to others). **504**.

Reynolds, Henry Muskett (1853–1948). Sotheby, 4 May 1914. **519**.

Roth, Bernard Mathias Simon (1852–1915). Sotheby, 19 July 1917. **756**. Sotheby, 14 October 1918, **640**.

Ryan, Valentine John Eustace (1882–1947). Glendining, 22 January 1952. **510**.

Sheppard, Rev. John Lewin (1794–1821). Sotheby, 14 January 1861. **201**.

Stretton, William (1755–1828). Sotheby, 17 March 1855. **526**.

Thorburn, Henry William (1846–1918). Sotheby, 27 November 1918. **205, 218**.

Walters, Frederick Arthur (1849–1931). Sotheby, 24 October 1932. **451, 615, 790**.

Wells, William Charles (1870–1949). Coins acquired from him by Willoughby Gardner. **549** (by exchange), **565, 580, 734A**.

Wheeler, Ernest Henry (1876–1933). Sotheby, 12 March 1930. **473, 577, 619, 640**. He also owned **530**.

Williams, Lieut.-Col. Alan. Gifts, 1953 and 1955. **710, 711, 782**.

Young, Joseph (*c.* 1844–1918). Sotheby, 5 February 1919. **110, 354, 634**. He also owned **746**.

(Unidentified Property). Sotheby, 12 June 1899. **288**.

(Unidentified Property) 'Glendining, August 1913' (so stated on ticket, but reference wrong: no Glendining sale in August 1913). **478**.

(Unidentified Property). Glendining, 23 July 1923. **559**.

(Unidentified Property). Sotheby, 15 December 1931. **86, 194, 324**.

DEALERS

A. H. Baldwin & Sons Ltd, London. **18, 29, 41, 47, 48, 59, 85, 89, 93, 97, 100, 135, 167, 178, 192, 195, 198, 205, 305, 327, 334, 340, 341, 353, 361, 451, 475, 479, 480, 559, 590, 591, 620, 635, 637, 701, 714, 738, 747, 750, 751, 762, 773, 774, 775, 776, 778, 788, 790, 791, 794**. Some of the coins are accompanied by the Baldwin firm's original tickets.

J. H. Dormer, London. **201**

L. S. Forrer, London. **302, 436, 638**.

D. H. Hess, Baton Rouge, Louisiana, USA. **786**.

W. S. Lincoln Ltd, London. **43, 60, 62, 66, 68, 70, 94, 96, 105, 151, 156, 166, 171, 173, 179, 181, 186, 199, 200, 244, 253, 267, 307, 311, 312, 321, 329, 351, 352, 358, 363, 429, 514, 520, 524, 629, 718, 760**. Some of the coins are accompanied by the Lincoln firm's original tickets.

S. & B. Coins (Simon Monks and Brian Reeds), Amersham. **707**.

B. A. Seaby Ltd, London. **7, 14 (?), 17, 69, 111, 112, 137, 140, 142, 153, 177, 436, 549, 630, 705, 728, 736 (?), 740, 741, 748**. Some of the coins are accompanied by the Seaby firm's original tickets.

Spink & Son Ltd, London (with *NCirc* numbers): **19, 34, 36, 37, 38, 46, 50, 67, 71, 87, 91, 163, 168, 176, 182, 188, 189, 193, 196, 202, 204, 206, 248, 269, 273, 287, 302, 328, 331, 343, 350, 355, 361, 437, 506, 509, 538, 542, 555, 572, 618, 639, 743, 780, 781, 793, 806, 807**. Other: **58, 94, 98, 187, 197, 256, 264, 323, 332, 342, 345, 362, 366, 422, 450, 474, 513, 519, 578, 598, 642, 647, 704, 727, 736 (?), 745**. With one possible exception (**328**, apparently ex Grant Francis), none of the coins are accompanied by the Spink firm's tickets. This would suggest that coins posted to Willoughby Gardner by Spink were customarily sent out without their accompanying tickets; if that was Spink's policy with all clients, that would account for the poor survival rate of older Spink coin tickets generally.

ABBREVIATIONS AND BIBLIOGRAPHY

Allen 1971	D. F. Allen, 'British potin coins: a review', in *The Iron Age and Its Hill-Forts. Papers Presented to Sir Mortimer Wheeler*, ed. M. Jesson and D. Hill (Southampton, 1971), pp. 127–48.
Archibald 1967	M. M. Archibald, 'Disposition of the Chester (1950) hoard', *BNJ* 36 (1967), 189.
BD	*see* Blunt and Dolley 1954.
Bean 2007	S. Bean, 'The coins', in *Meols: the Archaeology of the North Wirral Coast. Discoveries and Observations in the 19th and 20th Centuries, with a Catalogue of Collections*, G. Griffiths *et al.*, (Oxford, 2007), pp. 295–350.
Blackburn 1981	M. A. S. Blackburn, 'An imitative workshop active during Æthelred II's *Long Cross* issue', in *Studies in Northern Coinages of the Eleventh Century*, ed. C. J. Becker (Copenhagen, 1981), pp. 29–88.
Blackburn and Lyon 1986	M. A. S. Blackburn and C. S. S. Lyon, 'Regional Die-Production in Cnut's Quatrefoil issue', in *Anglo-Saxon Monetary History: Essays in Memory of Michael Dolley*, ed. M. A. S. Blackburn (Leicester, 1986), pp. 223–72.
Blackburn and Pagan 1986	M. A. S. Blackburn and H. Pagan, 'A revised check-list of coin hoards from the British Isles *c.* 500–1100', in *Anglo-Saxon Monetary History: Essays in Memory of Michael Dolley*, ed. M. A. S. Blackburn (Leicester, 1986), pp. 291–313 (updated on-line version available at www.medievalcoins.org).
Blunt 1973	C. E. Blunt, 'The coinage of Athelstan, king of England 924–39', *BNJ* 42 (1973), 35–160.
Blunt and Dolley 1954	C. E. Blunt and R. H. M. Dolley, 'The Chester (1950) hoard', *BNJ* 27 (1954), 125–60.
Blunt, Stewart and Lyon 1986	*see CTCE.*
BMC	C. F. Keary and H. A. Grueber, *A Catalogue of English Coins in the British Museum. Anglo-Saxon Series*, 2 vols. (London, 1887–93).

	G. C. Brooke, *A Catalogue of English Coins in the British Museum. The Norman Kings*, 2 vols. (London, 1916).
	D. F. Allen, *A Catalogue of English Coins in the British Museum. The Cross-and-Crosslets ('Tealby') Type of Henry II* (London, 1951).
BNJ	*British Numismatic Journal.*
Boon 1986	G. C. Boon, *Welsh Hoards 1979–1981* (Cardiff, 1986).
BP	*see* Blackburn and Pagan 1986.
Brooke 1916	*see BMC.*
Coin Hoards	*annual section in each volume of NC since 1994.*
CTCE	C. E. Blunt, B. H. I. H. Stewart and C. S. S. Lyon, *Coinage in Tenth-Century England* (Oxford, 1989).
Dolley 1961	R. H. M. Dolley, 'The Anglo-Saxon coins from Meols Sands', *Transactions of the Historic Society of Lancashire and Cheshire* 113 (1961), 197–201.
Dolley and Morrison 1962	R. H. M. Dolley and K. F. Morrison, 'A note on four "type immobilisé" coins of Melle from British finds', *NC*[7] 2 (1962), 157–60.
Dolley and Pirie 1964	R. H. M. Dolley and E. J. E. Pirie, 'The repercussions on Chester's prosperity of the viking descent on Cheshire in 980', *BNJ* 33 (1964), 39–44.
Eaglen 1999	R. J. Eaglen, 'The Mint of Huntingdon', *BNJ* 69 (1999), 47–145.
Gannon and Williams 2001	A. Gannon and G. Williams, 'Two small hoards of William I', *BNJ* 71 (2001), 162–4 and plate 36.
Graham-Campbell 2001	J. Graham-Campbell, 'The dual economy of the Danelaw', *BNJ* 71 (2001), 49–59.
Grierson and Blackburn 1986	P. Grierson and M. A. S. Blackburn, *Medieval European Coinage, with a Catalogue of the Coins in the Fitzwilliam Museum, Cambridge. Vol. 1: The Early Middle Ages (5th–10th Centuries)* (Cambridge, 1986).
Hild.	B. E. Hildebrand, *Anglosachsiska mynt i Svenska Kongliga Myntkabinettet*, rev. ed. (Stockholm, 1881).
Hill 1920	G. F. Hill, 'A find of coins of Eadgar, Eadweard II, and Æthelred II at Chester', *NC*[4] 20 (1920), 141–65.
Hughes 1864	T. Hughes, 'On some Anglo-Saxon coins discovered in the foundations of St John's church, Chester', *Journal of the Architectural, Archaeological and Historic Society of the County, City and Neighbourhood of Chester* 2 (1864), 289–308.

Hughes and Measom 1880 — T. Hughes and G. S. Measom, *The Stranger's Handbook to Chester* (Chester, 1880).

Jonsson 1986 — K. Jonsson, *Viking-Age Hoards and Late Anglo-Saxon Coins: a Study in Honour of Bror Emil Hildebrand's Anglosachsiska mynt* (Stockholm, 1986).

Jonsson 1987 — K. Jonsson, *The New Era: the Reformation of the Late Anglo-Saxon Coinage*, Commentationes de nummis saeculorum IX–XI in Suecia repertis: nova series 1 (Stockholm, 1987).

Keary and Grueber 1887 — *see BMC.*

Kruse and Tait 1992 — S. E. Kruse and J. Tait, 'XRF analysis of Viking-age silver ingots', *Proceedings of the Society of Antiquaries of Scotland* 122 (1992), 295–328.

Longbottom 1908 — F. W. Longbottom, 'A few notes on the coins of the Potter-Meols collection, found on the Cheshire shore, and presented to the Chester and North Wales Archaeological Society by Mr. T. S. Gleadowe', *Journal of the Architectural, Archaeological, and Historic Society for the County and the City of Chester, and North Wales*[2] 14 (1908), 5–17.

Mack 1967 — R. P. Mack, 'St John's church, Chester, hoard of 1864', *BNJ* 36 (1967), 36–9.

MEC 1 — *see* Grierson and Blackburn 1986.

Mossop 1970 — H. R. Mossop, *The Lincoln Mint, c. 890–1279* (Newcastle-upon-Tyne, 1970).

NC — *Numismatic Chronicle.*

NCirc — Spink's *Numismatic Circular.*

O'Donovan 1964 — M. A. O'Donovan, 'The Vatican hoard of Anglo-Saxon pennies', *BNJ* 33 (1964), 7–29.

Pagan 1995 — H. Pagan, 'Mints and moneyers in the West Midlands and at Derby in the reign of Eadmund (939–946)', *NC* 155 (1995), 139–64.

Peacock 1862 — J. Peacock, 'Saxon coins found at Chester', *NC*[2] 2 (1862), 305–6.

Peacock 1866 — J. Peacock, 'Find of Saxon coins at Chester', *NC*[2] 6 (1866), 322.

Pirie 1996 — E. J. E.Pirie, *Coins of the Kingdom of Northumbria c. 700-867 in the Yorkshire collections* (Llanfyllin, 1996).

Purvey 1969 — P. F. Purvey, 'Six remarkable late 10th-century pennies', *Seaby's Coin and Medal Bulletin* 609 (May 1969), 151–5.

Rigold 1977 — S. E. Rigold, 'The principal series of English *Sceattas*', *BNJ* 47 (1977), 21–30.

Saccocci 2009 — A. Saccocci, 'Un denario veneziano di Ottone III imperatore (996–1002) dagli scavi del monasterio di Santa Maria in valle a Cividale', *Forum Iulii* 33 (2009), 139–47.

SCBI 1 — P. Grierson, *Sylloge of Coins of the British Isles, vol. 1: Fitzwilliam Museum, Cambridge* (London, 1958).

SCBI 2 — A. S. Robertson, *Sylloge of Coins of the British Isles, vol. 2: Huntarian and Coats Collections, University of Glasgow, part I: Anglo-Saxon Coins* (London, 1961).

SCBI 4 — G. Galster, *Sylloge of Coins of the British Isles, vol. 4: Royal Collection of Coins and Medals, National Museum Copenhagen, part I: Ancient British and Anglo-Saxon Coins before Æthelred II* (London, 1964).

SCBI 5 — E. J. E. Pirie, *Sylloge of Coins of the British Isles, vol. 5: Grosvenor Museum, Chester part I: the Willoughby Gardner Collection of Coins with the Chester Mint Signature* (London, 1964).

SCBI 6 — R. B. K. Stevenson, *Sylloge of Coins of the British Isles, vol. 6: National Museum of Antiquities of Scotland, part I: Anglo Saxon Coins (with Associated Foreign Coins)* (London, 1966).

SCBI 9 — J. D. A. Thompson, *Sylloge of Coins of the British Isles, vol. 9: The Ashmolean Museum, Oxford* (London, 1967).

SCBI 16 — C. E. Blunt, F. Elmore Jones and R. P. Mack, *Sylloge of coins of the British Isles, vol. 16: Collection of Ancient British, Romano-British and English Coins Formed by Mrs Emery May Norweb of Cleveland, Ohio, USA: Part 1: Ancient British, Romano-British, Anglo-Saxon and Post-Conquest Coins to 1180* (London, 1971).

SCBI 17 — A. J. H. Gunstone, *Sylloge of Coins of the British Isles, vol. 17: Ancient British, Anglo-Saxon and Norman Coins in Midlands Museums* (London, 1971).

SCBI 20 — R. P. Mack, *Sylloge of Coins of the British Isles, vol. 20: Ancient British, Anglo-Saxon and Norman Coins in the Collection formed by Commander R. P. Mack R.N.* (London, 1973).

SCBI 21 — E. Pirie, *Sylloge of Coins of the British Isles, vol. 21: Coins in Yorkshire Museums* (London, 1975).

SCBI 26 — T. H. McK. Clough, *Sylloge of Coins of the British Isles, vol. 26: Museums in East Anglia* (London, 1980).

SCBI 27 — A. Gunstone, *Sylloge of Coins of the British Isles, vol. 27: Lincolnshire Collections* (London,1981).

SCBI 29 — M. Warhurst, *Sylloge of Coins of the British Isles, vol. 29: Merseyside County Museums* (London, 1982).

SCBI 30 — J. D. Brady, *Sylloge of Coins of the British Isles, vol. 30: Ancient British, Anglo-Saxon and Norman Coins in American Collections* (London, 1982).

SCBI 34 — M. M. Archibald and C. E. Blunt, *Sylloge of Coins of the British Isles, vol. 34: British Museum, Anglo-Saxon Coins V, Athelstan to the Reform of Edgar 924–c. 973* (London, 1986).

SCBI 36 — B. Kluge, *Sylloge of Coins of the British Isles, vol. 36: State Museum, Berlin Coin Cabinet, Anglo-Saxon, Anglo-Norman, and Hiberno-Norse Coins* (London, 1987).

SCBI 50 — V. M. Potin, *Sylloge of Coins of the British Isles, vol. 50: Hermitage Museum, St Petersburg* (Oxford, 1999).

SCMB — Seaby's *Coin and Medal Bulletin.*

Thompson 1956 — J. D. A. Thompson, *Inventory of British Coin Hoards A.D. 600–1500*, Royal Numismatic Society Special Publications 1 (Oxford, 1956).

Turner 1944 — T. M. Turner, 'A find of coins of Eadred, Eadwig and Eadgar at Chester', *BNJ* 24 (1941–4), 47–9.

Van Arsdell — R. D. Van Arsdell, *Celtic Coinage of Britain* (London, 1989).

Webster 1953 — G. W. Webster, 'A Saxon treasure hoard found at Chester, 1950', *Antiquaries Journal* 33 (1953), 22–32.

PLATES

IRON AGE

BRITISH POTIN COINAGE

	Weight g	Weight gr.	Die-Axis	
1.	1.21	18.6	–	Allen 1971 class H; Van Arsdell 129. Willoughby Gardner (via Mrs Gardner 1963).

EASTERN AND CENTRAL REGIONS (CATUVELLAUNI AND TRINOVANTES)

CUNOBELIN

	g	gr.	Die-Axis	
2.	2.00	31.0	180°	CVNOBELIN/TASCIO. AE, Van Arsdell 2097. Willoughby Gardner (via Mrs Gardner 1963).

SOUTH-WESTERN REGIONS (DUROTRIGES)

	g	gr.	Die-Axis	
3.	5.35	82.7	–	White gold or AR stater, Van Arsdell 1235. Willoughby Gardner (via Mrs Gardner 1963).

EAST ANGLIA (ICENI)

	g	gr.	Die-Axis	
4.	1.13	17.5	–	ANTED. AR, Van Arsdell 711. Willoughby Gardner (via Mrs Gardner 1963).
5.	1.21	18.7	–	ECE. AR, Van Arsdell 762. Willoughby Gardner (via Mrs Gardner 1963).

ANGLO-SAXON

ANGLO-SAXON AND FRISIAN SILVER 'SCEATTAS'

The series classification is that of Rigold 1977.

	g	gr.	Die-Axis	
6.	1.18	18.2	–	Series A, type 2a. Willoughby Gardner.
7.	1.28	19.6	–	Series B, type 27. Willoughby Gardner; ex Seaby; ex Grantley 710.
8.	0.92	14.2	–	Series E ('porcupine'). Willoughby Gardner.
9.	0.86	13.2	–	Series E (derivative). Willoughby Gardner.

KINGDOM OF NORTHUMBRIA

BASE SILVER AND COPPER 'STYCAS'

EANRED (810–41?)

	g	gr.	Die-Axis	
10.	1.22	18.8	315°	Eadvini (*Eadwine*). Dies not in Pirie 1996. Willoughby Gardner.
11.	1.24	19.2	270°	Fordred (*Fordræd*). Same dies as Pirie 1996, 1321. Willoughby Gardner.
12.	1.34	20.7	0°	Hvætred (*Hwætræd*). Dies not in Pirie 1996. Willoughby Gardner.

ÆTHELRED II (first reign, 841–4?)

	g	gr.	Die-Axis	
13.	1.17	18.0	0°	Vvlfsig (*Wulfsige*). Same dies as Pirie 1996, 1720 (wrongly assigned to Æthelred II's second reign). Willoughby Gardner.

ARCHBISHOPS OF YORK

WIGMUND (*c.* 837–54)

	g	gr.	Die-Axis	
14.	1.28	19.7	0°	Coenred (*Coenræd*). Same obv. die as Pirie 1996, 400–1; same rev. die as Pirie 1996, 411. Willoughby Gardner (via Mrs Gardner 1963); ex 'Seaby 50707' (*sic* in Moore typescript, but it seems more likely that this is a Spink number from *NCirc*).

[*continued overleaf*]

PLATE 1

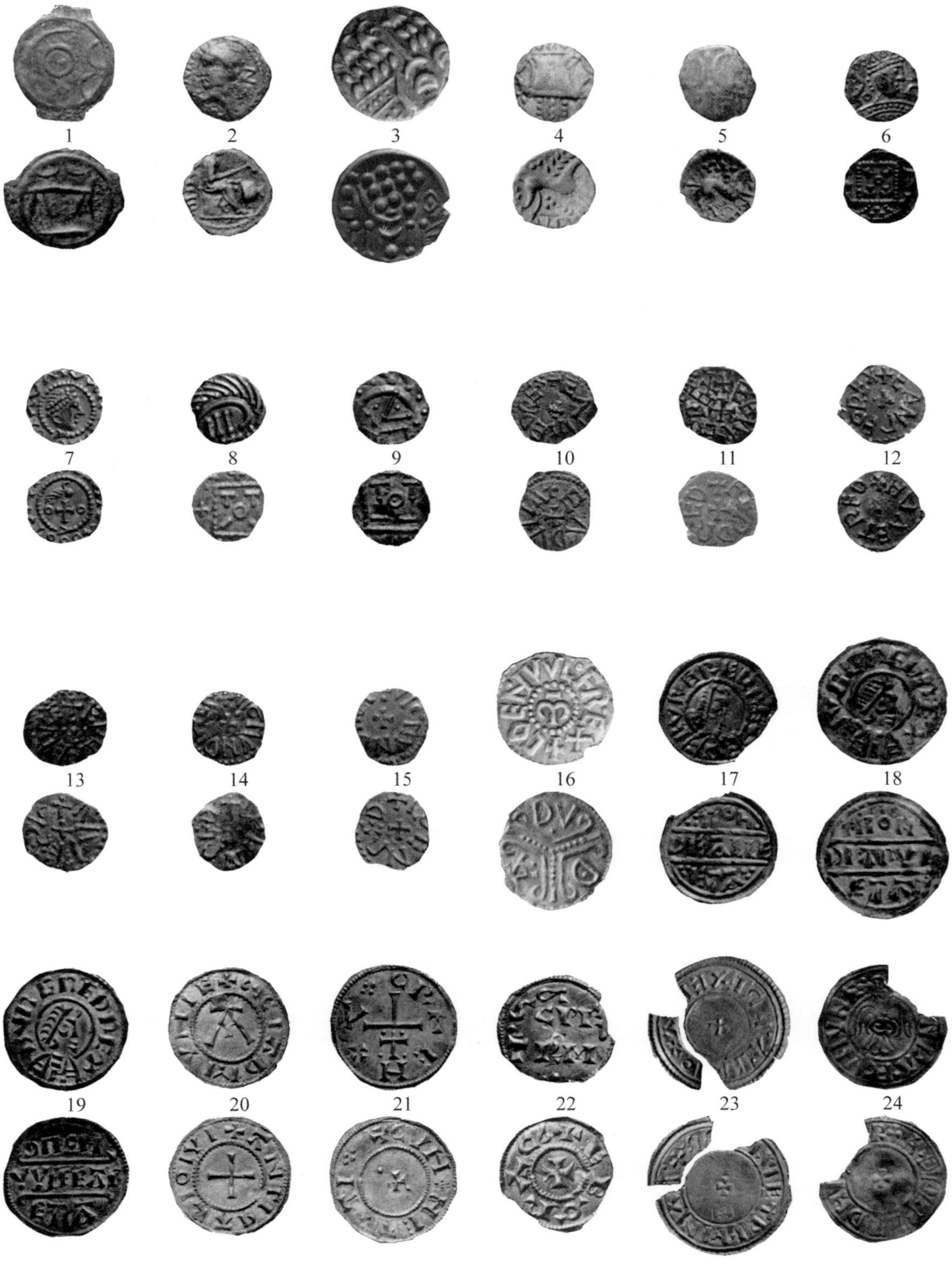

WIGMUND (*cont.*)

	Weight g	*Weight* gr.	*Die-Axis*	
15.	1.48	22.9	180°	Coenred (*Coenræd*). Obv. die not in Pirie 1996; same rev. die as previous coin. Willoughby Gardner.

KINGDOM OF MERCIA

COENWULF (796–821)

Canterbury, M/Tribrach issue (797/8–805): North 342

16.	1.10 slightly chipped	16.9	180°	Duda. No provenance.

BURGRED (852–74)

London, Bust/Lunette issue: Reverse variety *BMC* type A

17.	1.06 chipped	16.4	270°	Dealle (*Dealla*). Willoughby Gardner; ex Seaby; ex Grantley (1944) 870, 'found under Westminster Bridge', i.e. ex Westminster Bridge hoard. The only known coin for Burgred on which the moneyer's name is spelled thus (another coin exists on which it is spelled DEALGE).
18.	1.03	15.9	180°	Diarvlf (*Deorwulf*). Willoughby Gardner (via Mrs Gardner 1963); ex Baldwin (with Baldwin stock ticket B5118).

Reverse variety *BMC* type D

19.	1.31	20.2	90°	Vvlfeard (*Wulfheard*). Willoughby Gardner (via Mrs Gardner 1963); ex Spink (*NCirc* Sep–Oct 1920, 85566) (C. M. Crompton-Roberts collection); and ex Montagu (1895) 276.

VIKING KINGDOMS

EAST ANGLIA

ST EDMUND MEMORIAL COINAGE

Pre-Cuerdale issue (*c.* 895–905): North 483

20.	1.26	19.4	270°	Ansigar. Willoughby Gardner (via Mrs Gardner 1963).

VIKINGS OF NORTHUMBRIA

Unless otherwise stated the mint is presumed to be York.

CNUT (*c.* 900–5)

21.	1.30	20.1	90°	Rev. CVNNETTI. Willoughby Gardner. North 501.

ST PETER, SWORDLESS (*c.* 905–15)

22.	1.07 chipped	16.5	90°	EBORACO. Purchased 1975; ex Mack (1975) 102 (*SCBI 20*, 689); ex Chester (1862) hoard (Hughes no.12).

ANLAF GUTHFRITHSSON (939–41)

Circumscription Cross

23.	– two fragments	–	–	(Derby), no moneyer's name. Retrograde obv. legend and meaningless rev. legend, with M in field. Chester (1950) hoard, no. 518.

Raven/Cross

24.	1.04 badly chipped	16.1	0°	Athelferth (*Æthelferth*). Chester (1950) hoard, no. 517.

ANLAF SIHTRICSSON (941–4)

Triquetra/Standard

	Weight g	gr.	Die-Axis	
25.	– small fragment	–	–	[ ]rm[ ] (*Farman*). Chester (1950) hoard, no. 516.
Cross Moline/Cross(?)				
26.	– small fragment	–	–	[ ]dul[ ] (*Rædwulf*). Chester (1950) hoard, not in published list

ERIC BLOODAXE (first reign 947–8)

Sword/Cross

27.	– small fragment	–	–	[ ]adul[ ] (*Rædwulf*). Chester (1950) hoard, not in published list.

KINGDOM OF WESSEX

ALFRED (871–99)

Horizontal Pellet

28.	– three fragments	–	–	*Canterbury* ([ ]RO), [ ]iarvald (*Deorweald*). Chester (1950) hoard, no. 1.
Horizontal blank				
29.	1.57	24.2	270°	Aethered (*Æthelræd*). Winchester style. Willoughby Gardner (via Mrs Gardner 1963); ex Baldwin.

EDWARD THE ELDER (899–924)

Coin-types are as used in *CTCE*.

Bust diademed

30.	1.55 chipped	23.9	0°	Rægenulf (*Rægenwulf*). Winchester style. Willoughby Gardner; ex Glendining 13 Nov 1930, lot 51; ex 'Vatican' hoard (O'Donovan 1964, 446).
Horizontal Cross				
31.	1.26 badly chipped	19.4	180°	[ ]advvold (*Eadweald*). North West Midlands style (Chester?). Purchased 1975; ex Mack (1975) 116 (*SCBI 20*, 745); ex Chester (1862) hoard (Hughes no.2). Same obv. die as *SCBI 20*, 764, Tower (Reliquary) type, moneyer Eadwald.
Horizontal Trefoil				
32.	1.44	22.2	0°	Beahstan (*Beagstan*)). London style. Chester (1950) hoard, no. 3.
33.	1.52 slightly chipped	23.4	180°	Deora. London style. Willoughby Gardner.
34.	1.57 slightly chipped	24.2	180°	Abba. North West Midlands style (Chester?). Willoughby Gardner; ex Spink (*NCirc* Jun 1910, 76517) (Sir John Evans collection); ex Co. Dublin (1883) hoard.
35.	1.35 chipped	20.8	270°	Abba. North West Midlands style (Chester?). Willoughby Gardner; perhaps ex P. Carlyon-Britton (1916) 948 (lot purchased by Gantz); perhaps ex 'Astronomer' (F. McLean) (1906) 161.
36.	1.57	24.2	180°	Abba. North West Midlands style (Chester?). Willoughby Gardner; ex Spink (*NCirc* Nov–Dec 1921, 98525) (C. M. Crompton-Roberts collection).
37.	1.55 slightly chipped	23.9	–	Beorard. North West Midlands style (Chester?). Willoughby Gardner; ex Spink (*NCirc* Mar 1906, 25062).
38.	1.51 chipped	23.3	90°	Eadmund. North West Midlands style (Chester?). Willoughby Gardner; ex Spink (*NCirc* Sep-Oct 1920, 85586) (C. M. Crompton-Roberts collection).
39.	1.62	25.0	180°	Tiot(es). North West Midlands style (Chester?). Willoughby Gardner; ex Grantley (1944) 1032. Same obv. die as next.
40.	1.60	24.7	0°	Tiot(es). North West Midlands style (Chester?). Willoughby Gardner; ex P. Carlyon-Britton (1916) 952; ex 'Astronomer' (F. McLean) (1906) 161. Same obv. die as last.

[*continued overleaf*]

PLATE 2

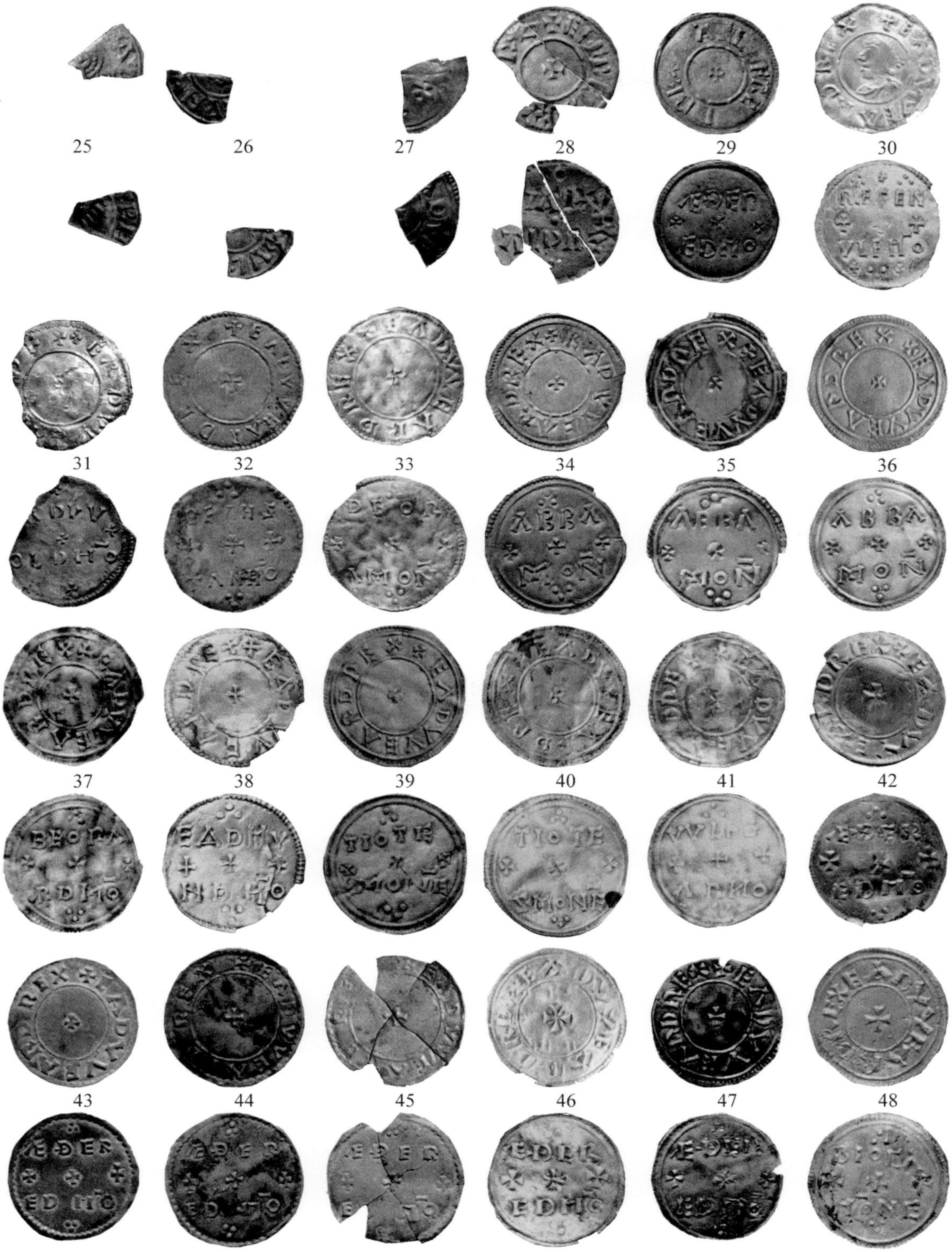

Plate 2 (*cont.*)

EDWARD THE ELDER (*cont.*)

Horizontal Trefoil (*cont.*)

	Weight *g*	*gr.*	*Die-Axis*	
41.	2.14	33.0	90°	Vvlfgar (*Wulfgar*). North West Midlands style (Chester?). Willoughby Gardner; ex Baldwin. The weight suggests that the coin might be a cast, but, if so, the original from which the cast was made is not known today.
42.	1.48 slightly chipped	22.8	270°	Æthered (*Æthelræd*). Winchester style. Willoughby Gardner.
43.	1.60	24.7	0°	Æthered (*Æthelræd*). Winchester style. Willoughby Gardner; ex Lincoln ex Glendining 13 Nov 1930, lot 66; ex 'Vatican' hoard (O'Donovan 1964, 75, 76 or 78).
44.	1.57	24.2	180°	Æthered (*Æthelræd*). Winchester style. Willoughby Gardner.
45.	– fragmentary	–	–	Æthered (*Æthelræd*). Winchester style. Chester (1950) hoard, 1975 parcel coin 1.
46.	1.53	23.6	270°	Æthered (*Æthelræd*). Winchester style. Willoughby Gardner; ex Spink (*NCirc* Sep–Oct 1920, 85585) (C. M. Crompton-Roberts collection); ex Nunn (1896) 91; ex Marsham (1888) 157.
47.	1.23 circular chip at edge, where originally pierced	19.0	270°	Æthered (*Æthelræd*). Winchester style. Willoughby Gardner; ex Baldwin.
48.	1.56	24.1	0°	Bioca (*Boga*). Winchester style. Willoughby Gardner; ex Baldwin; ex Glendining 13 Nov 1930, lot 77; ex 'Vatican' hoard (O'Donovan 1964, 171, where moneyer's name incorrectly given as Boica).

EDWARD THE ELDER (*cont.*)

Horiztonal Trefoil (*cont.*)

	Weight g	Weight gr.	Die-Axis	
49.	1.39 chipped	21.4	180°	Eadmund. Winchester style. Willoughby Gardner; ex Glendining 16 May 1929, lot 79; ex 'Vatican' hoard (O'Donovan 1964, 225).
50.	1.61	24.8	270°	Rægenulf (*Rægenwulf*). Winchester style. Willoughby Gardner; ex Spink (*NCirc* Mar–Apr 1922, 3634) (P. Carlyon-Britton collection).
51.	0.83 fragment	12.8	270°	[ ]ed. Winchester style. Chester (1950) hoard, no. 7.
52.	0.84 fragment	12.9	180°	[ ]bold. Winchester style. Chester (1950) hoard, no. 358 (where incorrectly attributed to reign of Eadwig).
Horizontal Cross Trefoil				
53.	1.55	23.9	0°	Æthered (*Æthelræd*). Winchester style. Willoughby Gardner; ex Glendining 13 Nov 1930, lot 67; ex 'Vatican' hoard (O'Donovan 1964, 94). Same obv. die as next.
54.	1.64	25.3	270°	Æthered (*Æthelræd*). Winchester style. Willoughby Gardner; ex Glendining 13 Nov 1930, lot 67; ex 'Vatican' hoard (O'Donovan 1964, 93). Same obv. die as last.
Horizontal Quatrefoil Trefoil				
55.	1.59	24.5	180°	Eadmund. South East Midlands style. Willoughby Gardner; ex Glendining 16 May 1929, lot 79; ex 'Vatican' hoard (O'Donovan 1964, 227).
Horizontal Pellet				
56.	– broken in two pieces	–	–	Æð[ ]ed (*Æthelræd*). Winchester style. Chester (1950) hoard, no. 2.
57.	1.54	23.7	90°	Æthered (*Æthelræd*). Winchester style. Willoughby Gardner.
58.	1.48	22.8	90°	Æthered (*Æthelræd*). Winchester style. Willoughby Gardner; ex Spink.
59.	1.55	23.9	90°	Æthered (*Æthelræd*). Winchester style. Willoughby Gardner; ex Baldwin.
60.	1.60	24.7	225°	Æthered (*Æthelræd*). Winchester style. Willoughby Gardner; ex Lincoln, ex Bruun (1925) 84. Same rev. die as next.
61.	1.62	25.0	180°	Æthered (*Æthelræd*). Winchester style. Willoughby Gardner; ex Glendining 13 Nov 1930, lot 67; ex 'Vatican' hoard (O'Donovan 1964, 85 or 86). Same rev. die as last.
62.	1.45 chipped	22.3	180°	Æthered (*Æthelræd*). Winchester style. Willoughby Gardner; ex Lincoln.
63.	1.60	24.7	0°	Æthered (*Æthelræd*). Winchester style. Willoughby Gardner; ex Glendining 13 Nov 1930, lot 65; ex 'Vatican' hoard (O'Donovan 1964, 79, 80, 84 or 92).
64.	1.36	21.0	0°	Oslac. Winchester style. Willoughby Gardner; ex P. Carlyon-Britton (1916) 952; perhaps ex 'Astronomer' (F. McLean) (1906) 161. The style is Winchester-derived rather than that of Winchester proper.
65.	1.57 slightly chipped	24.2	0°	Rægenulf (*Rægenwulf*). Winchester style. Willoughby Gardner; ex Gantz; ex Glendining 16 May 1929, lot 95; ex 'Vatican' hoard (O'Donovan 1964, 316 or 325).
66.	1.54	23.7	135°	Rægenulf (*Rægenwulf*). Winchester style. Willoughby Gardner; ex Lincoln (?).
67.	1.67	25.7	270°	Rægenulf (*Rægenwulf*). Winchester style. Willoughby Gardner; ex Spink (*NCirc* Nov 1907, 46897). Same obv. die as next.
68.	1.61	24.8	90°	Rægenulf (*Rægenwulf*). Winchester style. Willoughby Gardner; ex Lincoln. Same obv. die as last.
69.	1.66	25.6	0°	Rægenulf (*Rægenwulf*). Winchester style. Willoughby Gardner; ex Seaby; ex Grantley (1944) 1032.
70.	1.63	25.1	270°	Rægenulf (*Rægenwulf*). Winchester style. Willoughby Gardner; ex Lincoln (?).
71.	1.59	24.5	180°	Rægenulf (*Rægenwulf*). Winchester style. Willoughby Gardner; ex Spink (*NCirc* Nov–Dec 1921, 98529) (C. M. Crompton-Roberts collection).
72.	1.62	25.0	180°	Rægenulf (*Rægenwulf*). Winchester style. Willoughby Gardner; ex Gantz; ex Glendining 16 May 1929, lot 95; ex 'Vatican' hoard (O'Donovan 1964, 316 or 325).

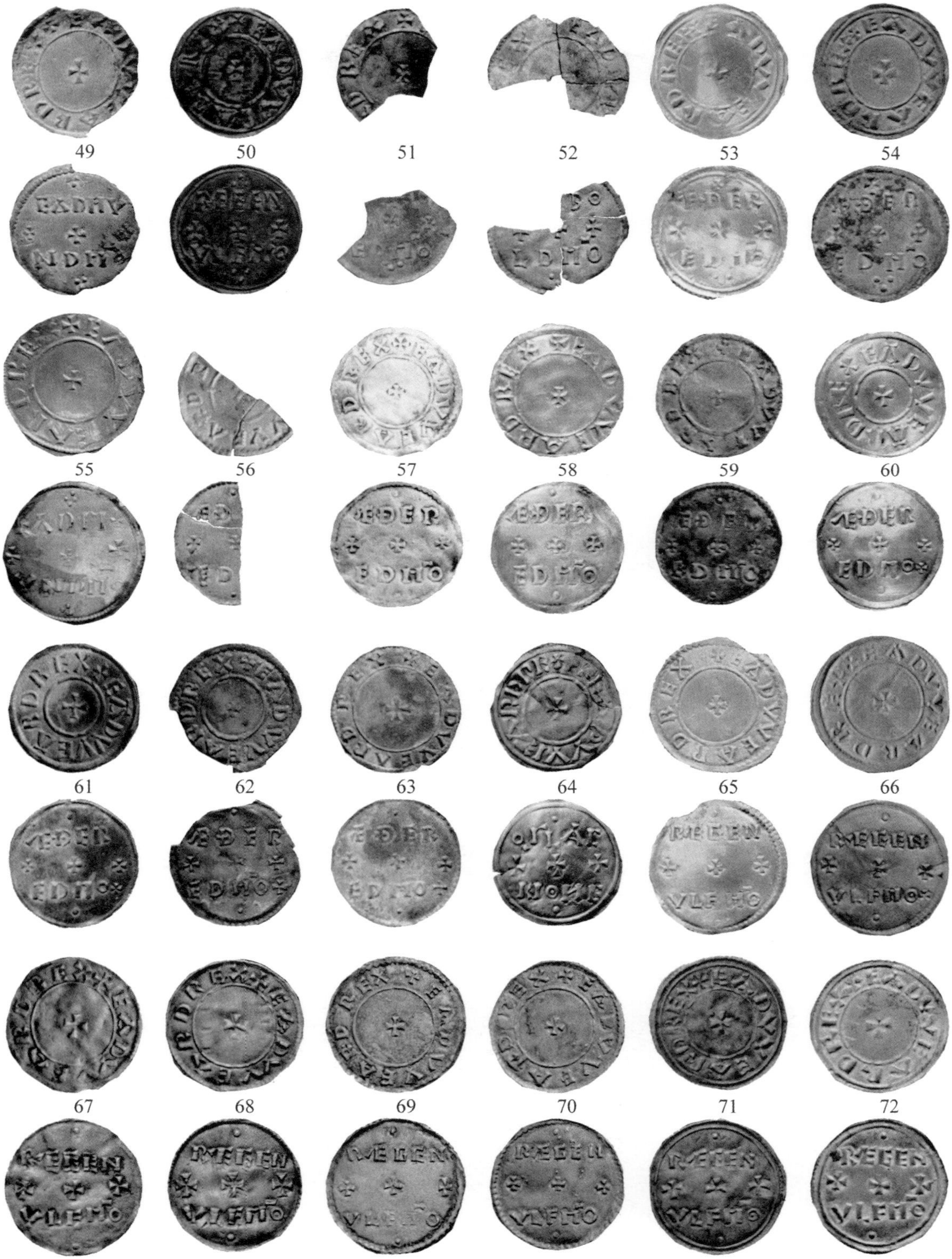

49 50 51 52 53 54

55 56 57 58 59 60

61 62 63 64 65 66

67 68 69 70 71 72

EDWARD THE ELDER (*cont.*)

Horizontal Pellet (*cont.*)

	Weight g	Weight gr.	Die-Axis	
73.	1.57.	24.2	270°	Vvlfred (*Wulfræd*). Winchester style. Chester (1950) hoard, no. 6. Central cross in middle line of rev. is a cross made up of five pellets.

Tower (Reliquary)

	Weight g	Weight gr.	Die-Axis	
74.	1.30 fragment	20.1	180°	Ea[ ]mnd (*Eadmund*). North West Midlands style (Chester?). Willoughby Gardner; ex P. Carlyon-Britton (1918) 1665; probably ex Rashleigh (1909) 240; and if so perhaps ex Cuff (1854) 482*.
75.	1.28 chipped	19.7	0°	Vvlfsige (*Wulfsige*). North West Midlands style (Chester?). Purchased 1977; ex Mack (1977) 88 (*SCBI 20*, 767); ex Chester (1862) hoard (but not listed by Hughes).

Spray

	Weight g	Weight gr.	Die-Axis	
76.	1.13 fragment	17.4	270°	Boiga (*Boga*). North West Midlands style (Chester?). Willoughby Gardner; ex Grantley (1944) 1039; perhaps ex Sotheby 26 Jul 1892, lot 98; perhaps ex Lindsay (1867) 48; ex Co.Tipperary hoard.

Hand

	Weight g	Weight gr.	Die-Axis	
77.	1.28 chipped	19.7	0°	Eared (*Eadred*). North West Midlands style (Shrewsbury?). Purchased 1975; ex Mack (1975) 119 (*SCBI 20*, 762); ex Chester (1862) hoard (Hughes no. 3).

Horizontal (imitative)

	Weight g	Weight gr.	Die-Axis	
78.	1.28 slightly chipped	19.7	0°	+ERDVVEARD E+ (retrograde). East Anglian style. Willoughby Gardner (via Mrs Gardner 1963); ex Henry Lawrence (1923) 49.
79.	– two fragments	–	–	[ ]VVEARD RE[ ]. East Anglian style. Chester (1950) hoard, no. 8.

Small fragments, probably of coins of Edward the Elder

	Weight g	Weight gr.	Die-Axis	
80.	– broken in three pieces	–	–	[ ]od. The fragment is of Horizontal type and has an obv. inscription commencing +EA. The absence of an inner outer circle on the rev. makes an attribution to Edward the Elder probable. Chester (1950) hoard, not in published list.
81.	–	–	–	[ ]er[ ]. The fragment is of Horizontal type and has an obv. inscription commencing +EA. The absence of an inner outer circle on the rev. makes an attribution to Edward the Elder probable. Chester (1950) hoard, not in published list.
82.	–	–	–	(moneyer's name illegible). The fragment is of Horizontal type and has an obv. inscription including the consecutive letters DRE. The absence of an inner outer circle on the rev. makes an attribution to Edward the Elder probable. Chester (1950) hoard, not in published list.
83.	–	–	–	(moneyer's name illegible). The fragment is of Horizontal type and the absence of an inner outer circle on the rev. makes an attribution to Edward the Elder probable. Chester (1950) hoard, no. 361 (where coin is attributed to the reign of Eadwig).

ÆTHELSTAN (924–39)

Horizontal Trefoil

	Weight g	Weight gr.	Die-Axis	
84.	1.59	24.5	270°	Abba. Chester style. Willoughby Gardner; ex P. Carlyon-Britton (1913) 375. Perhaps same rev. die as next, and as *SCBI 34*, 3.
85.	1.62	25.0	90°	Abba. Chester style. Willoughby Gardner; ex Baldwin (with their stock ticket B9274). Perhaps same rev. die as last, and as *SCBI 34*, 3.
86.	1.41	21.7	0°	Abba. Chester style. Willoughby Gardner; ex Sotheby 15 Dec 1931, lot 142. Same obv. die as next.
87.	1.56	24.1	180°	Abba. Chester style. Willoughby Gardner; ex Spink (*NCirc* Jun 1910, 76530) (Sir John Evans collection); ex Killyon Manor hoard. Same obv. die as last.
88.	– three fragments	–	–	[ ]ba (*Abba*). Chester style. Chester (1950) hoard, no. 9.

[*continued overleaf*]

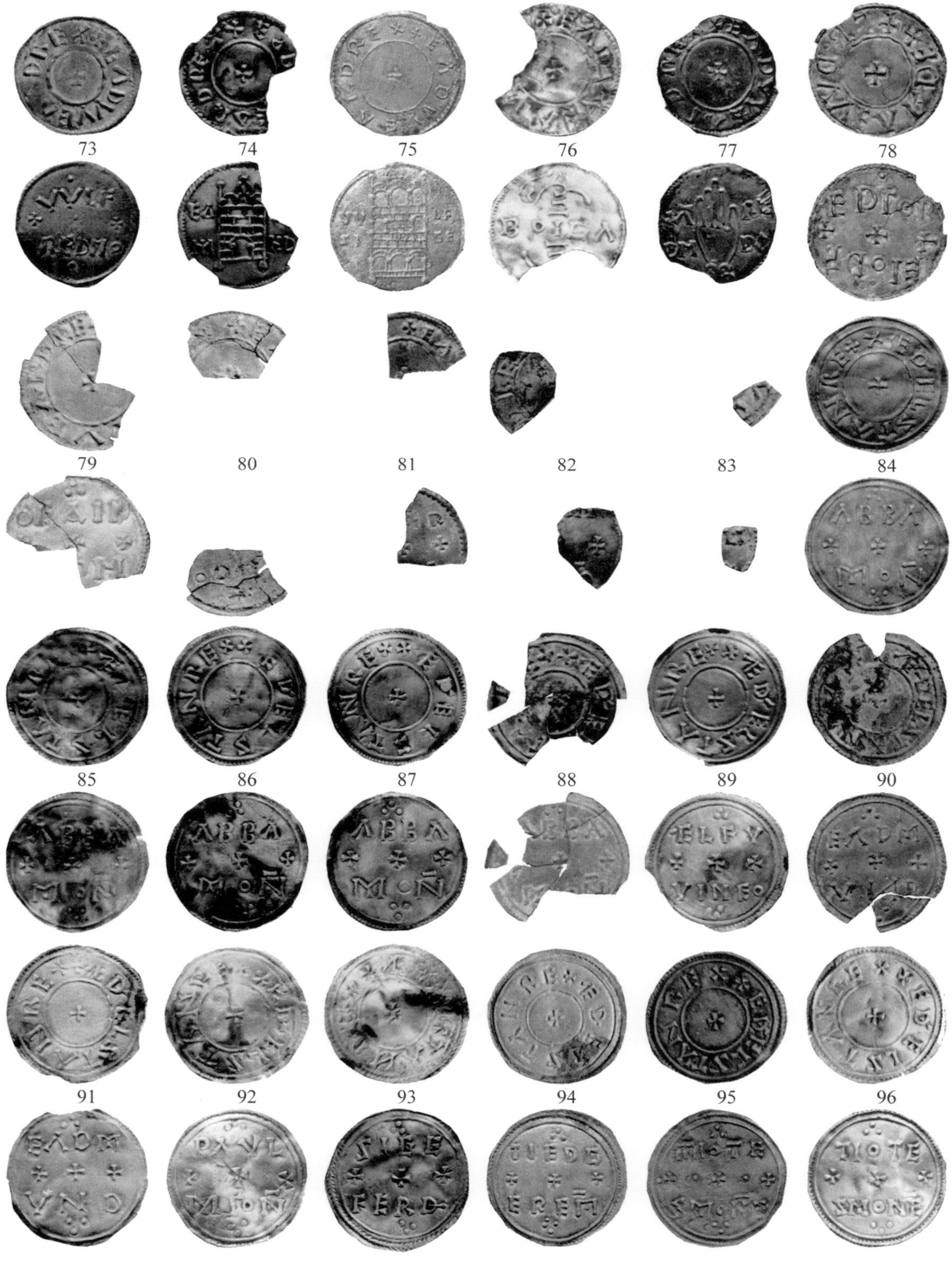

73 74 75 76 77 78 79 80 81 82 83 84 85 86 87 88 89 90 91 92 93 94 95 96

Plate 4 (*cont.*)

ÆTHELSTAN (*cont.*)
Horizontal Trefoil (*cont.*)

	Weight *g*	*gr.*	*Die-Axis*	
89.	1.50	23.1	270°	Ælfvvine (*Ælfwine*). Chester style. Willoughby Gardner; ex Baldwin; ex Glendining 13 Nov 1930, lot 108; ex 'Vatican' hoard (O'Donovan 1964, 483). Perhaps same obv. die as *SCBI 34*, 5.
90.	1.55 two fragments	24.0	180°	Eadmund. Chester style. Chester (1950) hoard, no. 15.
91.	1.50	23.1	270°	Eadmund. Willoughby Gardner; ex Spink (*NCirc* Jun 1910, 76531) (Sir John Evans collection); ex Castle Freke (1799) hoard. Perhaps same dies as *SCBI 1*, 570.
92.	1.49	23.0	90°	Paul (*Paulus*). Chester style. Willoughby Gardner; gift from R. C. Lockett 1925.
93.	1.51	23.3	0°	Sigeferth. Chester style. Willoughby Gardner; ex Baldwin. Overstruck on coin of Edward the Elder?
94.	1.62	25.0	180°	Tiedgere (*Tidgar*). Chester style. Willoughby Gardner; ex Lincoln; ex P. Carlyon-Britton (1913) 397; ex Sir John Evans; ex Castle Freke (1799) hoard.
95.	1.55	23.9	270°	Tiot(es). Chester style. Willoughby Gardner; ex P. Carlyon-Britton (1916) 983. Overstrike.
96.	1.57	24.2	270°	Tiot(es). Chester style. Willoughby Gardner; ex Lincoln; ex Hazlitt (1909) 1037.

ÆTHELSTAN (*cont.*)

Horizontal Trefoil (*cont.*)

	Weight *g*	*gr.*	*Die-Axis*	
97.	1.59	24.5	45°	Bioca (*Boga*). Winchester style. Willoughby Gardner; ex Baldwin; ex Glendining 13 Nov 1930, lot 107; ex 'Vatican' hoard (O'Donovan 1964, 492 or 493). Die-duplicate of Fitzwilliam Museum Cambridge ex Blunt, and of *SCBI 30*, 331.
98.	1.57	24.2	180°	Rægenulf (*Rægenwulf*). Winchester style. Willoughby Gardner; ex Spink; ex P. Carlyon-Britton (but not in sales ?). Die-duplicate of Forum hoard, no. 229.
99.	1.53 fragmentary	23.6	180°	Ead[ ]nd (*Eadmund*). Southern/Midlands style. Chester (1950) hoard, no. 16.
100.	1.60	24.7	0°	Eadmund. Southern/Midlands style. Willoughby Gardner; ex Baldwin; ex Glendining 16 May 1929, lot 108; ex 'Vatican' hoard (O'Donovan 1964, 499).
101.	1.45	22.3	90°	Iohann. Southern/Midlands style. Chester (1950) hoard, no. 19.
102.	1.28	19.7	90°	Vvealdhelm (*Wealdhelm*). Southern/Midlands style. Chester (1950) hoard, no. 24.
103.	1.45	22.3	270°	Clac(l) (*Klakkr*). Central East Midlands (NE I style). Chester (1950) hoard, no. 14.
104.	1.59	24.5	270°	Oda. Central East Midlands (NE I style). Chester (1950) hoard, no. 22. Same dies as *SCBI 34*, 228 and 229.
105.	1.55	23.9	0°	Osulf (*Asulfr/Oswulf*). Central East Midlands (NE I style). Willoughby Gardner; ex Lincoln 19/7/1909 (*sic*). Although the dies are of general NE I character, neither die is of the classic NE I style.
106.	1.59	24.5	90°	Stefanus. Central East Midlands (NE I style). Chester (1950) hoard, no. 23.
107.	1.33 slightly chipped	20.5	0°	Winele. Central East Midlands (NE I style). Willoughby Gardner.
108.	1.50	23.1	0°	Winele. Central East Midlands (NE I style). Chester (1950) hoard, no. 25.
109.	– fragment	–	–	(moneyer's name illegible). The fragment is of Horizontal type, NE1 style, with M as the last letter in the first line of the rev. inscription. It seems possible that it is of the moneyer Are, for whom similar coins are known with ARE M as the first line on the rev. Chester (1950) hoard, no. 27.
Horizontal Quatrefoil				
110.	1.46	22.5	0°	Wiard. Central East Midlands (NE II style). Willoughby Gardner; ex Joseph Young (1919) 24.
Circumscription Cross				
111.	1.57	24.2	315°	*Chester* (LEGECF), Abba. Purchased 1967 (GM 29.C.67); ex Seaby (on Seaby ticket with their acquisition date 1950).
112.	– fragmentary	–	–	*Chester* ([ ]GECFI), Ælfvine (*Ælfwine*). Willoughby Gardner (via Mrs Gardner 1963); ex Seaby.
113.	1.40 chipped	21.6	315°	*Chester* (LEGC), Eadmund. Found near Oswestry, Shropshire 1999
114.	1.55 slightly chipped	23.9	0°	*Chester* (LEGF), Maeldomen (*Mældomen*). Willoughby Gardner (via Mrs Gardner 1963). Die-duplicate of *SCBI 5*, 18, perhaps same obv die as *SCBI 20*, 778.
115.	1.36	21.0	0°(?)	*Oxford* (OX VRBIS), Ingelri (*Ingalric*). Chester (1950) hoard, 1975 parcel coin 2.
116.	1.47 fragmentary	22.7	270°	*Shrewsbury* ([ ]CROB), Berhtelm (*Beorhthelm*). Chester (1950) hoard, no. 43.
117.	1.43	22.1	180°	*York* (EFORPIC), Regnald. Chester (1950) hoard, no. 51.
118.	– fragment	–	–	*York* ([ ]), [ ]gnal[ ] (*Regnald*). Chester (1950) hoard, no. 50.
119.	1.55	23.9	0°	*York* (EFORPIC), Regnald. Chester (1950) hoard, no. 48.
120.	– fragmentary	–	225°	*York* (E[ ]), Regnald. Chester (1950) hoard, no. 49.

PLATE 5

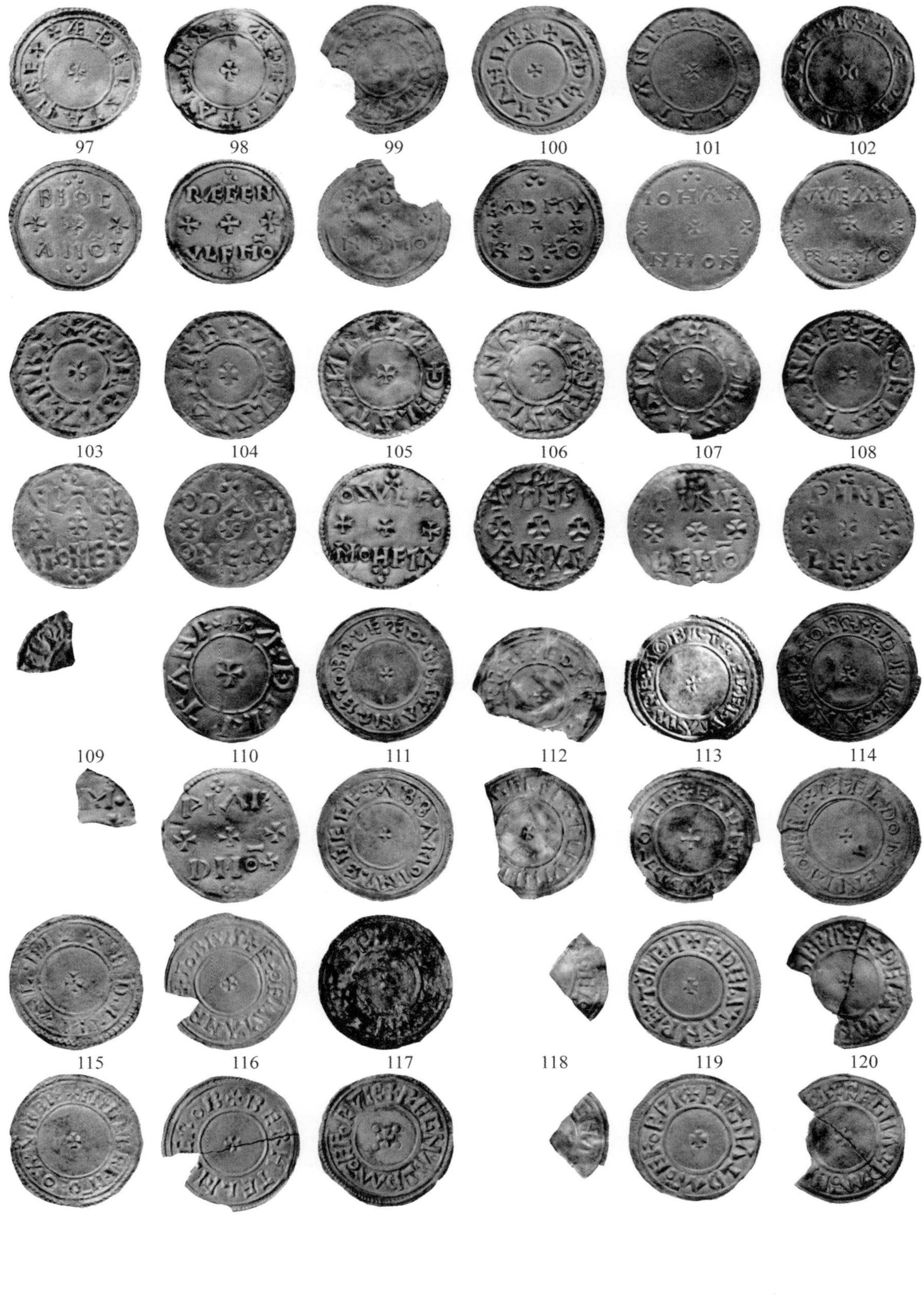

97 98 99 100 101 102

103 104 105 106 107 108

109 110 111 112 113 114

115 116 117 118 119 120

ÆTHELSTAN (*cont.*)

Circumscription Cross (*cont.*)

	Weight g	Weight gr.	Die-Axis	
Circumscription Cross (variant)				
121.	1.63	25.1	90°	*Chester* (LEGEFE), Cenapa (*Cnapa*). Chester (1950) hoard, 1975 parcel coin 3. Cross on obv. is composed of four limbs meeting at a central pellet, while rev. type is similar, but with rays in each angle of the cross.
Circumscription Rosette				
122.	– fragmentary	–	–	*Chester* (LE[ ]), [ ]d (*Eadmund*). Chester (1950) hoard, not in published list.
Circumscription type (exact variety uncertain)				
123.	– small fragment	–	–	*London* (LVN [ ]), moneyer's name missing. Chester (1950) hoard, not in published list.
Bust Crowned				
124.	1.43 badly chipped	22.1	90°	*Norwich* ([ ]PIC), Manticen. Chester (1950) hoard, no. 31. Die-duplicate of *SCBI 34*, 147.
125.	1.19 chipped	18.3	90°	Wiard. North-East Midlands style. Purchased (or given ?) 1958; ex Lockett (1958) 2741; ex Rashleigh (1909) 249.
Circumscription Cross (imitative)				
126.	0.87 slightly chipped	13.4	0°	Imitation of coin of *Chester* (DEORERD MON EIECIEI). Willoughby Gardner; ex Grantley (1944) 1052. Cross in field on obv. and rev. Die-duplicate of *SCBI 34*, 272.
127.	1.32	20.3	0°	Imitation of coin of *Chester*; similar legend to previous coin, but more blundered. Chester (1950) hoard, no. 36. Cross in field on obv. and rev.
Horizontal and Circumscription fragments attributable to Æthelstan				
128.	–	–	–	Fragment of coin of Horizontal type reading]ELS[on obv. and]DMO in bottom line of rev. (but no pellets beneath?). Chester (1950) hoard, no. 28.
129.	–	–	–	Fragment of coin of Horizontal type (?), reading]DE[on obv., rev. hard to make out. Chester (1950) hoard, not in published list.
130.	– two fragments	–	–	Fragment of coin of Horizontal type, reading]AN[on obv.,]AD[ ]/[ ]++/[ ]MO. Chester (1950) hoard, not in published list.
131.	–	–	–	Fragment of coin of Horizontal type, reading]DELS[on obv.,]MO[on rev., trefoil of pellets beneath. Chester (1950) hoard, no. 29.
132.	–	–	–	Fragment of coin of Circumscription type, reading]RE[on obv.,]EC[on rev. Chester (1950) hoard, not in published list.
133.	–	–	–	Fragment of coin of Circumscription type, reading +Æ [ ]R on obv.,]LEI[on rev. Chester (1950) hoard, not in published list.

EDMUND (939–46)

HT1 type

	g	gr.	Die-Axis	
134.	1.58	24.4	270°	Paul(es) (*Paulus*). Chester style. Willoughby Gardner; ex P. Carlyon-Britton (1916) 990; perhaps ex Montagu (1895) 665 (but lot purchased at Montagu sale by Bearman, whose collection is not believed to have come on the market until after 1916). Same rev. die as next three coins.
135.	1.53	23.6	180°	Paul(es) (*Paulus*). Chester style. Willoughby Gardner; ex Baldwin 1923. Die-duplicate of next two coins, and of *SCBI 34*, 330 and *SCBI 6*, 209. Same rev. die as preceding coin.
136.	1.55	23.9	225°	Paul(es) (*Paulus*). Chester style. Willoughby Gardner (via Mrs Gardner 1963). Die-duplicate of preceding coin and of next. Same rev. die as coin 134.
137.	1.32 badly chipped	20.3	90°	Paul(es) (*Paulus*). Chester style. Willoughby Gardner (via Mrs Gardner 1963); ex Seaby no. 5327, 1948 (on Seaby ticket with their acquisition date 1944). Die-duplicate of preceding two coins. Same rev. die as coin 134.
138.	1.56	24.1	135°	Ælfstan. Southern/Midlands style. Chester (1950) hoard, no. 58. Same obv. die as *SCBI* 34, 279.
139.	1.64	25.3	270°	Ælfstan. Southern/Midlands style. Chester (1950) hoard, no. 59.

[*continued overleaf*]

PLATE 6

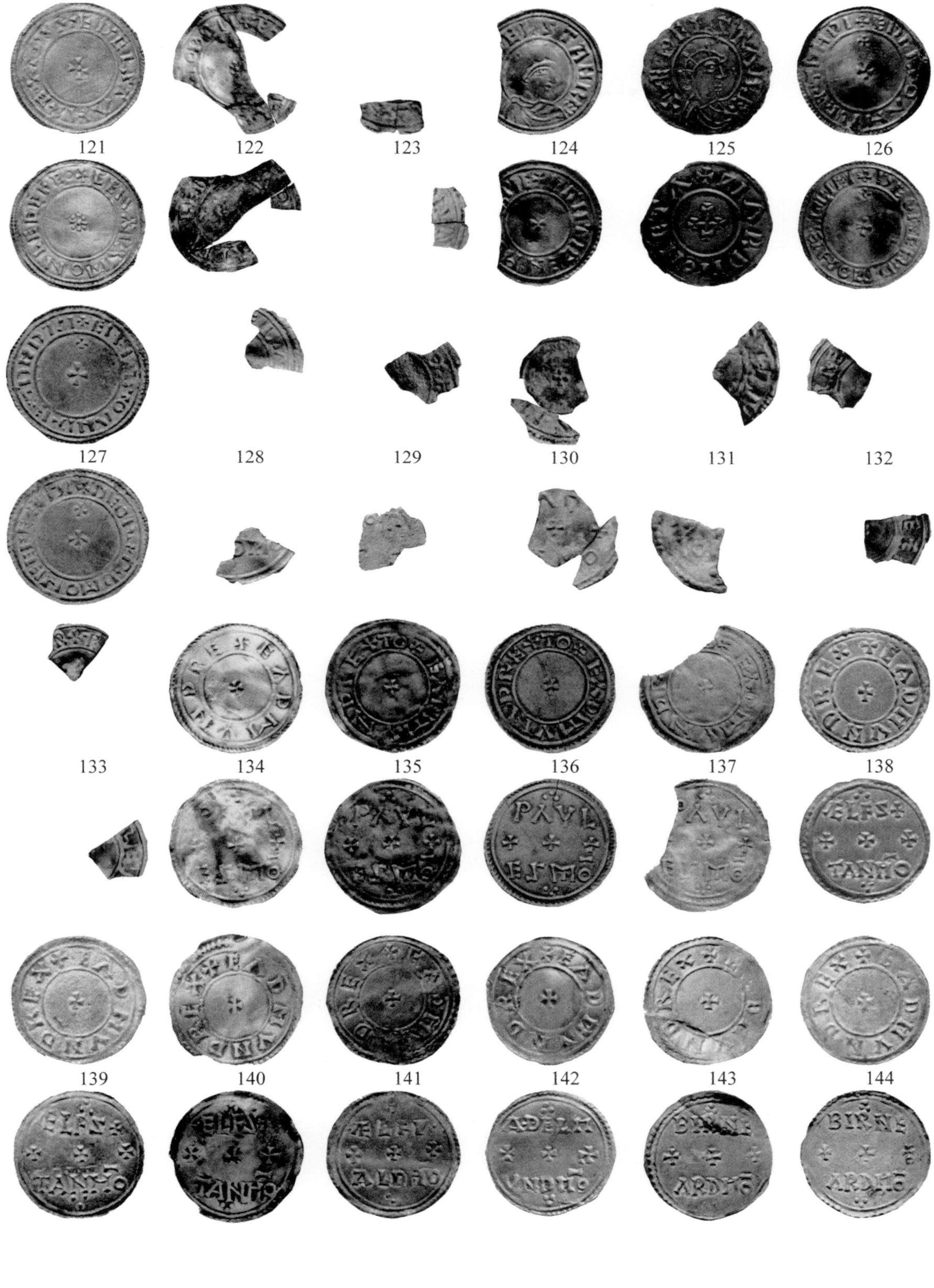
121 122 123 124 125 126
127 128 129 130 131 132
133 134 135 136 137 138
139 140 141 142 143 144

Plate 6 (*cont.*)

EDMUND (*cont.*)

HT1 type (*cont.*)

	Weight *g*	*gr.*	*Die-Axis*	
140.	1.41 slightly chipped	21.7	270°	Ælfstan. Southern/Midlands style. Willoughby Gardner; ex Seaby (with Seaby ticket, their acquisition date 1940).
141.	1.56	24.1	180°	Ælfwald (*Ælfweald*). Southern/Midlands style. Chester (1950) hoard, no. 63.
142.	1.64	25.3	270°	Athelmund (*Æthelmund*). Southern/Midlands style. Willoughby Gardner; ex Seaby. Die-duplicate of *SCBI 34*, 286.
143.	1.56	24.1	135°	Birneard. Southern/Midlands style. Chester (1950) hoard, no. 67. Perhaps same rev. die as next two, and as *SCBI 6*, 204.
144.	1.49	23.0	135°	Birneard. Southern/Midlands style.Chester (1950) hoard, no. 68. Perhaps same rev. die as above and next, and as *SCBI 6*, 204.

EMDUND (*cont.*)

HT1 Type

	Weight		Die-	
	g	*gr.*	*Axis*	
145.	1.48	22.8	180°	Birneard. Southern/Midlands style. Chester (1950) hoard, no. 69. Perhaps same rev. die as previous two, and as *SCBI 6*, 204.
146.	1.53	23.6	0°	Burnwald (*Beornweald*). Southern/Midlands style. Chester (1950) hoard, no. 71.
147.	1.45	22.3	180°	Burnwald (*Beornweald*). Southern/Midlands style. Chester (1950) hoard, no. 73.
148.	1.43	22.1	270°	Heremod. Southern/Midlands style. Chester (1950) hoard, no. 85.
149.	1.51	23.3	0°	Heremod. Southern/Midlands style. Chester (1950) hoard, no. 84. Same rev. die as *SCBI 34*, 310.
150.	1.43	22.1	0°	Herewig. Southern/Midlands style. Chester (1950) hoard, no. 86.
151.	1.57	24.2	270°	Osulf (*Asulfr*/*Oswulf*). Southern/Midlands style. Willoughby Gardner; ex Lincoln.
152.	1.53	23.6	90°	Rægnold (*Rægenweald*). Southern/Midlands style. Chester (1950) hoard, no. 102.
153.	1.57	24.2	45°	Rægenulf (*Rægenwulf*). Southern/Midlands style. Willoughby Gardner; ex Seaby; ex Grantley (1944) 1065; ex Montagu (1895) 666.
154.	1.56	24.1	270°	Siedeman (*Sidumann*). Southern/Midlands style. Chester hoard (1950), no.104. Same rev. die as, and perhaps die-duplicate of, coin in Rome, ex Forum hoard.
155.	1.37	21.1	0°	Wigeard (*Wigheard*). Southern/Midlands style. Chester hoard (1950), no. 110. Perhaps same obv. die as coin in Manx Museum, ex Ballaqueeny hoard.
156.	1.51	23.3	0°	Wigeard (*Wigheard*). Southern/Midlands style. Willoughby Gardner; ex Lincoln; ex Montagu (1895) 667. Die-duplicate of *SCBI* 1, 587 and of coin in Rome, ex Forum hoard. Same obv. die as *SCBI* 34, 341 and 342.
157.	1.29 slightly chipped	19.9	0°	Ingelgar (*Ingalgar*). York style. Chester (1950) hoard, no. 88.
158.	1.54	23.7	0°	Ingelgar (*Ingalgar*). York style. Chester (1950) hoard, no. 87.
159.	1.30	20.1	45°	Boge (*Boga*). Central East Midlands style (NE I). Willoughby Gardner; ex Spink (*NCirc* Sept–Oct 1919, 74718).

HP1 type

160.	1.53	23.6	0°	Byrneard (*Beornheard*). Southern style. Chester (1950) hoard, no. 70.
161.	1.57 slightly chipped	24.2	90°	Eadred (*Eadræd*). Southern style. Chester (1950) hoard, no.80. Die-duplicate of *SCBI 34*, 353.
162.	1.58	24.4	0°	Eardulf (*Eardwulf*). Southern style. Chester (1950) hoard, no. 83. Triangle of pellets in rev. field.

HC1 type

163.	1.49	23.0	90°	Elfric (*Ælfric*). Southern style. Chester (1950) hoard, no. 57. Compare dies of *SCBI 30*, 349.

HR1 type

164.	1.57	24.2	180°	Elfwald (*Ælfweald*). Chester style. Chester (1950) hoard, no. 61. Same obv. die as next, and *SCBI 34*, 402.
165.	1.56	24.1	180°	Ælfval (*Ælfweald*). Chester style. Chester (1950) hoard, no. 62. Same obv. die as last, and same rev. die as Spink sale 58 (30 Apr 1987), lot 21.
166.	1.56	24.1	315°	Ælfvine (*Ælfwine*). Chester style. Willoughby Gardner; ex Lincoln; ex 'A Gentleman', Sotheby, 21 Nov 1911, lot 582. Perhaps die-duplicate of coin in Rome ex Forum hoard.
167.	1.57	24.2	0°	Ælfvine (*Ælfwine*). Chester style. Willoughby Gardner; ex Baldwin; ex Henry Lawrence (1923) 50. Die-duplicate of *SCBI* 6, 211. Same obv. die as Spink sale 58 (30 Apr 1987), lot 21, a coin of the moneyer Ælfweald (see coin 165 above).
168.	1.43 chipped	22.1	0°	Cnapa. Chester style. Willoughby Gardner; ex Spink (*NCirc* Oct 1908, 58391). Same rev. die as *SCBI 34*, 413.

PLATE 7

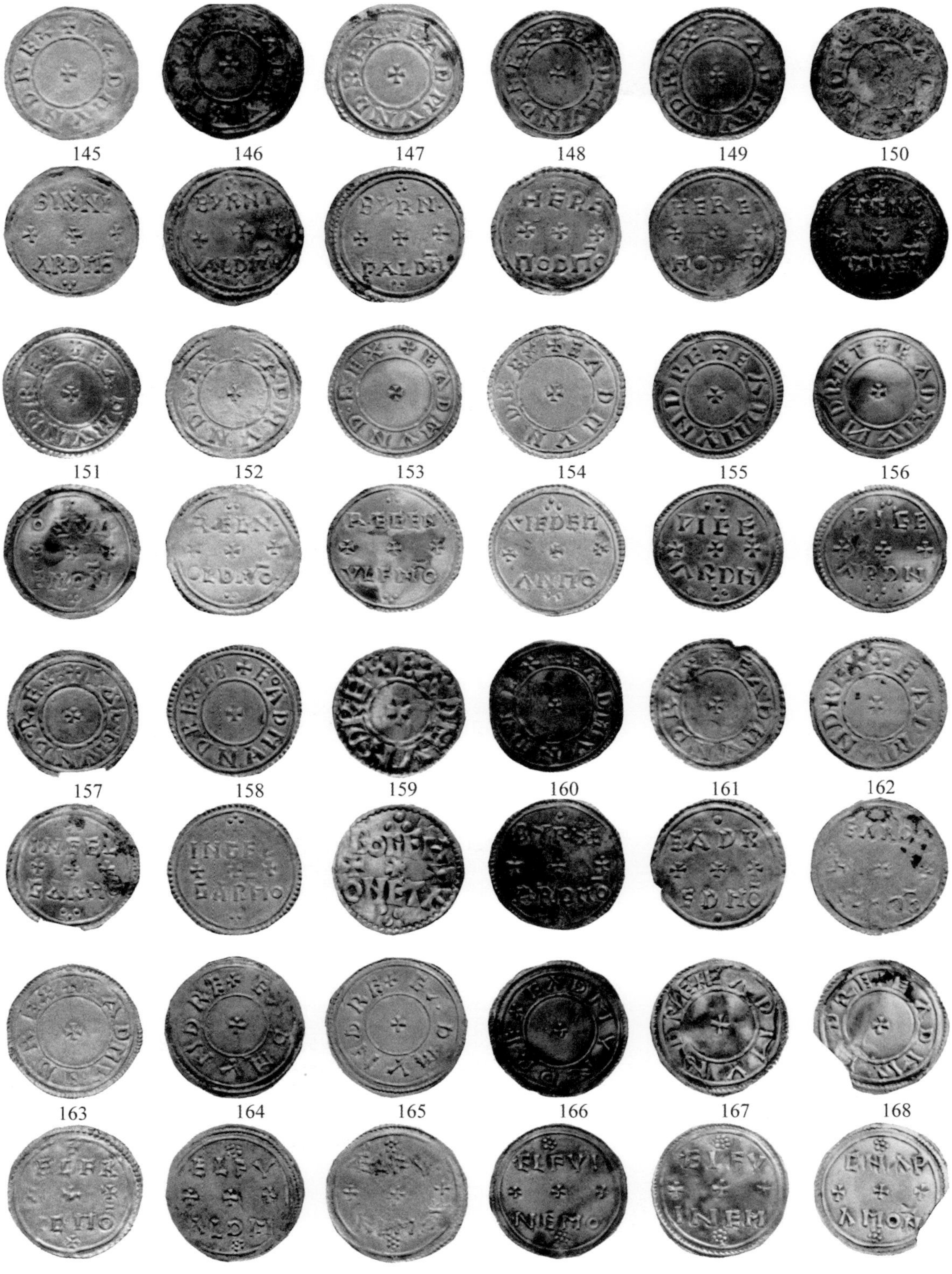

145 146 147 148 149 150 151 152 153 154 155 156 157 158 159 160 161 162 163 164 165 166 167 168

EDMUND (*cont.*)

HR1 type (*cont.*)

	Weight *g*	*gr.*	*Die-Axis*	
169.	1.58	24.4	315°	Dorulf(e) (*Deorwulf*). Chester style. Willoughby Gardner; ex Duart-Smith (1945) 70 (associated ticket says ex Lincoln, but coin is on wrong ticket), probably ex Dawnay (1922) 26 (lot bought by 'Smith'). Die-duplicate of *SCBI 34*, 417 and of *NCirc* Dec 1990, 7560.
	slightly chipped			
170.	1.52	23.4	0°	Dorulf (*Deorwulf*). Chester style. Chester (1950) hoard, no. 77.
171.	1.56	24.1	90°	Dorulf (*Deorwulf*). Chester style. Willoughby Gardner; ex Lincoln. Die-duplicate of coin 172, same obv. die as coin 173.
172.	1.54	23.7	315°	Dorulf (*Deorwulf*). Chester style. Chester (1950) hoard, no. 79. Die-duplicate of coin 171, same obv. die as coin 173.
173.	1.62	25.0	90°	Dorulf (*Deorwulf*). Chester style. Willoughby Gardner; ex Lincoln; ex 'A Collector' (R. D. Bain), Sotheby 8 May 1928, lot 218. Same obv. die as previous two coins.
174.	1.43	22.1	180°	Dorulf (*Deorwulf*). Chester style. Willoughby Gardner (on new ticket saying ex Glendining sale, 1945, i.e. Duart-Smith sale, but the Duart-Smith coin is coin 165 above). Die-duplicate of next coin, and of *SCBI 6*, 212. Same obv. die as coin 176 and *SCBI 34*, 416. Letter M in obv. legend is engraved upside down.
175.	1.55	23.9	90°	Dorulf (*Deorwulf*). Chester style. Chester (1950) hoard, no. 78. Die-duplicate of previous coin, and of *SCBI 6*, 212. Same obv. die as coin 176 and *SCBI 34*, 416.
176.	1.39	21.4	180°	Dorulf (*Deorwulf*). Chester style. Willoughby Gardner; ex Spink (*NCirc* June 1910, 76539) (Sir John Evans collection); ex Castle Freke (1799) hoard. Die-duplicate of *SCBI* 34, 416. Same obv. die as previous two coins.
	slightly chipped			
177.	1.54	23.7	270°	Dorulf (*Deorwulf*). Chester style. Willoughby Gardner; ex Seaby 23 Aug 1927 (if coin is on right ticket). Die-duplicate of *SCBI 34*, 418 and of *SCBI 6*, 213.
178.	1.55	23.9	45°	Eadmund. Chester style. Willoughby Gardner; ex Baldwin (with their stock ticket A.1042). Die-duplicate of *SCBI 34*, 420 and 421 and probably of *SCBI 17*, 148. Same obv. die as coins 218–19 below.
179.	1.60	24.7	45°	Eadmund. Chester style. Willoughby Gardner; ex Baldwin (with their stock ticket A.1042). Die-duplicate of *SCBI 34*, 420–21 and probably of *SCBI 17*, 148. Same obv. die as coins 218–19 below.
180.	1.24	19.1	270°	Erod (*Eroth*). Chester style. Willoughby Gardner; ex P. Carlyon-Britton (1916) 986.
	slightly chipped			
181.	1.57	24.2	180°	Frard. Chester style. Willoughby Gardner; ex Lincoln; ex Ready (1920) 95.
182.	1.55	23.9	45°	Frard. Chester style. Willoughby Gardner; ex Spink (*NCirc* Apr 1916, 39406). Die-duplicate of *SCBI 34*, 429. Same rev. die as *SCBI 34*, 430.
183.	1.64	25.3	45°	Frard. Chester style. Willoughby Gardner. Same rev. die as *SCBI 36*, 177.
184.	1.53	23.6	180°	Mældomen. Chester style. Willoughby Gardner; ex R. C. Lockett (gift); ex P. Carlyon-Britton (1916) 991; ex 'Nobleman' (Marquess of Ailesbury) (1903) 1; presumptively found with the unique coin of Hywel Dda which figured in the same lot. Die-duplicate of coin in National Museum of Ireland, ex Smarmore hoard, and of fragment in Fitzwilliam Museum, Cambridge, CM 1990-1-540, ex Blunt. Probably same obv. die as next.
185.	1.50	23.1	90°	Mældomen. Chester style. Chester (1950) hoard, no. 93. Probably same obv. die as last.
186.	1.56	24.1	180°	Mærten(e) (*Martin*). Chester style. Willoughby Gardner; ex Lincoln. Die-duplicate of *SCBI 34*, 435, *SCBI 6*, 216, and coin in Rome, ex Forum hoard.
187.	1.59	24.5	270°	Mærten(e) (*Martin*). Chester style. Willoughby Gardner; ex Spink (but not from *NCirc* June 1910 where other coins of Eadmund with this provenance offered); ex Sir John Evans; ex Killyon Manor hoard. Same rev. die as next.

[*continued overleaf*]

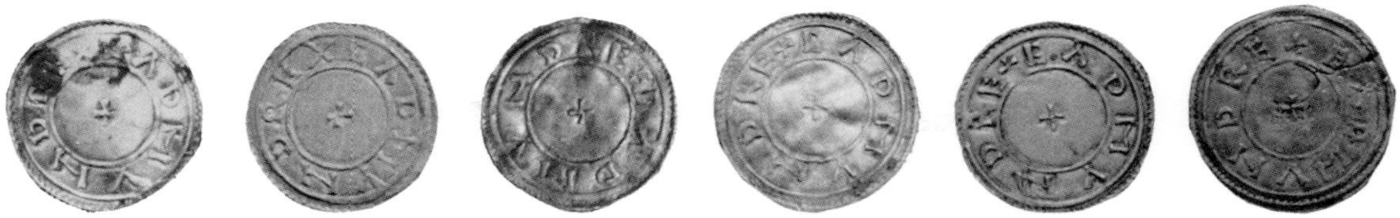

169 170 171 172 173 174

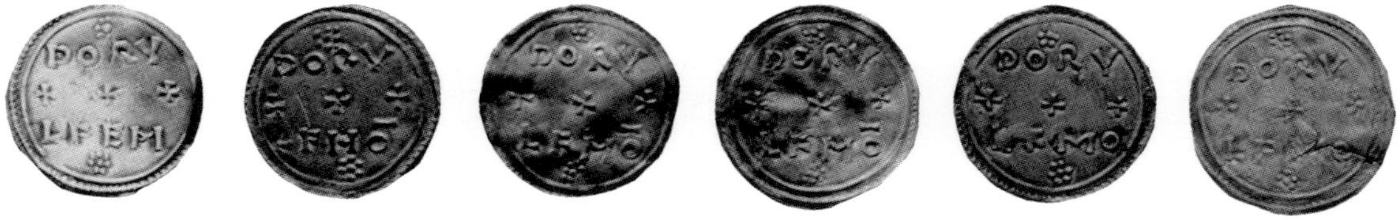

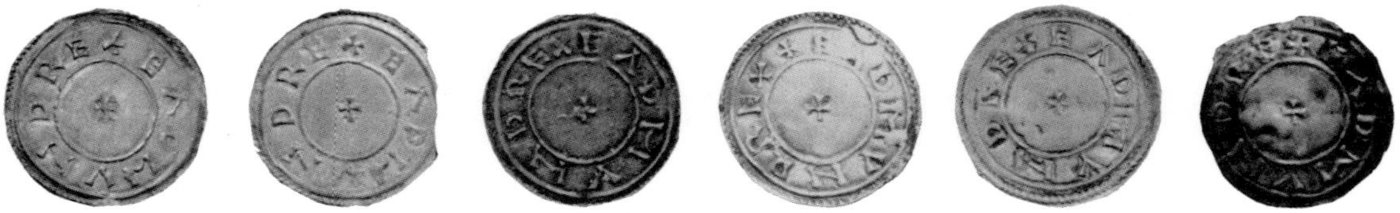

175 176 177 178 179 180

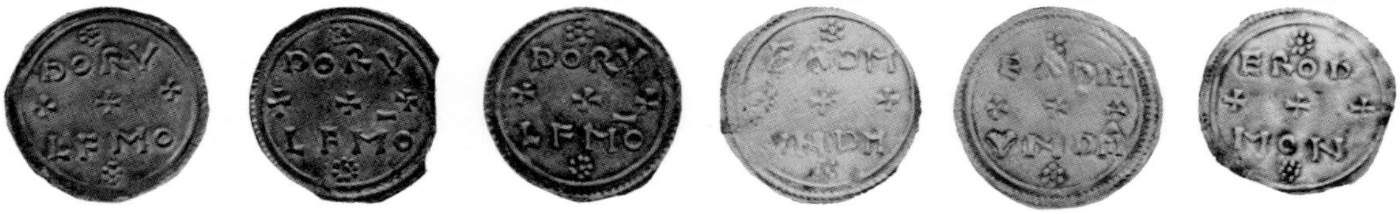

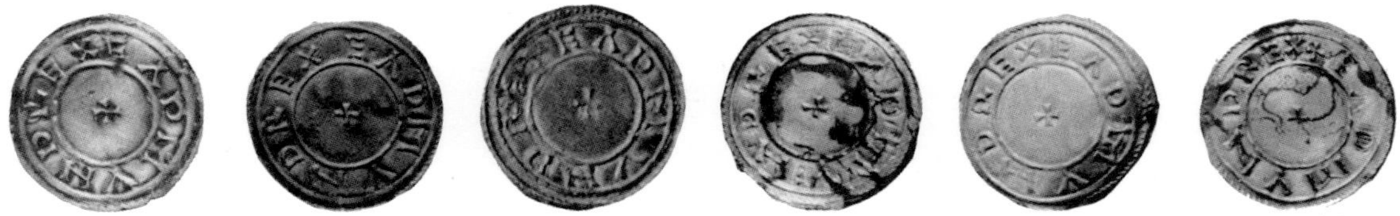

181 182 183 184 185 186

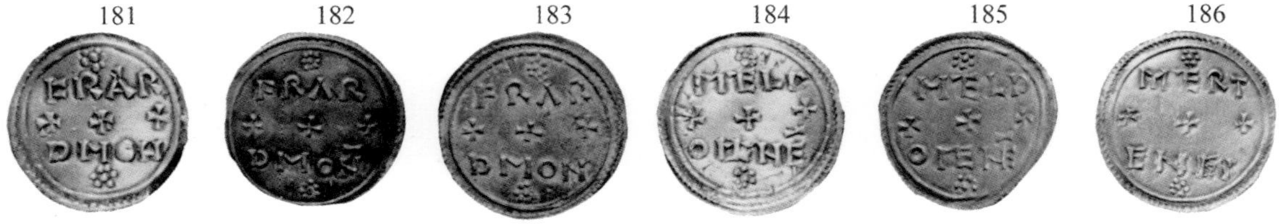

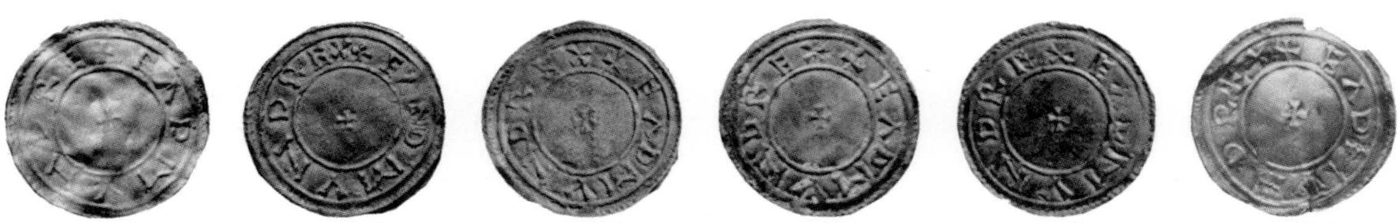

187 188 189 190 191 192

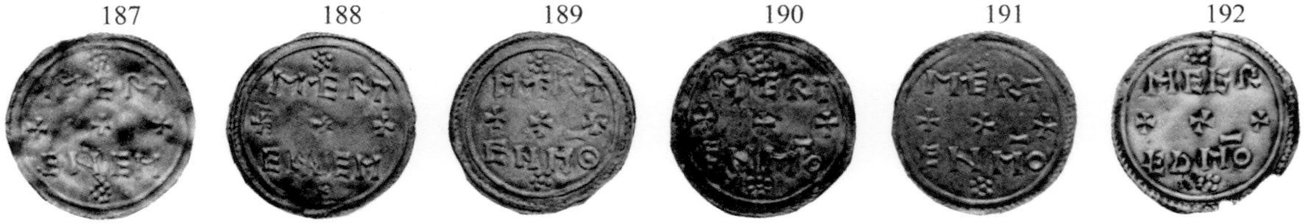

Plate 8 (*cont.*)

EDMUND (*cont.*)
HR1 type (*cont.*)

	Weight		*Die-*	
	g	*gr.*	*Axis*	
188.	1.58	24.4	90°	Mærten(e) (*Martin*). Chester style. Willoughby Gardner; ex Spink (*NCirc* Nov–Dec 1921, 98537) (C. M. Crompton-Roberts collection); ex Peace (1894) 38. Probably same obv. die as *SCBI 34*, 434–5. Same rev. die as last.
189.	1.47	22.7	45°	Mærten (*Martin*). Chester style. Willoughby Gardner; ex Spink (*NCirc* Sep–Oct 1920, 85601) (C. M. Crompton-Roberts collection). Same obv. die as next and *SCBI 34*, 433.
190.	1.55	23.9	225°	Mærten (*Martin*). Chester style. Chester (1950) hoard, no. 95. Same obv. die as last and *SCBI 34*, 433.
191.	1.56	24.1	270°	Mærten (*Martin*). Chester style. Chester (1950) hoard, no. 96.
192.	1.57 chipped	24.2	180°	Megred (*Mægenræd*). Chester style. Willoughby Gardner; ex Baldwin (with their stock ticket A.1041); ex Maynard (1885)8. Die-duplicate of Fitzwilliam Museum, Cambridge, CM 1990-1-492; ex Blunt.

EDMUND (*cont.*)

HR1 type (*cont.*)

	Weight		Die-	
	g	*gr.*	*Axis*	
193.	1.48	22.8	225°	Osulf (*Asulfr/Oswulf*). Chester style. Willoughby Gardner; ex Spink (*NCirc* Sep–Oct 1920, 85605) (C. M. Crompton-Roberts collection); evidently ex Briggs (1893) 202; and therefore ex Howard (1874) 15. Same rev. die as next and *SCBI 34*, 439.
194.	1.47	22.7	180°	Osulf (*Asulfr/Oswulf*). Chester style. Willoughby Gardner; ex Sotheby 15 Dec 1931, lot 143. Same rev. die as last and *SCBI 34*, 439.
195.	1.38 slightly chipped	21.3	135°	Regnulf (*Rægenwulf*). Chester style. Willoughby Gardner; ex Baldwin. Die-duplicate of next coin and of *SCBI 34*, 442 and 443.
196.	1.68	25.9	135°	Regnulf (*Rægenwulf*). Chester style. Willoughby Gardner (via Mrs Gardner 1963); ex Spink (*NCirc* June 1910, 76540) (Sir John Evans collection). Die-duplicate of previous coin and of *SCBI 34*, 443.
197.	1.60	24.7	45°	Regnulf (*Rægenwulf*). Chester style. Willoughby Gardner; ex Spink. Die-duplicate of coin in C. S. S. Lyon collection, also of *SCBI 9*, 354.
198.	1.54	23.7	135°	Thrmod(e) (*Thormothr*). Chester style. Willoughby Gardner; no provenance stated on Gardner's ticket but older accompanying ticket seems to be a Baldwin one. Die-duplicate of *SCBI 6*, 218. Same rev. die as *SCBI 34*, 452.
199.	1.56	24.1	135°	Thrmod(e) (*Thormothr*). Chester style. Willoughby Gardner; ex Lincoln ex Ready (1920) 94.
200.	1.61	24.8	45°	Thrmod (*Thormothr*). Chester style. Willoughby Gardner; ex Lincoln. Same obv. die as *SCBI 34*, 452.
201.	1.09 chipped at edges	16.8	270°	Thrmod (*Thormothr*). Chester style. Willoughby Gardner; ex J. H. Dormer (dealer); presumably ex Dudman (1913) 234 (lot bt by Dormer); ex Allen (1898) 229; ex Lewin Sheppard (1861) 110. Second line of rev. inscription retrograde.
202.	1.57	24.2	225°	Thrmod (*Thrormothr*). Chester style. Willoughby Gardner; ex Spink (*NCirc* Nov–Dec 1921, 98539) (C. M. Crompton-Roberts collection); ex Bateman Heirlooms (1893) 304. Die-duplicate of *SCBI 4*, 730, and of Spink sale 1 (11 Oct 1978), lot 112.
203.	1.72	26.5	180°	Vvlfstan (*Wulfstan*). Chester style. Chester (1950) hoard, no. 113. Same rev. die as, and possibly die-duplicate of, coin in National Museum of Dublin, ex Smarmore hoard.
204.	1.53	23.6	180°	Vvlfstan (*Wulfstan*). Chester style. Willoughby Gardner; ex Spink (*NCirc* May 1937, 61166). Die-duplicate of *SCBI 50*, 237. Same rev. die as *SCBI 34*, 459.
205	1.50	23.1	180°	Vvlfstan (*Wulfstan*). Chester style. Willoughby Gardner; ex Baldwin; ex Thorburn (1918) 61. Die-duplicate of *SCBI 50*, 238.
206.	1.53	23.6	0°	Vvlfstan (*Wulfstan*). Chester style. Willoughby Gardner; ex Spink (*NCirc* Mar–Apr 1924, 28950 (Gardner wrongly recorded number as 28953)). Same obv. die as *SCBI 34*, 459.
207.	1.57	24.2	45°	Wlfstan (*Wulfstan*). Chester style. Willoughby Gardner; ex Parsons.
208.	1.34	20.7	90°	Demence. Chester hoard (1950), no. 75.
209.	1.41	21.7	0°	Othelric(es) (*Othilric*). Derby style. Chester (1950) hoard, no. 101. Die-duplicate of coin in Rome; ex Forum hoard.
210.	0.79 fragment	12.1	–	Sica[ ] (*Sigegar*). Derby style. Chester (1950) hoard, no. 105.
211.	1.25	19.3	45°	Sigwold(es) (*Sigeweald*). Derby style. Chester (1950) hoard, no. 107.
212.	1.38	21.3	270°	Wuccgar(es) (*Wulfgar*). Derby style. Chester (1950) hoard, no. 112. Same rev. die as Spink sale 6 (10 Oct 1979), lot 269.
213.	1.35	20.8	270°	Athelulf (*Æthelwulf*). Unlocated Midlands style. Chester (1950) hoard, no. 65. Same rev. die as *SCBI 34*, 406. Reverse inscription retrograde.
214.	1.41 chipped	21.7	135°	Cenb[ ]rht (*Coenbeorht*). Unlocated Midlands style. Chester (1950) hoard (but not in published list).
215.	1.62	25.0	180°	Eadstan. Uncertain Midlands style. Chester (1950) hoard, no. 81. Same rev. die as *SCBI 34*, 423.
216.	- fragment	-		Eadst[ ](*Eadstan*). Uncertain Midlands style. Chester (1950) hoard, no. 82. Same rev. die as *SCBI 34*, 422.

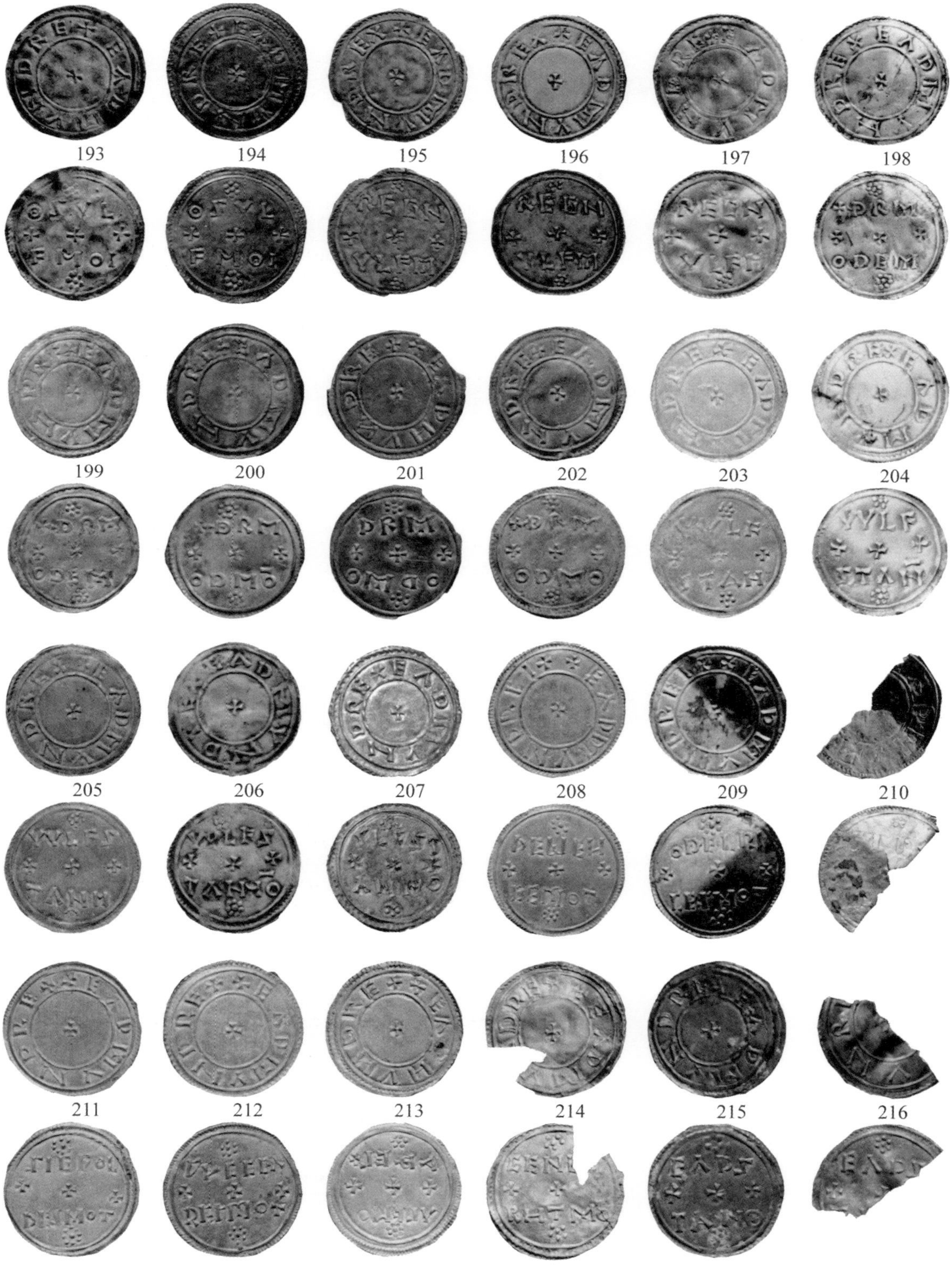

193 194 195 196 197 198

199 200 201 202 203 204

205 206 207 208 209 210

211 212 213 214 215 216

EDMUND (*cont.*)

R/HR1 type

	Weight g	Weight gr.	Die-Axis	
217.	1.47	22.7	180°	Amund(es) (*Æthelmund*?). Unlocated West Midlands style. Chester (1950) hoard, no. 117.

HM var (a) type

	g	gr.	Die-Axis	
218.	1.60	24.7	45°	Eadmund. Chester style. Willoughby Gardner; ex Thorburn (1918) 61; ex Montagu (1895) 664; ex Londesborough (1888) 870. Die-duplicate of next, and of *SCBI 50*, 233. Same obv. die as *SCBI 34*, 420 and 421.
219.	1.53	23.6	315°	Eadmund. Chester style. Willoughby Gardner; ex Parsons. Die-duplicate of last.

HR1 var (a) type

	g	gr.	Die-Axis	
220.	1.41	21.7	180°	Derby (**DER**) Afra. Chester (1950) hoard, 1975 parcel coin 4.

[Note that a fragmentary coin attributed to Edmund in the original publication of the Chester (1950) hoard, HT1 type, moneyer Leofric, no. 91, will be found listed below under the heading UNCERTAIN RULER.]

EADRED (946–55)

HT1 type

	g	gr.	Die-Axis	
221.	0.96 chipped	14.8	135°	Theodmaer (*Theodmær*). Derby style. Chester (1950) hoard, no. 225.
222.	1.41 slightly chipped	21.7	90°	Hunred (*Hunræd*). Northern East Midlands style. Chester (1950) hoard, no. 190.
223	1.47	22.7	180°	Hunred (*Hunræd*). Northern East Midlands style. Chester (1950) hoard, no. 192. Letter **O** in rev. inscription contains a small cross.
224.	1.52	23.4	90°	Hunred (*Hunræd*). Northern East Midlands style. Chester (1950) hoard, no. 193.
225.	0.80 broken half (?)	12.3	–	Hun[ ] (*Hunræd*). Northern East Midlands style. Chester (1950) hoard, no. 194.
226.	0.79 cut halfpenny (?)	12.2	0°	[ ]nr[ ](*Hunræd*). Northern East Midlands style. Chester (1950) hoard, no. 191.
227.	1.38	21.3	0°	Hunred (*Hunræd*). Northern East Midlands style. GM 276.55; ex Edward Davies.
228.	1.50 Wt given by Moore	23.1	–	Theodmaer (*Theodmær*). Northern East Midlands style (probably). Chester (1950) hoard, 1975 parcel coin 8. (*Not located or illustrated.*)
229.	1.55	23.9	180°	Athelmund (*Æthelmund*). Southern/Unlocated Midlands style. Chester (1950) hoard, no. 127. Apparently die-duplicate of coin in E. J. Harris collection. Same rev. die as *SCBI 34*, 498.
230.	1.51	23.3	0°	Athelmund (*Æthelmund*). Southern/Unlocated Midlands style. Chester (1950) hoard, no. 128.
231.	1.42	21.9	0°	Baldvvin (*Baldwin*). Southern/Unlocated Midlands style. Chester (1950) hoard, no. 139.
232.	1.28	19.8	180°	Baldvvin (*Baldwin*). Southern/Unlocated Midlands style. Chester (1950) hoard, no. 140.
233.	1.55	23.9	0°	Beahred (*Beagræd*). Southern/Unlocated Midlands style. Chester (1950) hoard, no. 142.
234.	1.24	19.1	270°	Bernehe (*Beornehere*). Southern/Unlocated Midlands style. Chester (1950) hoard, no. 145.
235.	1.55	23.9	315°	Biorhtulf (*Beorhtwulf*). Southern/Unlocated Midlands style. Chester (1950) hoard, no. 147. Die-duplicate of *SCBI 34*, 508.
236.	1.32	20.3	0°	Gislehelm. Southern/Unlocated Midlands style. Chester (1950) hoard, no. 176.
237.	1.39	21.4	0°	Grim (*Grimr*). Southern/Unlocated Midlands style. Chester (1950) hoard, no. 180. Die-duplicate of *SCBI 9*, 359.
238.	1.48	22.8	90°	Heremod. Southern/Unlocated Midlands style. Chester (1950) hoard, no. 182.
239.	1.52	23.4	180°	Heremod. Southern/Unlocated Midlands style. Chester (1950) hoard, no. 183. Same obv. die as *SCBI 34*, 525, same rev. die as coin in Manx Museum.
240.	1.49	23.0	270°	Heremod. Southern/Unlocated Midlands style. Chester (1950) hoard, no. 184.
241.	1.55	23.9	90°	Heremod. Southern/Unlocated Midlands style. Chester (1950) hoard, no. 185.

PLATE 10

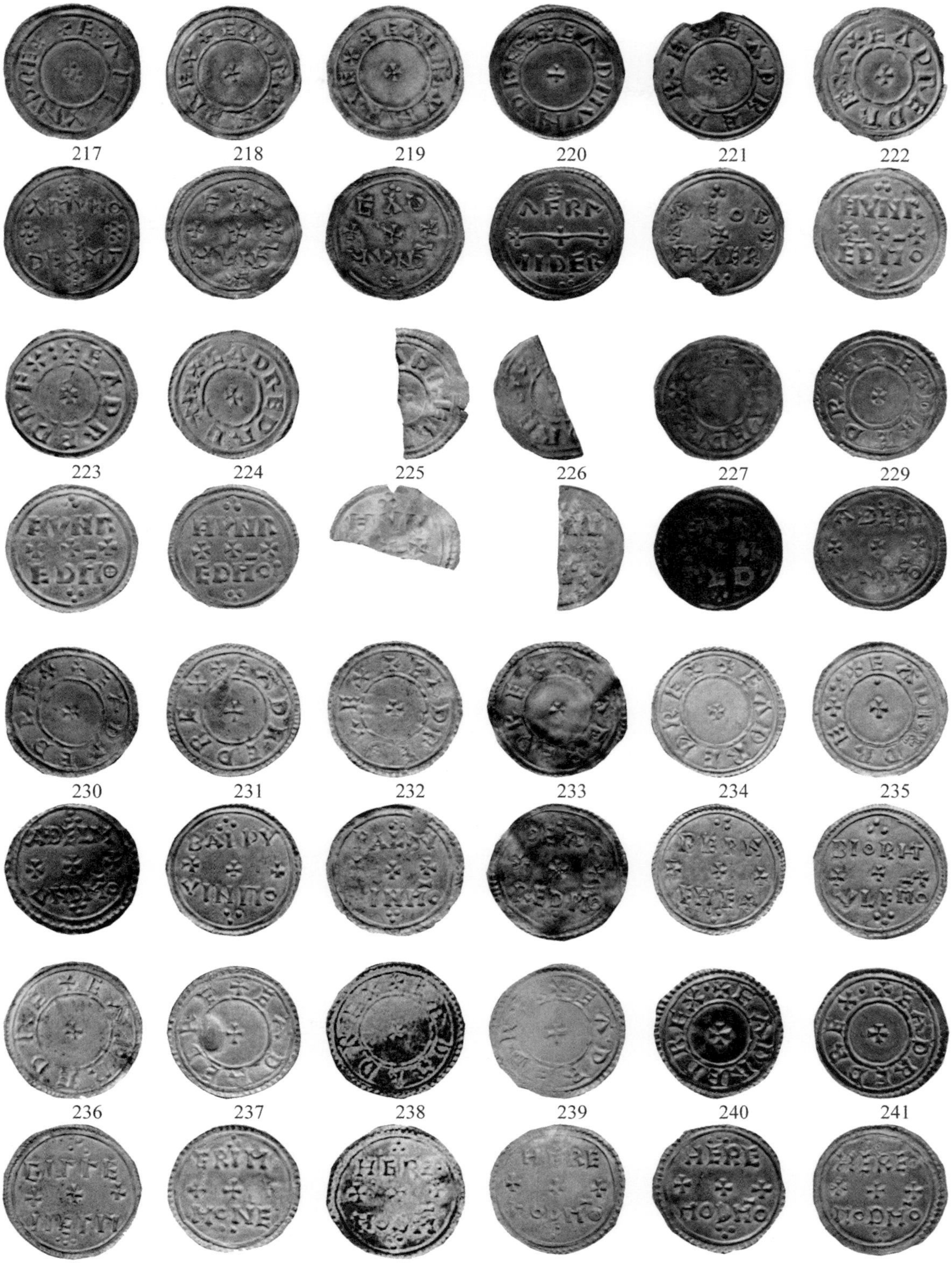

217 218 219 220 221 222

223 224 225 226 227 229

230 231 232 233 234 235

236 237 238 239 240 241

EADRED (*cont.*)

HT1 type (*cont.*)

	Weight *g*	*gr.*	Die-Axis	
242.	1.43	22.1	180°	Leofhelm. Southern/Unlocated Midlands style. Chester (1950) hoard, no. 197. Die-duplicate of next coin.
243.	1.51	23.3	180°	Leofhelm. Southern/Unlocated Midlands style. Chester (1950) hoard, no. 196. Die-duplicate of previous coin.
244.	1.07 chipped	16.5	180°	Leofstan. Southern/Unlocated Midlands style. Willoughby Gardner (via Mrs Gardner 1963); ex Lincoln.
245.	1.64	25.3	270°	Martin. Southern/Unlocated Midlands style. Willoughby Gardner; ex Grantley (1944) 1077. Same rev. die as *SCBI 34*, 321 and as coin from Winchester Cathedral Excavations, *BNJ* 47 (1977), p. 136, no. 4, both of which have Eadmund obv. dies.
246.	1.49	23.0	270°	Osefrth (*Osferth*). Southern/Unlocated Midlands style. Chester (1950) hoard, no. 204. Same rev. die as *SCBI 34* 323, which has an Eadmund obv. die.
247.	1.66	25.6	180°	Otic. Southern/Unlocated Midlands style. Chester (1950) hoard, no. 214.
248.	1.22	18.8	180°	Siefereth (*Sigeferth*). Southern/Unlocated Midlands style. Willoughby Gardner; ex P. Carlyon-Britton (1916) 999; ex Spink (*NCirc* Jun 1910, 76554) (Sir John Evans collection), 'from Ireland'.
249.	1.30	20.1	45°	Heriger (*Hereger*). York style. Chester (1950) hoard, no. 187.
HCT1 var type				
250.	1.53	23.6	90°	Osulf (*Asulfr/Oswulf*). Southern style. Chester (1950) hoard, no. 208. Pellets at each side of cross at top of rev.
HT1 type (NE I)				
251.	1.38	21.3	225°	Manna. Central East Midlands style. Chester (1950) hoard, no. 203.
252.	1.46 wt given by Moore	22.5	–	Wilebert (*Wilbeorht*). Central East Midlands style. Chester (1950) hoard, 1975 parcel coin 7. (*Not located or illustrated.*)
HR1 type				
253.	1.64	25.3	0°	Thurmod (*Thurmothr*). Chester style. Willoughby Gardner; ex Lincoln. Die-duplicate of *SCBI 34*, 635 and of coin in National Museum of Ireland ex Newtownlow hoard. Same obv. die as next.
254.	1.52	23.4	270°	Thurmod (*Thurmothr*). Chester style. Chester (1950) hoard, no. 228. Die-duplicate of *SCBI 6*, 287. Same obv. die as last.
255.	1.60 slightly chipped	24.7	270°	Vvlfstn (*Wulfstan*). Chester style. Willoughby Gardner; ex Gantz. Die-duplicate of *SCBI 34*, 645 and of *SCBI 2*, 659.
256.	1.26	19.4	0°	Æthered (*Æthelræd*). Derby/Unlocated East Midlands style. Willoughby Gardner; ex Spink; ex P. Carlyon-Britton (1913) 417. S in obv. field at 7 o'clock. Same rev. die as coin in National Museum of Ireland, ex Newtownlow hoard.
257.	1.27	19.6	270°	Agtard(es). Derby/Unlocated East Midlands style. Chester (1950) hoard, no. 131.
258.	1.45	22.3	315°	Agtard(es). Derby/Unlocated East Midlands style. Chester (1950) hoard, no. 134.
259.	1.22	18.8	45°	Agtard(es). Derby/Unlocated East Midlands style. Chester (1950) hoard, no. 133.
260.	1.26	19.5	0°	Agtard(es). Derby/Unlocated East Midlands style. Chester (1950) hoard, no. 132.
261.	1.53	23.6	225°	Bernard (*Beornheard*). Derby/Unlocated East Midlands style. Chester (1950) hoard, no. 144.
262.	1.21	18.6	225°	Boga(es). Derby/Unlocated East Midlands style. Chester (1950) hoard, no. 149. Die-duplicate of *SCBI* 34, 604 and of next coin, probably also of *SCBI 6*, 274.
263.	1.46	22.5	0°	Boga(es). Derby/Unlocated East Midlands style. Willoughby Gardner; ex P. Carlyon-Britton (1916) 1003. Die-duplicate of previous coin.
264.	1.18 slightly chipped	18.2	270°	Boge(es) (*Boga*). Derby/Unlocated East Midlands style. Willoughby Gardner; ex Spink 3 Nov 1944.
265.	1.03	15.9	45°	Boiga(es) (*Boga*). Derby/Unlocated East Midlands style. Chester (1950) hoard, no. 148.
266.	1.21	18.6	45°	Boiga(es) (*Boga*). Derby/Unlocated East Midlands style. Chester (1950) hoard, no. 151.

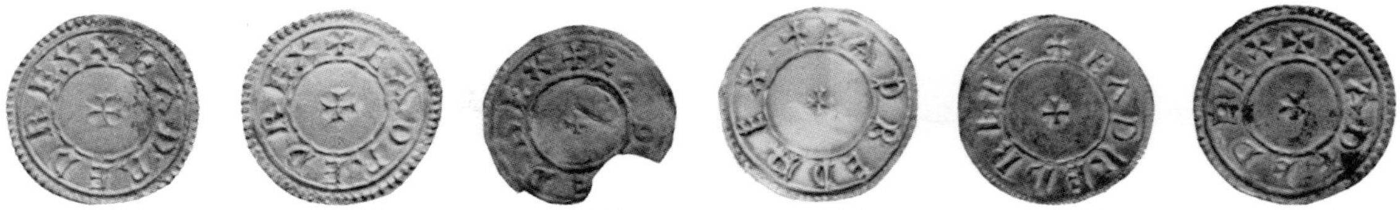

242 243 244 245 246 247

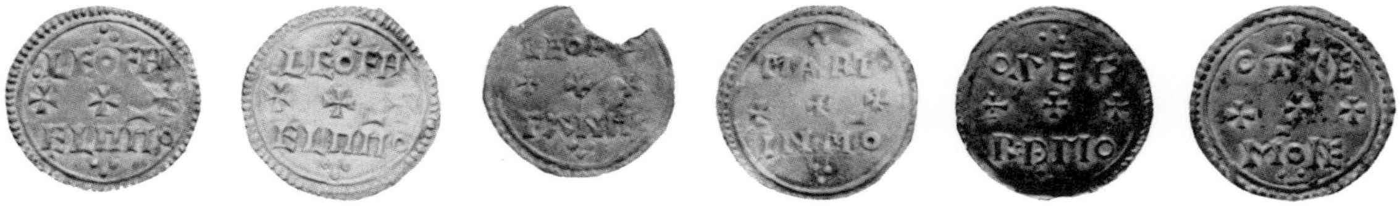

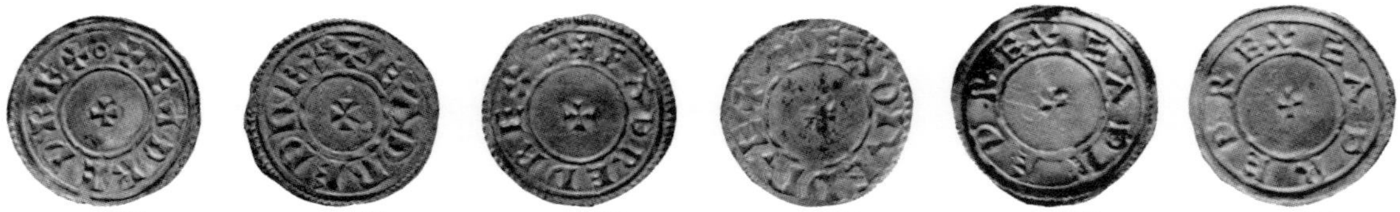

248 249 250 251 253 254

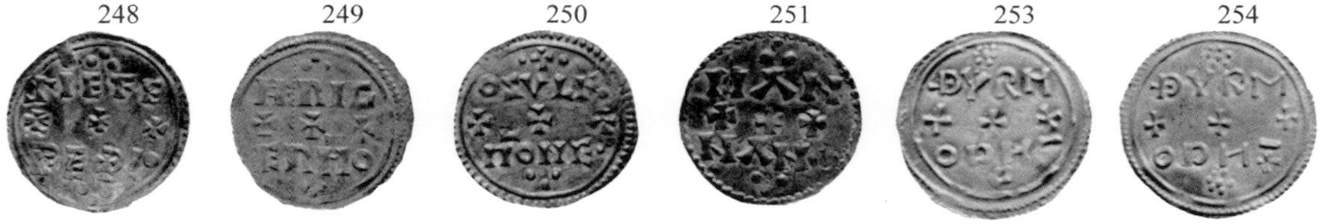

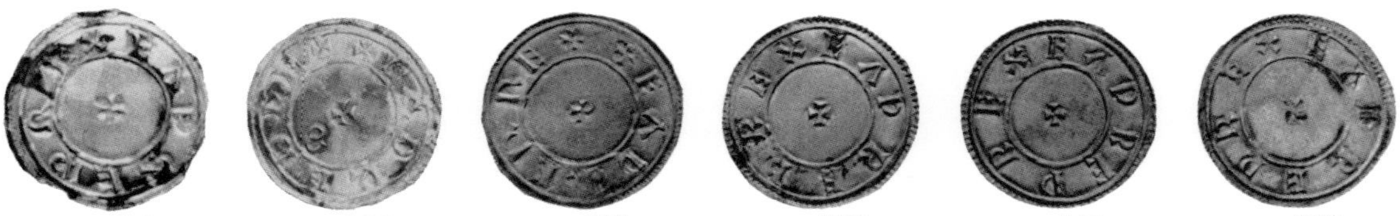

255 256 257 258 259 260

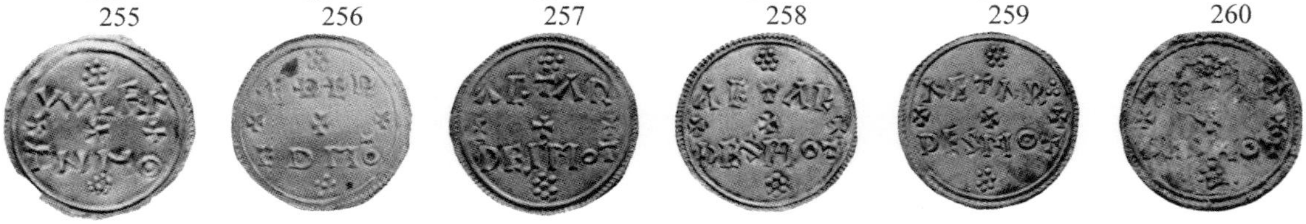

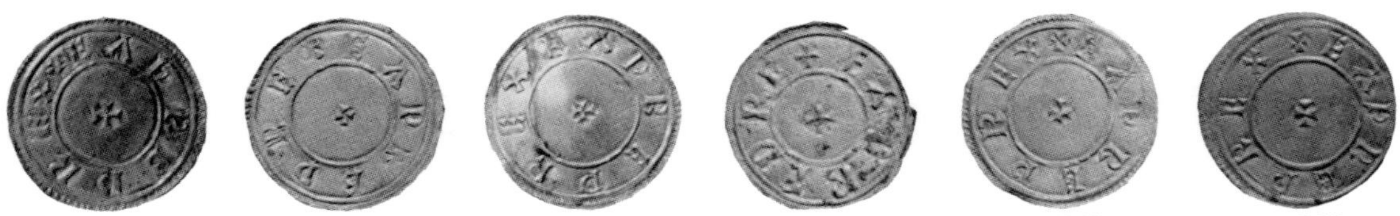

261 262 263 264 265 266

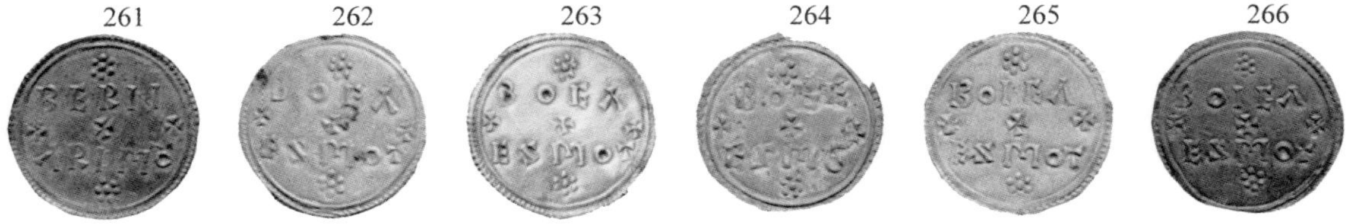

EADRED (*cont.*)

HR1 type (*cont.*)

	Weight g	*Weight* gr.	*Die-Axis*	
267.	1.05 slightly chipped	16.2	315°	Boiga(es) (*Boga*). Derby/Unlocated East Midlands style. Willoughby Gardner; ex Lincoln; ex Ready (1920) 96.
268.	1.11	17.1	0°	Boiga(es) (*Boga*). Derby/Unlocated East Midlands style. Willoughby Gardner; ex P. Carlyon-Britton (1916) 1003.
269.	1.43	22.1	180°	Boiga(es) (*Boga*). Derby/Unlocated East Midlands style. Willoughby Gardner; ex Spink (*NCirc* Jun 1910, 76556) (Sir John Evans collection); ex Killyon Manor hoard.
270.	1.46	22.5	90°	Boiga(es) (*Boga*). Derby/Unlocated East Midlands style. A. C. Hirons 1955 (gift, GM 29 M 55), found in Chester, 'near the amphitheatre', July 1951. M in obv. field at 2.30 o'clock.
271.	1.33	20.5	315°	Boiga(es) (*Boga*). Derby/Unlocated East Midlands style. Chester (1950) hoard, no. 150. Same obv. die and possibly same rev. die as *SCBI 6*, 273.
272.	1.08	16.6	180°	Boiga(i) (*Boga*). Derby/Unlocated East Midlands style. Chester (1950) hoard, no. 152. Die-duplicate of next.
273.	1.13	17.4	0°	Boiga(i) (*Boga*). Derby/Unlocated East Midlands style. Willoughby Gardner; ex Spink; ex P. Carlyon-Britton (not in sales). Die-duplicate of last.
274.	1.36	21.0	0°	Ethelulf(es) (*Æthelwulf*). Derby/Unlocated East Midlands style. Chester (1950) hoard, no. 129.
275.	1.19 slightly chipped	18.3	180°	Frethic(es) (*Freothuric/Fredric*). Derby/Unlocated East Midlands style. Willoughby Gardner; ex Gantz.
276.	1.31	20.2	0°	Frethic(es) (*Freothuric/Fredric*). Derby/Unlocated East Midlands style. Chester (1950) hoard, no. 163.
277.	1.40	21.6	225°	Frethic(es) (*Freothuric/Fredric*). Derby/Unlocated East Midlands style. Chester (1950) hoard, no. 164. Die-duplicate of *SCBI 20*, 789. M in obv. field at 10 o'clock.
278.	1.23	19.0	90°	Frethic(es) (*Freothuric/Fredric*). Derby/Unlocated East Midlands style. Chester (1950) hoard, no. 165. Perhaps die-duplicate of *SCBI 4*, 739.
279.	1.10	16.9	135°	Frethic(es) (*Freothuric/Fredric*). Derby/Unlocated East Midlands style. Chester (1950) hoard, no. 166.
280.	1.29 wt given by Moore	19.9	–	Frethic(es) (*Freothuric/Fredric*). Derby/Unlocated East Midlands style. Chester (1950) hoard, 1975 parcel coin 5. (*Not located or illustrated.*)
281.	1.24	19.1	315°	Frethic(s) (*Freothuric/Fredric*). Derby/Unlocated East Midlands style. Chester (1950) hoard, no. 167. Perhaps die-duplicate of *SCBI 34*, 613.
282.	1.17	18.1	0°	Gislemer (*Gislamar*). Derby/Unlocated East Midlands style. Chester (1950) hoard, no. 177.
283.	1.37	21.1	135°	Gislemer (*Gislamar*). Derby/Unlocated East Midlands style. Chester (1950) hoard, no. 178.
284.	1.30	20.1	90°	Grim(es) (*Grimr*). Derby/Unlocated East Midlands style. Chester (1950) hoard, no. 181.
285.	1.20	18.5	0°	Grim(es) (*Grimr*). Derby/Unlocated East Midlands style. Chester (1950) hoard, no. 179.
286.	1.28	19.7	270°	Man(es). Derby/Unlocated East Midlands style. Chester (1950) hoard, no. 202.
287.	1.19 slightly chipped	18.3	0°	Oslac (*Aslakr*). Derby/Unlocated East Midlands style. Willoughby Gardner; ex Spink (*NCirc* Sep–Oct 1920, 85613) (C. M. Crompton-Roberts collection); evidently ex Briggs (1893) 204; and therefore ex Howard (1874) 17.
288.	1.34	20.7	90°	Osulf(es) (*Asulfr/Oswulf*). Derby/Unlocated East Midlands style. Willoughby Gardner; ex P. Carlyon-Britton (1916) 1005; perhaps ex Sotheby 12 Jun 1899, lot 287; ex Ballaquayle hoard. M in obv. field at 3 o'clock. Same obv. die as *SCBI 34*, 599, moneyer Arnulf, and coin in Oslo, moneyer Oban.
289.	1.43	22.1	135°	Othelric(es) (*Othilric*). Derby/Unlocated East Midlands style. Chester (1950) hoard, no. 210. M in obv. field at 1 o'clock. Apparently from same obv. die as *SCBI 16*, 161, moneyer Elfred.
290.	1.35	20.8	45°	Othelric(es) (*Othilric*). Derby/Unlocated East Midlands style. Chester (1950) hoard, no. 212.
291.	1.36	21.0	90°	Othelric(es) (*Othilric*). Derby/Unlocated East Midlands style. Chester (1950) hoard, no. 213. Same rev. die as *SCBI 34*, 628 and *SCBI 4*, 750.

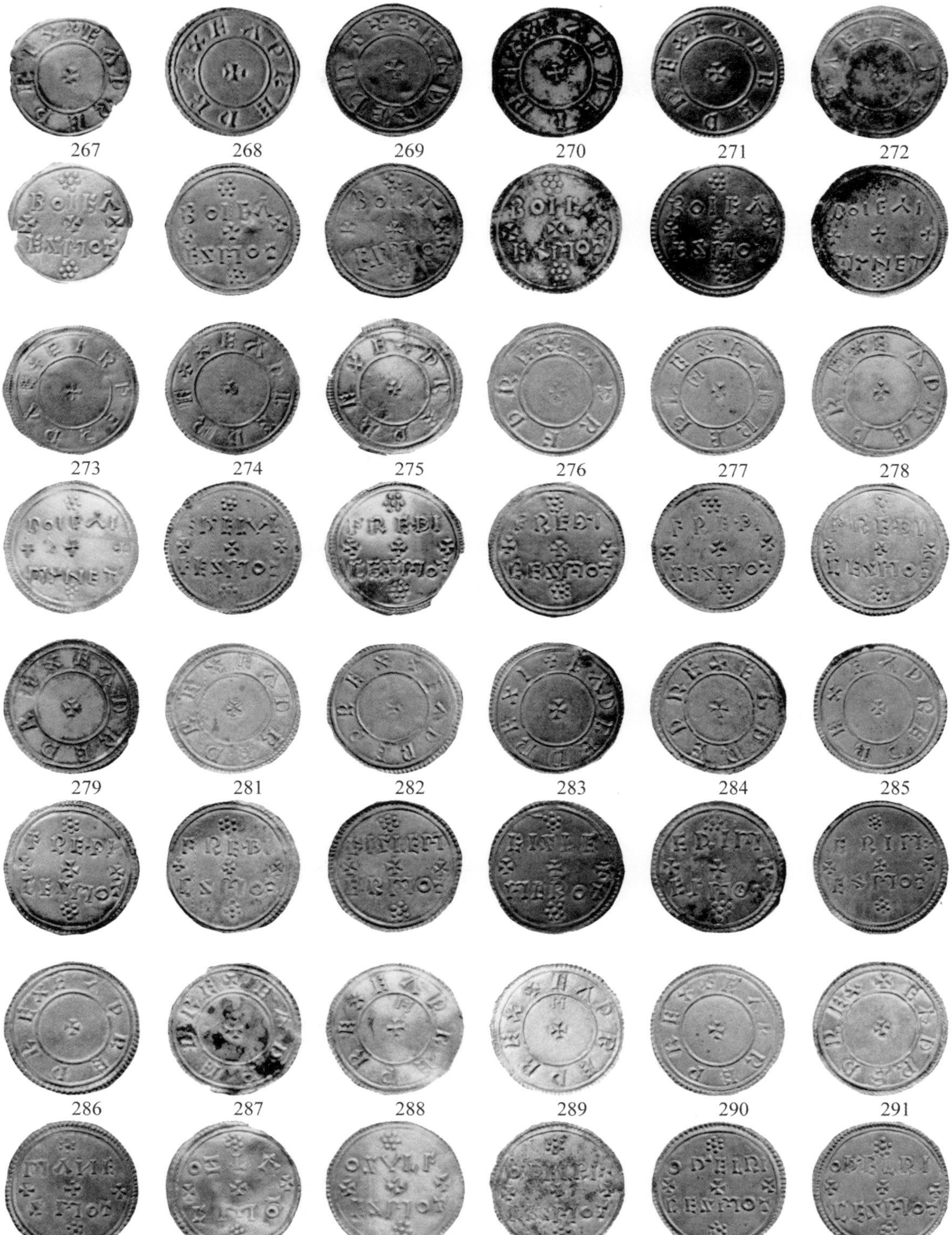

267 268 269 270 271 272

273 274 275 276 277 278

279 281 282 283 284 285

286 287 288 289 290 291

EADRED (*cont.*)

HR1 type (*cont.*)

	Weight g	*Weight* gr.	*Die-Axis*	
292.	1.48	22.8	0°	Othelric(es) (*Othilric*). Derby/Unlocated East Midlands style. Chester (1950) hoard, no. 211.
293.	1.35 wt given by Moore	20.8	–	Othelric(es) (*Othilric*). Derby/Unlocated East Midlands style. Chester (1950) hoard, 1975 parcel coin 13. (*Not located or illustrated.*)
294.	1.38	21.3	225°	Redwine (*Rædwine*). Derby/Unlocated East Midlands style. Chester (1950) hoard, no. 215.
295.	1.51	23.3	315°	Regther(es). Derby/Unlocated East Midlands style. Chester (1950) hoard, no. 217.
296.	1.47	22.7	270°	Regther(es). Derby/Unlocated East Midlands style. Chester (1950) hoard, no. 218.
297.	1.48	22.8	270°	Regther(es). Derby/Unlocated East Midlands style. Chester (1950) hoard, no. 216. M in obv. field at 5 o'clock.
298.	1.42	21.9	90°	Sfear (*Sigegar*?). Derby/Unlocated East Midlands style. Chester (1950) hoard, no. 222. Apparently die-duplicate of coin in Dresden.
299.	1.23	19.0	225°	Sigar (*Sigegar*). Derby/Unlocated East Midlands style. Chester (1950) hoard, no. 221. Same obv. die as *SCBI 34*, 634.
300.	1.31	20.2	180°	Sigar(es) (*Sigegar*). Derby/Unlocated East Midlands style. Chester (1950) hoard, no. 223.
301.	1.43	22.1	0°	Sigar(es) (Sigegar). Derby/Unlocated East Midlands style. Chester (1950) hoard, no. 224. Same rev. die as *SCBI 50*, 249.
302.	1.26	19.4	45°	Dermod (*Thormothr*?). Derby/Unlocated East Midlands style. Willoughby Gardner; ex L. S. Forrer; ex Virgil Brand; ex P. Carlyon-Britton (1913) 418; presumably ex Spink (*NCirc* Apr 1907, 38988); and ex 'A Gentleman', Sotheby 18 Feb 1907, lot 88 (lot bought by Spink). M in obv. field at 6 o'clock.
303.	1.38	21.3	315°	Wulfgar(es). Derby/Unlocated East Midlands style. Willoughby Gardner; ex P. Carlyon-Britton (1913) 422. M in obv. field at 9 o'clock.
304.	1.17 slightly chipped	18.1	45°	Wulfgar(es). Derby/Unlocated East Midlands style. Willoughby Gardner.
305.	1.40 slightly chipped	21.6	225°	Wulfgar(es). Derby/Unlocated East Midlands style. Willoughby Gardner; ex Baldwin; ex Henry Lawrence (1923) 50.
306.	1.36	21.0	45°	Wulfgar(es). Derby/Unlocated East Midlands style. Chester (1950) hoard, no. 237.
307.	0.96 fragment	14.8	90°	Wulfgar(es). Derby/Unlocated East Midlands style. Willoughby Gardner; ex Lincoln. M in obv. field at 3 o'clock. Same obv. die as *SCBI 6*, 285.
308.	1.31	20.2	0°	Wulgar(es). Derby/Unlocated East Midlands style. Chester (1950) hoard, no. 239.
309.	1.30	20.1	180°	Wulgar(es). Derby/Unlocated East Midlands style. Chester (1950) hoard, no. 238.
310.	1.27	19.6	0°	Wulgar(es). Derby/Unlocated East Midlands style. Chester (1950) hoard, no. 236.
311.	1.50	23.1	270°	Wulgar(es). Derby/Unlocated East Midlands style. Willoughby Gardner; apparently ex Lincoln.
312.	1.22 chipped	18.8	45°	Wulfstan. Derby/Unlocated East Midlands style. Willoughby Gardner; ex Lincoln; ex Ready (1920) 98.
313.	1.46	22.5	90°	Amund(es). Unlocated Midlands style. Chester (1950) hoard, no. 135.
314.	1.17 slightly chipped	18.1	180°	Baldc (*Baldric*?). Unlocated Midlands style. Chester (1950) hoard, no. 137.
315.	1.33 broken in two pieces	20.5	90°	Baldric. Unlocated Midlands style. Chester (1950) hoard, no. 138.
316.	1.34 chipped	20.7	315°	Cenbe[ ]ht (*Coenbeorht*). Unlocated Midlands style. Chester (1950) hoard, no. 153.

PLATE 13

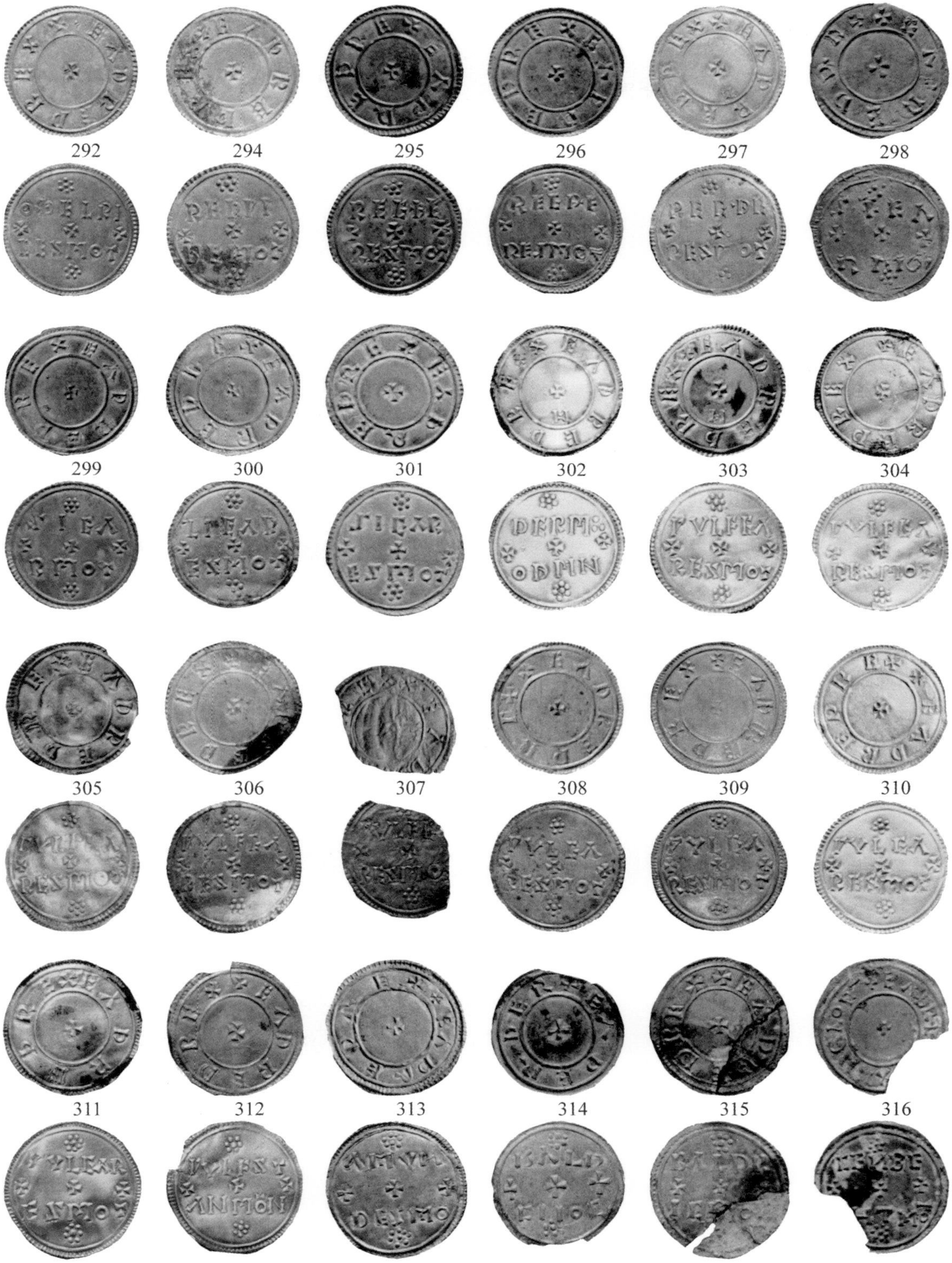

292 294 295 296 297 298

299 300 301 302 303 304

305 306 307 308 309 310

311 312 313 314 315 316

EADRED (*cont.*)

HR1 type (*cont.*)

	Weight *g*	Weight *gr.*	Die-Axis	
317.	1.44	22.2	270°	Dudid (*Duding*?). Unlocated Midlands style. Chester (1950) hoard, no. 158.
318.	1.64	25.3	90°	Hildulf (*Hildulfr*). Unlocated Midlands style. Chester (1950) hoard, no. 188. Die-duplicate of *SCBI 34*, 618 and of *SCBI 4*, 743.

HR2 type

	Weight *g*	Weight *gr.*	Die-Axis	
319.	1.62	25.0	0°	Ælfsie (*Ælfsige*). Chester style. Chester (1950) hoard, no. 124.
320.	1.54	23.7	135°	Ælfsige. Chester style. Chester (1950) hoard, no. 125.
321.	1.55	23.9	270°	Deorulf (*Deorwulf*). Chester style. Willoughby Gardner; ex Lincoln.
322.	0.81 fragment	12.5	180°	[ ]lf (*Deorwulf*?). Chester style. Chester (1950) hoard, no. 520.
323.	1.61	24.8	0°	Dorulf (*Deorwulf*). Chester style. Willoughby Gardner; ex Spink; ex P. Carlyon-Britton (1913) 423. Die-duplicate of *SCBI 34*, 650. Same obv. die as coin of HR 2 var c. type below.
324.	1.45 slightly chipped	22.3	90°	Duran (*Durand*). Chester style. Willoughby Gardner; ex Sotheby 15 Dec 1931, lot 143. Die-duplicate of *SCBI 6*, 289 and of *SCBI 4*, 737 and 737a.
325.	1.51	23.3	225°	Eadmun (*Eadmund*). Chester style. Chester (1950) hoard, no. 161.
326.	1.55	23.9	225°	Eadmun (*Eadmund*). Chester style. Willoughby Gardner; ex P. Carlyon-Britton (1916) 1007. Same rev. die as previous coin.
327.	1.62	25.0	0°	Eadmund. Chester style. Willoughby Gardner; ex Baldwin (with Baldwin ticket, stock no. 5260).
328.	1.52	23.4	180°	Eoroth (*Iorothr*). Chester style. Willoughby Gardner; ex Spink (*NCirc* Mar–Apr 1915, 28753); ex 'G.R.F.2.15' (presumably to be interpreted as ex Grant Francis, February 1915). Possibly die-duplicate of coin in Manx Museum, Douglas.
329.	1.60	24.7	135°	Eroth (*Iorothr*). Chester style. Willoughby Gardner; ex Lincoln.
330.	1.47	22.7	0°	Frard (*Eoferheard*?). Chester style. Willoughby Gardner; ex Sir John Evans (but not from *NCirc* Jun 1910, where other Evans coins of Eadred offered); ex Montagu (1895) 686. Same rev. die as next two coins.
331.	1.45	22.3	0°	Frard (*Eoferheard*?). Chester style. Willoughby Gardner; ex Spink (*NCirc* Sep–Oct 1920, 85611) (C. M. Crompton-Roberts collection); evidently ex Briggs (1893) 205. Die-duplicate of *SCBI 34*, 653 and of *SCBI 50*, 246. Same rev. die as previous coin and as next coin.
332.	1.45 slightly chipped	22.3	90°	Frard (*Eoferheard*?). Chester style. Willoughby Gardner; ex Spink; ex Bascom (1914) 66. Same rev. die as previous two coins.
333.	1.54 wt given by Moore	23.7	–	Frar(a?)d (*Eoferheard*?). Chester style. Chester (1950) hoard, 1975 parcel coin 6. Legends recorded by Moore as +EADRED RE and FRARAD MO, but reverse reading should no doubt be FRARD MO. (*Not located or illustrated*).
334.	1.49 slightly chipped	23.0	90°	Frothric (*Freothuric/Fredric*). Chester style. Willoughby Gardner; ex Baldwin. Die-duplicate of next coin, and of *SCBI 6*, 291.
335.	1.57	24.2	180°	Frothric (*Freothuric/Fredric*). Chester style. Chester (1950) hoard, no. 173. Die-duplicate of previous coin.
336.	1.70	26.2	270°	Frothric (*Freothuric/Fredric*). Chester style. Chester (1950) hoard, no. 170. Same obv. die as *SCBI 6*, 292, same rev. die as *SCBI 4*, 741.
337.	1.59	24.5	180°	Frothric (*Freothuric/Fredric*). Chester style. Chester (1950) hoard, no. 171.
338.	1.54	23.7	180°	Frothric (*Freothuric/Fredric*). Chester style. Chester (1950) hoard, no. 172. Die-duplicate of *SCBI 9*, 368 and probably of *SCBI 30*, 358.
339.	1.47	22.7	90°	Frothric (*Freothuric/Fredric*). Chester style. Willoughby Gardner; ex Spink (*NCirc* Sep–Oct 1920, 85612) (C. M. Crompton-Roberts collection); evidently ex Briggs (1893) 204. Possibly die-duplicate of *SCBI 9*, 369.
340.	1.58	24.4	90°	Frothric (*Freothuric/Fredric*). Chester style. Willoughby Gardner; ex Baldwin.
341.	1.58	24.4	135°	Frothric (*Freothuric/Fredric*). Chester style. Willoughby Gardner; ex Baldwin; ex Parsons (1929) 107 (c).

PLATE 14

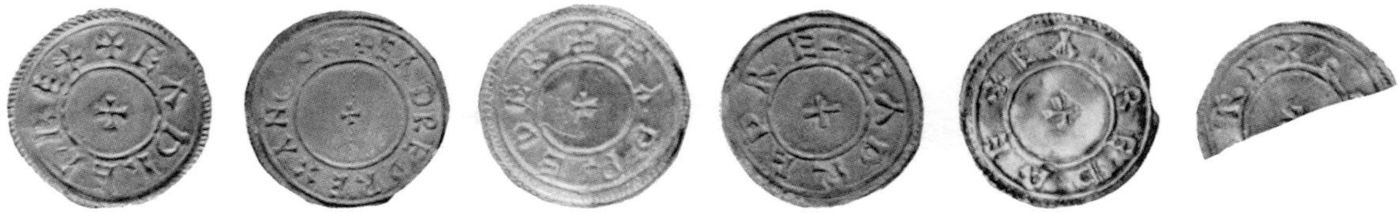

317 318 319 320 321 322

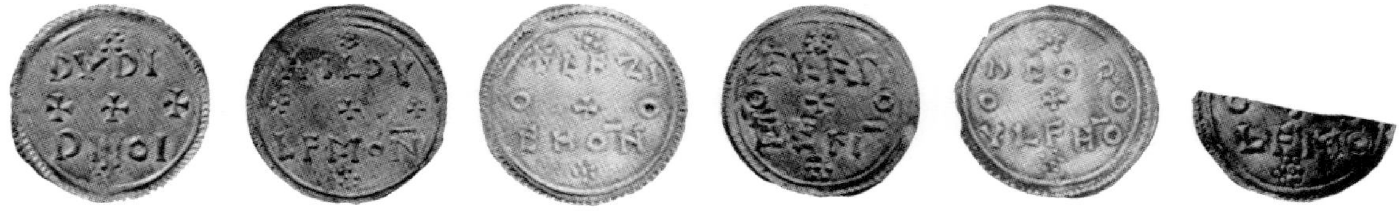

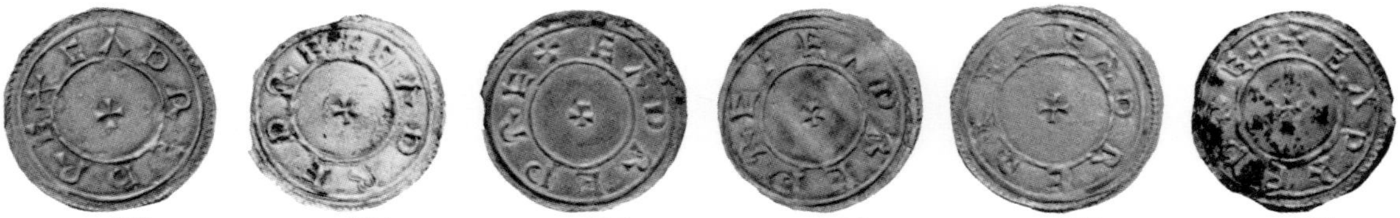

323 324 325 326 327 328

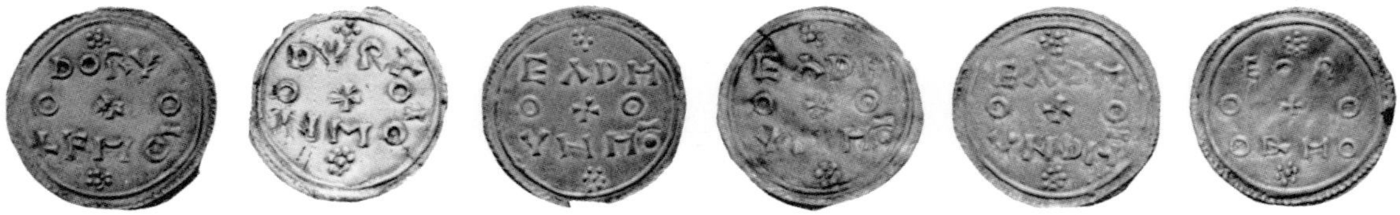

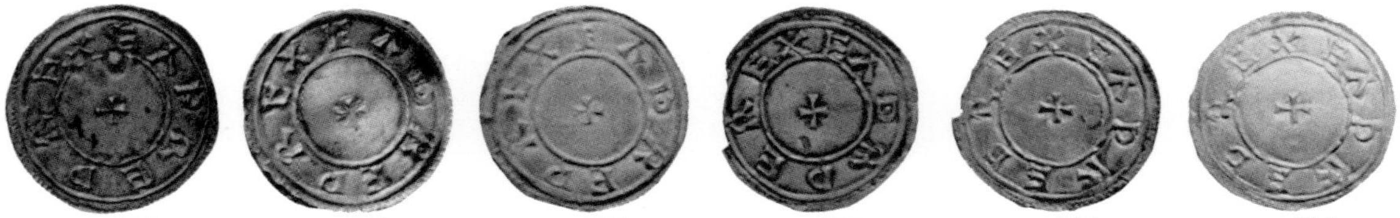

329 330 331 332 334 335

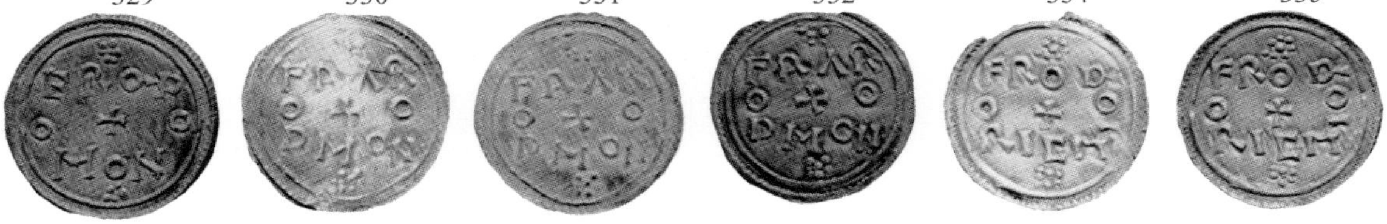

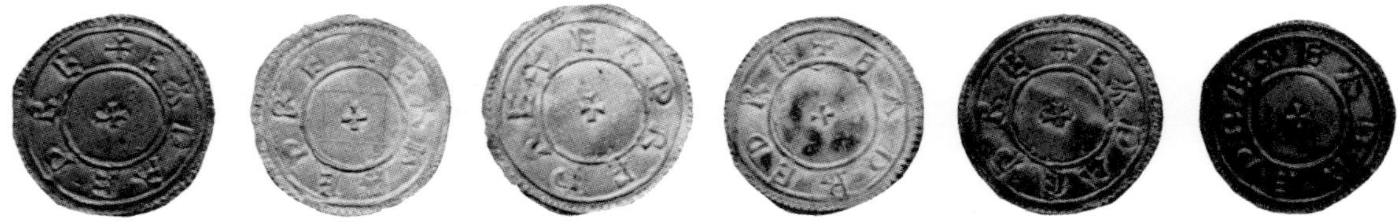

336 337 338 339 340 341

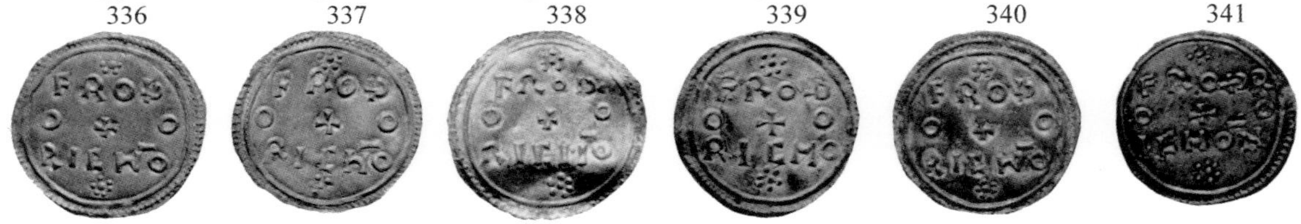

EADRED (*cont.*)

HR2 type (*cont.*)

	Weight g	Weight gr.	Die-Axis	
342.	1.59	24.5	45°	Gilles (*Gillys*). Chester style. Willoughby Gardner; ex Spink (but not from *NCirc* Jun 1910, where other coins of Eadred ex Evans offered); ex Sir John Evans; ex Killyon Manor hoard.
343.	1.43 slightly chipped	22.1	90°	Gilyl (*Gillys*). Chester style. Willoughby Gardner; ex Spink (*NCirc* Mar 1906, 25107).
344.	1.29	19.9	315°	Gilys (*Gillys*). Chester style. Willoughby Gardner; ex Gantz.
345.	1.59	24.5	180°	Siferth (*Sigeferth*). Chester style. Willoughby Gardner; ex Spink, ex P. Carlyon-Britton (1913) 425. Perhaps from same rev. die as coin in Manx Museum, Douglas.
346.	– fragmentary	–	–	Siferth (*Sigeferth*). Chester style. Chester (1857) hoard, Newstead Eadred no. 3.
347.	1.59	24.5	0°	Thurmod (*Thormothr*). Chester style. Chester (1950) hoard, no. 229.
348.	1.55 badly cracked	23.9	45°	Thurmod (*Thormothr*). Chester style. Chester (1950) hoard, no. 230.
349.	1.58	24.4	0°	Thurmod (*Thormothr*). Chester style. Chester (1950) hoard, no. 231.
350.	1.59	24.5	0°	Thurmod (*Thormothr*). Chester style. Willoughby Gardner; ex Spink (*NCirc* Mar–Apr 1922, 3653).
351.	1.41 broken in two pieces	21.7	180°	Thurmod (*Thormothr*). Chester style. Willoughby Gardner; ex Lincoln. Same rev. die as *SCBI 6*, 293.
352.	1.38 chipped	21.3	90°	Thurmod (*Thormothr*). Chester style. Willoughby Gardner; ex Lincoln.
353.	1.20 badly chipped	18.5	270°	Thurmod (*Thormothr*). Chester style. Willoughby Gardner (no explicit provenance but with original ticket of a dealer, perhaps Baldwin).
354.	1.38	21.3	270°	Thrmod (*Thormothr*). Chester style. Willoughby Gardner; ex Young (and therefore Joseph Young (1919) 30?). Die-duplicate of Noble (1975) 397. Same obv. die as next coin.
355.	1.37	21.1	45°	Thrmod (*Thormothr*). Chester style. Willoughby Gardner (via Mrs Gardner 1963); ex Spink (*NCirc* Sep–Oct 1920, 85614) (C. M. Crompton-Roberts collection); evidently ex Briggs (1893) 204. Same obv. die as previous coin.
356.	1.58	24.4	90°	Vverstan (*Wærstan*). Chester style. Chester (1950) hoard, no. 234. Die-duplicate of *SCBI 34*, 665.
357.	1.65	25.5	225°	Vvilaf (*Wiglaf*). Chester style. Chester (1950) hoard, no. 235. Probably die-duplicate of *SCBI 34*, 666. Same rev. die as coin in National Museum of Ireland, Dublin, ex Smarmore hoard.
358.	1.42	21.9	315°	Vvlfstan (*Wulfstan*). Chester style. Willoughby Gardner; ex Lincoln. Die-duplicate of *SCBI 34*, 668 and of *SCBI 2*, 660. Same obv. die as *SCBI 34*, 643–4, which have HR1 reverses. Same rev. die as next coin.
359.	1.44	22.2	180°	Vvlfstan (*Wulfstan*). Chester style. Chester (1950) hoard, no. 241. Same rev. die as previous coin.
360.	1.57	24.2	315°	Vvlfstan (*Wulfstan*). Chester style. Willoughby Gardner. Same obv. die as *NCirc* Feb 1990, 192. Same obv. die as next coin.
361.	1.44	22.2	0°	Vvlfstan (*Wulfstan*). Chester style. Willoughby Gardner (on an original Baldwin stock ticket no.5259 (but possibly ex Spink (*NCirc* Jun 1910, 76561) (Sir John Evans collection); ex Killyon Manor hoard).

HR2 var (a) type

	g	gr.	Die-Axis	
362.	1.52	23.4	270°	Gilles (*Gillys*). Chester style. Willoughby Gardner; ex Spink; ex P. Carlyon-Britton (1913) 423. Die-duplicate of *SCBI 34*, 672 and of *SCBI 21*, 1005.

HR2 var (b) type

	g	gr.	Die-Axis	
363.	1.42 slightly chipped	21.9	0°	Frothric (*Freothuric/Fredric*). Chester style. Willoughby Gardner; ex Lincoln. Die-duplicate of *SCBI 34*, 671, *SCBI 4*, 740, *SCBI 29*, 475, *SCBI 30*, 360, and of next two coins. Cross of five pellets above and below lines of rev. inscription.
364.	1.59	24.5	0°	Frothric (*Freothuric/Fredric*). Chester style. Chester (1950) hoard, no. 168. Die-duplicate of previous coin, and of next and of *SCBI 34*, 671, *SCBI 4*, 740, *SCBI 29*, 475 and *SCBI 30*, 360.
365.	1.49	23.0	180°	Frothric (*Freothuric/Fredric*). Chester style. Chester (1950) hoard, no. 169. Die-duplicate of previous two coins and of *SCBI 34*, 671, *SCBI 4*, 740, *SCBI 29*, 475 and *SCBI 30*, 360.

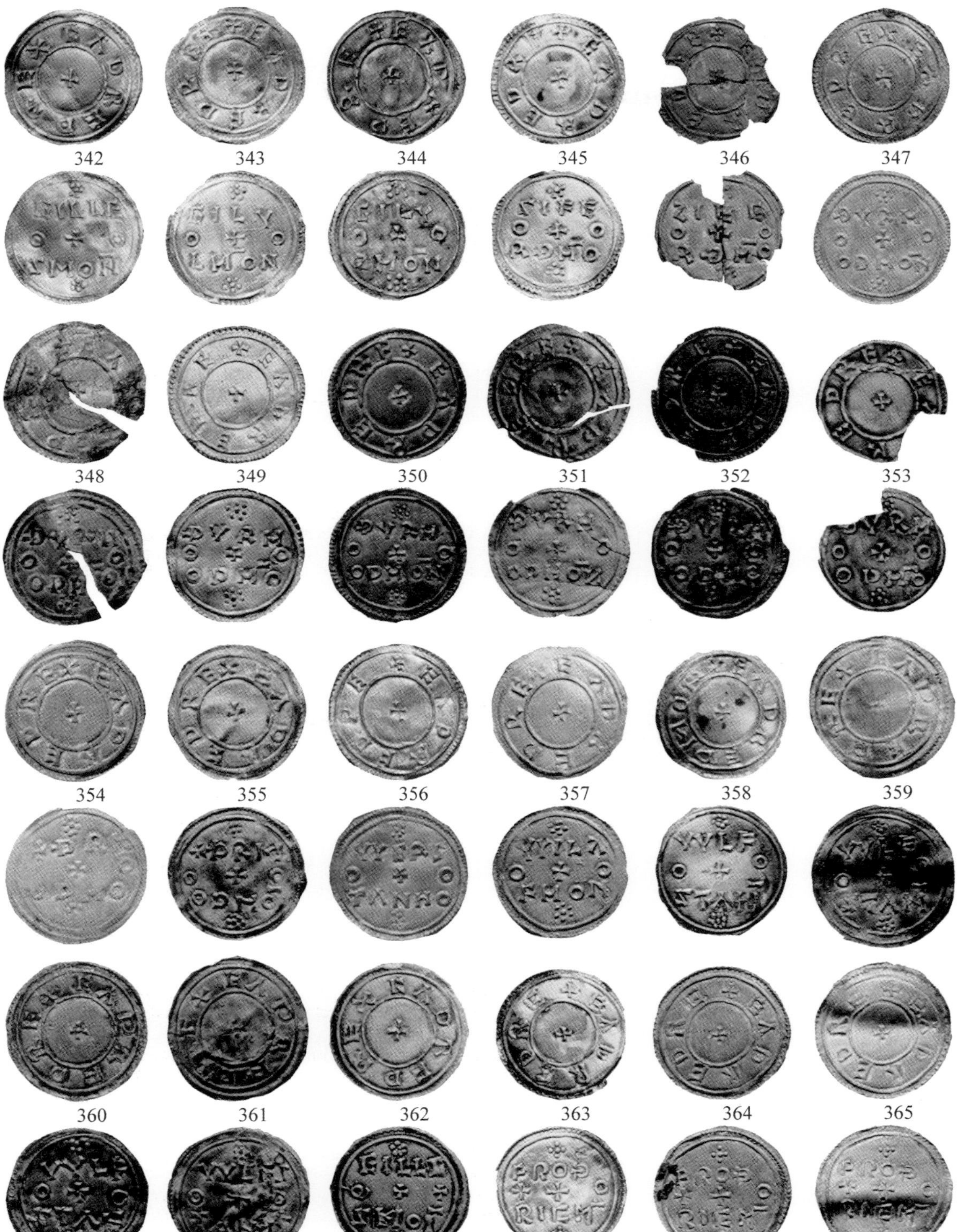

342 343 344 345 346 347

348 349 350 351 352 353

354 355 356 357 358 359

360 361 362 363 364 365

EADRED (*cont.*)

HR2 var (c) type

	Weight g	Weight gr.	Die-Axis	
366.	1.64	25.3	0°	Dorulf (*Deorwulf*). Chester style. Willoughby Gardner; ex Spink. Same obv. die as coin 323 above and as *SCBI 34*, 650.
R/HC4 type				
367.	1.64 wt given by Moore	25.3	-	Æthered (*Æthelræd*). Unlocated East Midlands style. Chester (1950) hoard 1975 parcel coin 14. Listed by Moore as being of this type, but Moore did not provide an explicit description of the coin's rev. design and it is possible that it may be of another related type. (*Not located or illustrated.*)
368.	1.54	23.7	0°	Oslac (*Aslakr*). Unlocated East Midlands style. Willoughby Gardner; ex P. Carlyon-Britton (1913) 425.
R/HR1 type				
369.	1.53	23.6	135°	Manne(es) (*Man/Manna*). Unlocated East Midlands style. Chester (1950) hoard, no. 245.
370.	1.48	22.8	90°	Manne(es) (*Man/Manna*). Unlocated East Midlands style. Chester (1950) hoard, no. 246. Die-duplicate of *SCBI 4*, 747 and of Lockett (1955) 597.
Crowned Bust type				
371.	1.22	18.8	180°	Manna. Unlocated East Midlands style. Chester (1950) hoard, no. 251.
372.	1.60	24.7	270°	Manna. Unlocated East Midlands style. Chester (1950) hoard, no. 250.
373.	1.25	19.3	45°	Sarvvrd (*Saraward*). Unlocated East Midlands style. Chester (1950) hoard, no. 255.
374.	1.45	22.3	90°	Vvilebert (*Wilbeorht*). Unlocated East Midlands style. Chester (1950) hoard, no. 257.
375.	1.49	23.0	225°	Vvilebert (*Wilbeorht*). Unlocated East Midlands style. Chester (1950) hoard, no. 258.
376.	0.99 fragment	15.3	–	[ ]r[ ]. Uncertain moneyer. Unlocated East Midlands style. Chester (1950) hoard, 1975 parcel coin 12. Although the end of the king's name is missing from the obv. inscription, the coin is attributable to Eadred's reign on stylistic grounds.

EADWIG (955–9)

HT1 type

	g	gr.	Die-Axis	
377.	1.42	21.9	90°	Brothar (*Brother*). Southern/Unlocated Midlands style. Chester (1950) hoard, no. 315. Die-duplicate of next coin.
378.	1.18	18.2	0°	Brothar (*Brother*). Southern/Unlocated Midlands style. Chester (1950) hoard, no. 316. Die-duplicate of previous coin.
379.	1.59	24.5	180°	Byrnferth (*Beornferth*). Southern/Unlocated Midlands style. Chester (1950) hoard, no. 311.
380.	1.24	19.1	0°	Clac (*Klakkr*). Southern/Unlocated Midlands style. Chester (1950) hoard, no. 320. Clac is recorded as a moneyer at NEWE (Newport Pagnell ?) in Eadwig's *HT3* type, and an attribution of this coin to the same mint is possible on stylistic grounds.
381.	1.03 slightly chipped	15.9	90°	Clac (*Klakkr*). Southern/Unlocated Midlands style. Chester (1950) hoard, no. 319. Die-duplicate of *SCBI 34*, 727. Attributable to the NEWE mint (see note on previous coin).
382.	1.47	22.7	270°	Cytel (*Ketill*). Southern/Unlocated Midlands style. Chester (1950) hoard, no. 321.
383.	0.95 chipped	14.6	270°	Eadulf (*Eadwulf*). Southern/Unlocated Midlands style. Chester (1950) hoard, no. 325. Perhaps same obv. die as *SCBI 34*, 729. Eadulf is recorded as a moneyer at HAN (Northampton ?) in Eadwig's *HT3* type, and an attribution of this coin to the same mint is possible on stylistic grounds.
384.	1.03	15.9	0°	Effrd (*Everard*). Southern/Unlocated Midlands style. Willoughby Gardner; ex Bliss (1916) 98; ex Ballaquayle hoard. Same obv. die as *SCBI 50*, 255.
385.	1.30	20.1	270°	Grhm (*Grimr*?). Southern/Unlocated Midlands style. Chester (1950) hoard, no. 330. Grim is recorded as a moneyer at BEDA (Bedford) in Eadwig's *HT3* type, but an attribution of this coin to the same mint is not obvious from its style.

[*continued overleaf*]

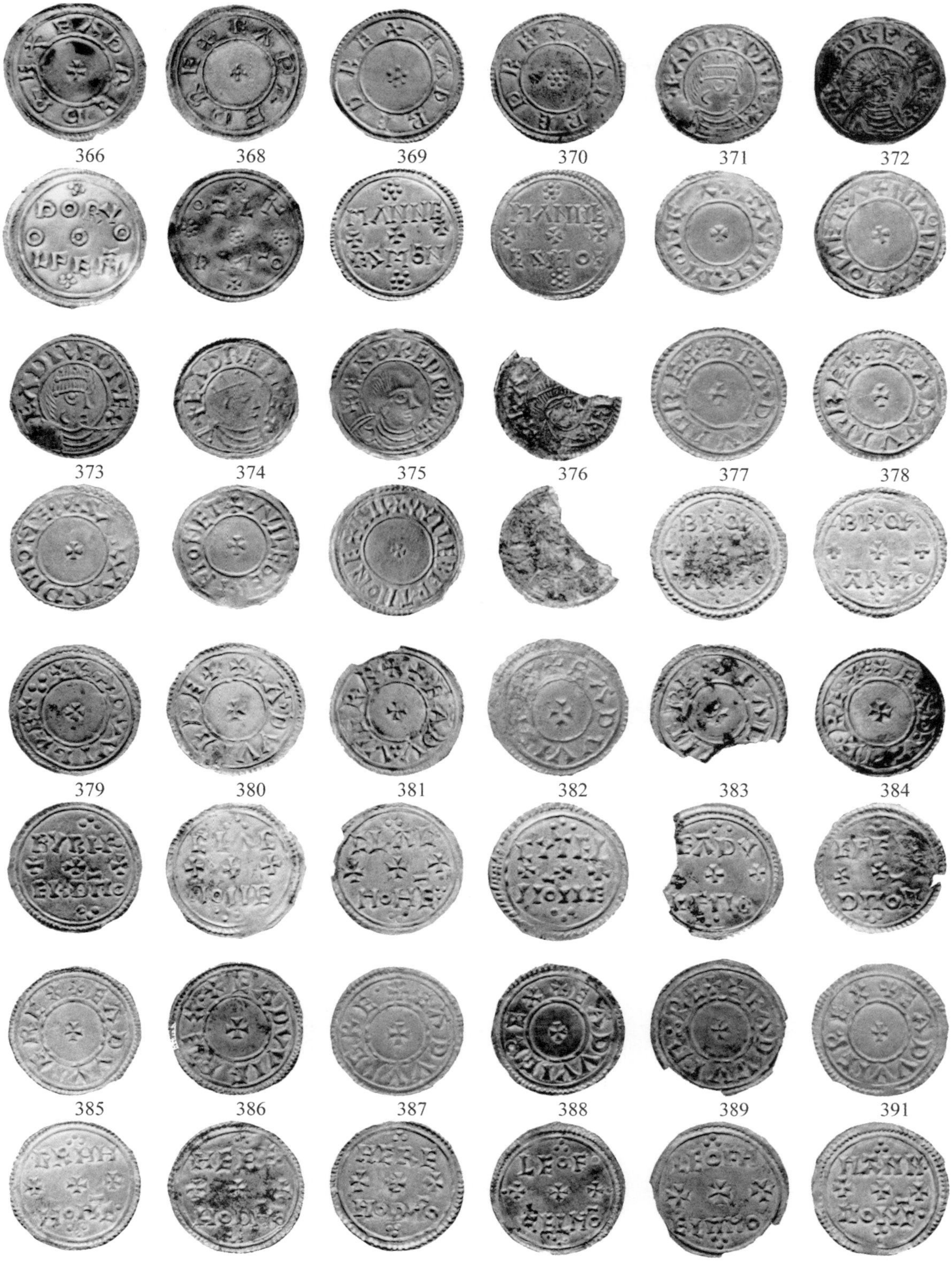

366 368 369 370 371 372

373 374 375 376 377 378

379 380 381 382 383 384

385 386 387 388 389 391

Plate 16 (*cont.*)

EADWIG (*cont.*)

HT1 type (*cont.*)

	Weight *g*	*gr.*	*Die-Axis*	
386.	1.50	23.1	90°	Heremod. Southern/Unlocated Midlands style. Chester (1950) hoard, no. 332.
387.	1.57	24.2	0°	Heremod. Southern/Unlocated Midlands style. Chester (1950) hoard, no. 333. Die-duplicate of *SCBI 4*, 766 and *SCBI 9*, 390. Same obv. die as *SCBI 34*, 736.
388.	1.46	22.5	0°	Leofhelm. Southern/Unlocated Midlands style. Chester (1950) hoard, no. 342.
389.	1.07 slightly chipped	16.5	0°	Leofhelm. Southern/Unlocated Midlands style. Chester (1950) hoard, no. 344.
390.	1.28 wt given by Moore	19.7	–	Leofhelm. Southern/Unlocated Midlands style (?). Chester (1950) hoard, 1975 parcel coin 9. (*Not located or illustrated.*)
391.	1.71	26.4	0°	Mann. Southern/Unlocated Midlands style. Chester (1950) hoard, no. 347.

EADWIG (*cont.*)

HT1 type (*cont.*)

No.	Weight g	Weight gr.	Die-Axis	
392.	1.30	20.1	315°	Mann. Southern/Unlocated Midlands style. Chester (1950) hoard, no. 346.
393.	1.04 badly chipped	16.1	180°	Winenon (*Wineman*?). Southern/Unlocated Midlands style. Chester (1950) hoard, no. 353. Rev. legend ends **HV**. Wineman is recorded as a moneyer at **HAN** (Northampton ?) in Eadwig's *HT3* type, and an attribution of this coin to the same mint is possible on stylistic grounds.
394.	1.32	20.3	180°	Æsculf (*Æscwulf*). York style. Chester (1950) hoard, no. 305.
395.	1.48	22.8	315°	Heriger (*Hereger*). York style. Chester (1950) hoard, no. 334.
396.	1.28	19.7	90°	Heriger (*Hereger*). York style. Chester (1950) hoard, no. 335.
397.	1.48	22.8	135°	Heriger (*Hereger*). York style. Chester (1950) hoard, no. 336.
398.	1.39 broken in two pieces	21.4	0°	Heriger (*Hereger*). York style. Chester (1950) hoard, no. 337.
399.	1.27	19.6	315°	Heriger (*Hereger*). York style. Chester (1950) hoard, no. 338.
400.	1.49	23.0	0°	Heriger (*Hereger*). York style. Chester (1950) hoard, no. 339.
HTC1 type				
401.	1.67	25.7	90°	Vvlfstan (*Wulfstan*). Southern/Unlocated Midlands style. Chester (1950) hoard, no. 357.
HP1 type				
402.	0.84 two fragments	12.9	225°	[ ]red. Southern/Unlocated Midlands style. Chester (1950) hoard, no. 359. This is the only recorded coin of *HP1* type for Eadwig.
HT1 type (*NE I*)				
403.	1.19	18.3	90°	Eaenulf (*Eanwulf*). Central East Midlands style. Chester (1950) hoard, no. 326.
HT1 type (*NE IV*)				
404.	1.55	23.9	315°	Levich (*Leofing*?). Lincoln style. Chester (1950) hoard, no. 345. Die-duplicate of *SCBI 6*, 334.
HT3 type				
405.	1.42	21.9	180°	*Bedford* (**BEDA**), Baldwine (*Baldwin*). Chester (1950) hoard, no. 265. Same rev. die as coin 407 (and *NCirc* Feb 1990, 195).
406.	1.47	22.7	180°	*Bedford* (**BEDA**), Baldwine (*Baldwin*). Chester (1950) hoard, no. 266.
407.	(1.26)	19.4	180°	*Bedford* (**BEDA**), Baldwine (*Baldwin*). Chester (1950) hoard, no. 264. Same rev. die as coin 405.
408.	1.43	22.1	0°	*Bedford* (**BEDA**), Boiga (*Boga*). Chester (1950) hoard, no. 267. Die-duplicate of *SCBI 34*, 797.
409.	1.57	24.2	270°	*Bedford* (**BEDA**), Frothgar (*Froteger*). Chester (1950) hoard, no. 268
410.	1.46	22.5	270°	*Bedford* (**BEDA**), Grim (*Grimr*). Chester (1950) hoard, no. 270. Die-duplicate of next coin and of *SCBI 34*, 800.
411.	1.43	22.1	270°	*Bedford* (**BEDA**), Grim (*Grimr*). Chester (1950) hoard, no. 271. Die-duplicate of last coin and of *SCBI 34*, 800.
412.	1.47	22.7	90°	*Bedford* (**BEDA**), Grim (*Grimr*). Chester (1950) hoard, no. 272.
413.	1.37	21.1	90°	*Bedford* (**BEDA**), Grim (*Grimr*). Chester (1950) hoard, no. 273.
414.	1.40	21.6	0°	*Bedford* (**BEDA**), Grim (*Grimr*). Chester (1950) hoard, no. 274.
415.	1.29	19.9	180°	*Bedford* (**BEDA**), Herewig. Chester (1950) hoard, no. 275. Same rev. die as next coin and as *SCBI 34*, 801. No pellets above and below lines of rev. inscription.

PLATE 17

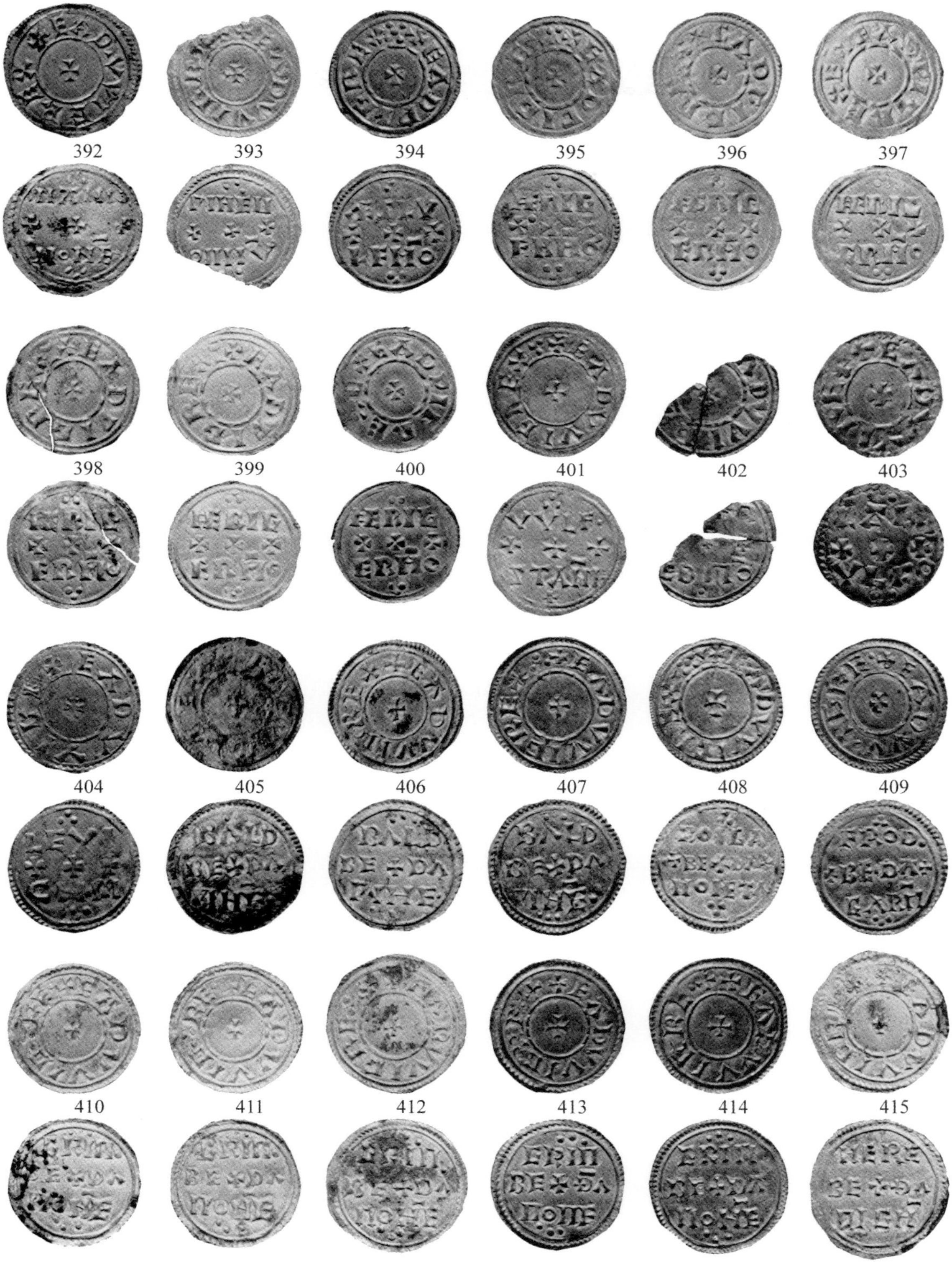

392 393 394 395 396 397

398 399 400 401 402 403

404 405 406 407 408 409

410 411 412 413 414 415

EADWIG (*cont.*)

HT3 type (*cont.*)

	Weight g	gr.	Die-Axis	
416.	1.40	21.6	270°	*Bedford* (BEDA), Herewig. Chester (1950) hoard, no. 276. Same rev. die as last coin and as *SCBI 34*, 801. No pellets above and below lines of rev. inscription.
417.	1.35	20.8	90°	*Bedford* (BEDA), Leofstain (*Leofstan*). Chester (1950) hoard, no. 277.
418.	1.30	20.1	315°	*Northampton* (HAN), Wærin. Chester (1950) hoard, no. 287.
419.	1.22	18.8	270°	*Northampton* (HAN), Wærin. Chester (1950) hoard, no. 286.
420.	1.30	20.1	0°	*Northampton* (HAN), Wineman. Chester (1950) hoard, no. 289. Same rev. die as *SCBI 34*, 809. Eaglen 1999 no. 5a (as possibly of Huntingdon).
421.	1.34	20.7	0°	*Southampton* (HAN), Mangod. Chester (1950) hoard, no. 284. Die-duplicate of *SCBI 30*, 371.
422.	0.98 chipped	15.1	45°	*Newport Pagnell* (?) (NEPE), Cilm. Willoughby Gardner; ex Spink; ex P. Carlyon-Britton (1918) 1701. Perhaps die-duplicate of *SCBI 34*, 814.
423.	1.47	22.7	270°	*Newport Pagnell* (?) (NEPE), Clac (*Klakkr*). Chester (1950) hoard, no. 280. Perhaps die-duplicate of *SCBI 2*, 666, and same rev. die as *SCBI 34*, 815.
424.	1.24	19.1	270°	*Newport Pagnell* (?) (NEPE), Clac (*Klakkr*). Chester (1950) hoard, no. 281.
HR1 type				
425.	1.45	22.3	180°	Agtard(es) (*Aithard*). Derby style. Chester (1950) hoard, no. 309. M in obv. field at 8 o'clock. Probably die-duplicate of Fitzwilliam Museum Cambridge CM 1990-1-565, ex Blunt. Same obv. die as *SCBI 30*, 370.
426.	1.34	20.7	270°	Boiga(es) (*Boga*). Derby style. Chester (1950) hoard, no. 313.
427.	1.34	20.7	180°	Boiga(es) (*Boga*). Derby style. Chester (1950) hoard, no. 314.
428.	1.47	22.7	180°	Frethic(es) (*Freothuric/Fredric*). Derby style. Chester (1950) hoard, no. 328. M in obv. field at 5 o'clock. Same obv. die as coin in E. J. Harris collection.
429.	1.15 chipped	17.7	270°	Leofmann (*Leofman*). Derby style. Willoughby Gardner; ex Lincoln; ex 'Astronomer' (F. McLean) (1906) 199; ex Bateman Heirlooms (1893) 305. M in obv. field at 12 o'clock.
HR3 type				
430.	1.43 slightly chipped	22.1	270°	Ælfsie (*Ælfsige*). Chester style. Chester (1950) hoard, no. 291. Same obv. die (?) as *SCBI 6*, 347, moneyer Wilsig. Same rev. die as Lockett (1955) 608.
431.	1.52	23.4	270°	Deorulf (*Deorwulf*). Chester style. Chester (1950) hoard, no. 292. Die-duplicate of *SCBI 34*, 831.
432.	– two fragments	–	–	Doru[ ]f (*Deorwulf*). Chester style. Chester (1857) hoard, 1981 parcel.
433.	1.58	24.4	270°	Eadmund. Chester style. Chester (1950) hoard, no. 293. Same rev. die as, and perhaps die-duplicate of *SCBI 34*, 834, and Fitzwilliam Museum, Cambridge, CM 1990-1-567, ex Blunt.
434.	1.54	23.7	0°	Eoferad (*Eoferheard*). Chester style. Chester (1950) hoard, no. 294. Die-duplicate of *SCBI 17*, 155 and 156, also Ryan (1952) 780.
435.	1.55	23.9	270°	Eoferad (*Eoferheard*). Chester style. Chester (1950) hoard, no. 295. Die-duplicate of *SCBI 34*, 835.
436.	1.49	23.0	0°	Eorod (*Iorothr*). Chester style. Willoughby Gardner; either ex L. S. Forrer (as per coin ticket); or ex Seaby (as per MS catalogue) 1947. Die-duplicate of *SCBI 34*, 836 and *SCBI 29*, 486. Same obv. die as *SCBI 29*, 487, moneyer Freotheric ; *SCBI 6*, 346, moneyer Thurmod ; and *SCBI 34*, 842, moneyer Werstan. Perhaps same obv. die as coin 447 below, Eadwig HR3/Eadred HR2 mule, moneyer Thurmod.
437.	1.30 broken	20.1	0°	Frard (*Everard*). Chester style. Willoughby Gardner; ex Spink; ex P. Carlyon-Britton (1918) 1701. Same obv. die as coin 448 below, Eadwig HR3/Edgar CR mule. Same rev. die as *SCBI 34*, 837 and *SCBI 16*, 163.
438.	1.55	23.9	270°	Frard (*Everard*). Chester style. Chester (1950) hoard, no. 297. Same obv. die as *SCBI 34*, 837 and *SCBI 16*, 163.
439.	1.55	23.9	0°	Freotheri (*Freothuric/Fredric*). Chester style. Chester (1950) hoard, no. 300. Same obv. die as *SCBI 34*, 830, moneyer Ælfsie.

PLATE 18

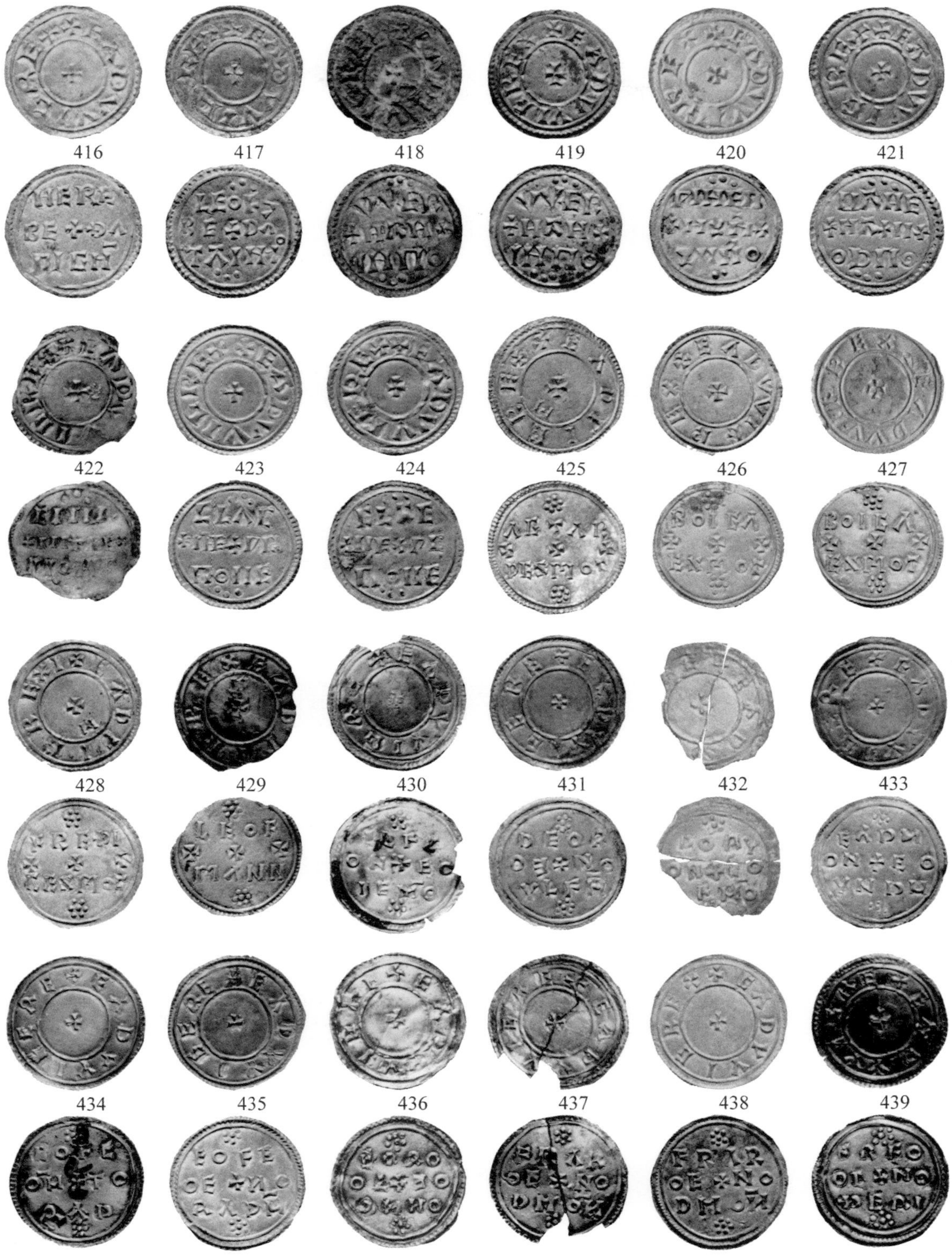

416 417 418 419 420 421

422 423 424 425 426 427

428 429 430 431 432 433

434 435 436 437 438 439

EADWIG (*cont.*)

HR3 type (*cont.*)

	Weight g	*Weight* gr.	*Die-Axis*	
440.	1.52	23.4	0°	Freotheri (*Freothuric*/*Fredric*). Chester style. Chester (1950) hoard, no. 299. Obverse double-struck. Same rev. die as *SCBI 34*, 839.
441.	1.59	24.5	270°	Vvilsig (*Wilsige*). Chester style. Chester (1950) hoard, no. 301. Die-duplicate of *SCBI 34*, 844, and same rev. die as *SCBI 6*, 348.

HR5 type

442.	1.58	24.4	180°	Manin (*Manning*). Unlocated East Midlands style. Chester (1950) hoard, no. 365. Die-duplicate of *SCBI 34*, 850. Same obv. die as HR1 coin of Manin, *SCBI 6*, 340.

Horizontal type, uncertain variety

443.	– small fragment	–	–	Small fragment with letters VV consecutively in obv. inscription and a visible letter E in rev. inscription. The presence of an inner outer circle on the rev. suggests that this is a fragment of a coin of Eadwig. Chester (1950) hoard, no. 360.

Ornamental type c

444.	1.38	21.3	270°	Oswald. Unlocated East Midlands style. Chester (1950) hoard, no. 367. Presumably die-duplicate of *SCBI 34*, 855 and *SCBI 9*, 384.

Ornamental type d

445.	1.65	25.4	270°	Æthelsige. Unlocated (perhaps Southern) style. Chester (1950) hoard, no. 372. Die-duplicate of *SCBI 34*, 856. Note the curved cross bars to the first and third crosses in the central line of the rev.

EADWIG-EADRED MULES

EADWIG HR3 type/*EADRED HR2* type

446.	1.57	24.2	270°	Sunu. Chester style. Chester (1950) hoard, no. 352. Same rev. die as coin of Eadred HR2 type, *SCBI 2*, 657.
447.	1.29 chipped	19.9	90°	Thurmod (*Thormothr*). Chester style. Willoughby Gardner. Perhaps same obv. die as coins of Eadwig HR3 type, moneyer Eoroth, *SCBI 34*, 836 and coin 436 above; moneyer Thurmod, *SCBI 9*, 346; and moneyer Werstan, *SCBI 34*, 842. Rev. die not so far recorded in conjunction with an obv. die of Eadred, but it may be presumed to be a reused die from Eadred's reign, as the HR2 type was not struck as a substantive type at Chester under Eadwig.

EADWIG-EDGAR MULE

EADWIG HR3 type/*EDGAR CR* type

448.	1.64	25.3	270°	Ælfsige. Chester style. Chester (1950) hoard, no. 370. Die-duplicate of *SCBI 34*, 858. Same obv. die as coin 437 above, moneyer Frard. Same rev. die as *SCBI 17*, 174 and as coin 599 below, which are both CR coins of Edgar.

EDGAR (959–75)

PRE-REFORM ISSUES

HT1 type

449.	1.45	22.3	270°	Grim(es) (*Grimr*). Southern/Unlocated Midlands style. Chester (1950) hoard, no. 402. Reverse double-struck. Die-duplicate of *SCBI 34*, 921, 922.
450.	1.66	25.6	0°	Martin. Southern/Unlocated Midlands style. Willoughby Gardner; ex Spink; ex Dawnay (1922) 28.
451.	1.26	19.4	180°	Sigefreth (*Sigeferth*). Southern/Unlocated Midlands style. Willoughby Gardner; ex Baldwin; ex Walters (1932) 70.
452.	1.33	20.5	270°	Adelaver (*Æthelweard*?). Lincoln (NE V) style. Chester (1950) hoard, no. 375.
453.	1.02 badly chipped	15.7	90°	Adelaver (*Æthelweard*?). Lincoln (NE V) style. Chester (1857) hoard, 1981 parcel.

[*continued overleaf*]

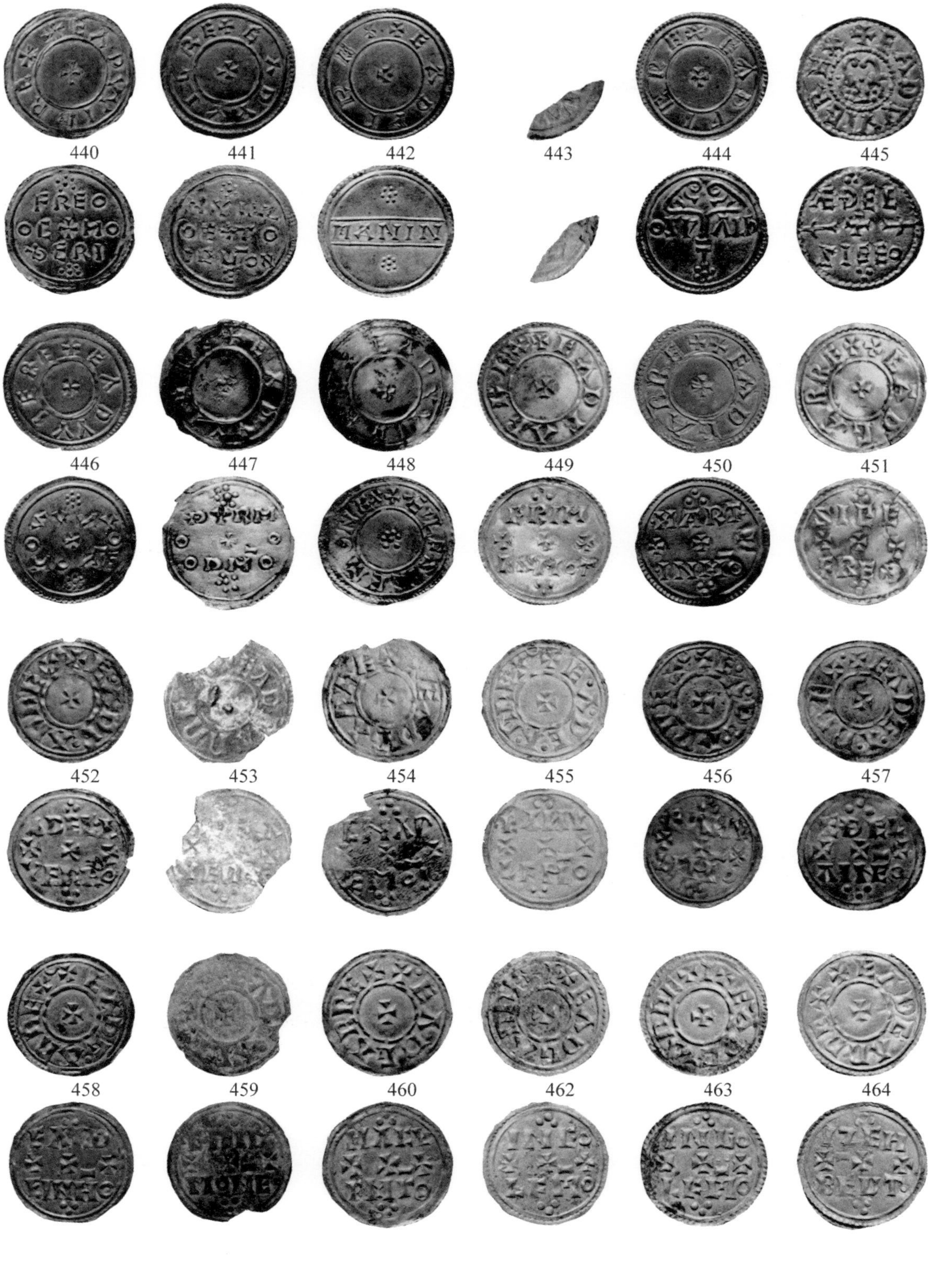

440 441 442 443 444 445

446 447 448 449 450 451

452 453 454 455 456 457

458 459 460 462 463 464

Plate 19 (*cont.*)

PRE-REFORM ISSUES (*cont.*)

HT1 type (*cont.*)

	Weight *g*	*gr.*	*Die-Axis*	
454.	1.13 chipped	17.4	90°	Cnape (*Cnapa*). Lincoln (NE V) style. Willoughby Gardner; ex Bliss (1916) 104.
455.	1.36	21.0	0°	Eanulf (*Eanwulf*). Lincoln (NE V) style. Chester (1950) hoard, no. 393.
456.	1.36	21.0	270°	Eanulf (*Eanwulf*). Lincoln (NE V) style. Willoughby Gardner (via Mrs Gardner 1963).
457.	1.32	20.3	180°	Ethelaine (*Æthelwine*). Lincoln (NE V) style. Willoughby Gardner (via Mrs Gardner 1963).
458.	1.43	22.1	225°	Fardein (*Farthegn*). Lincoln (NE V) style. Chester (1950) hoard, no. 397.
459.	1.00 chipped	15.4	90°	Grid (*Grith*). Lincoln (NE V) style. Willoughby Gardner (via Mrs Gardner 1963).
460.	1.40	21.6	0°	Hacuf. Lincoln (NE V) style. Chester (1950) hoard, no. 405.
461.	1.47	22.7	–	Harcer (*Hereger*). Lincoln (NE V) style. Chester (1950) hoard, 1975 parcel, coin 10. (*Not located or illustrated.*)
462.	1.34	20.7	180°	Ingolf (*Ingolfr*). Lincoln (NE V) style. Chester (1950) hoard, no. 421.
463.	1.39	21.4	315°	Ingolf (*Ingolfr*). Lincoln (NE V) style. Chester (1950) hoard, no. 422. Die-duplicate of *SCBI 34*, 940.
464.	1.42	21.9	90°	Isenbert (*Isenbert*). Lincoln (NE V) style. Chester (1950) hoard, no. 423.

EDGAR (*cont.*)

HT1 type (*cont.*)

	Weight *g*	*gr.*	Die-Axis	
465.	1.38	21.3	0°	Ive (*Ifa*). Lincoln (NE V) style. Chester (1950) hoard, no. 424.
466.	1.30	20.1	315°	Ive (*Ifa*). Lincoln (NE V) style. Chester (1950) hoard, no. 425.
467.	1.31	20.2	90°	Ive (*Ifa*). Lincoln (NE V) style. Chester (1950) hoard, no. 426.
468.	1.40	21.6	270°	Manai (*Man*/*Manna*). Lincoln (NE V) style. Chester (1950) hoard, no. 431.
469.	1.42	21.9	0°	Manan (*Man*/*Manna*). Lincoln (NE V) style. Chester (1950) hoard, no. 430.
470.	1.42	21.9	270°	Manolet. Lincoln (NE V) style. Chester (1950) hoard, no. 428.
471.	1.49	23.0	0°	Manolet. Lincoln (NE V) style. Chester (1950) hoard, no. 429.
472.	1.34	20.7	0°	Æsculf (*Æscwulf*). York style. Chester (1950) hoard, no. 382. Die-duplicate of *SCBI 34*, 989.
473.	1.22	18.8	315°	Durand. York style. Willoughby Gardner; ex Wheeler (1930) 31. Group of four pellets above and below lines of rev. inscription.
474.	1.44	22.2	90°	Durand. York style. Willoughby Gardner; ex Spink March 1914; ex P. Carlyon-Britton (1913) 442. Group of four pellets above and below lines of rev. inscription.
475.	1.21 slightly chipped	18.6	135°	Durand. York style. Willoughby Gardner; ex Baldwin. Perhaps die-duplicate of *SCBI 34*, 994.
476.	1.32	20.3	135°	Durand. York style. Willoughby Gardner.
477.	1.17	18.1	270°	Durand. York style. Willoughby Gardner; ex P. Carlyon-Britton (1916) 1024.
478.	1.15 cracked	17.7	225°	Durand. York style. Willoughby Gardner; ex Baldwin, ex Glendining 'Aug 1913' (*sic*, but no Glendining coin sale of this date).
479.	1.24	19.1	180°	Durand. York style. Willoughby Gardner; ex Baldwin.
480.	1.31 cracked	20.2	90°	Durand. York style. Willoughby Gardner; ex Baldwin.
481.	1.32	20.3	270°	Durand. York style. Willoughby Gardner (via Mrs Gardner 1963); ex Tetney hoard.
482.	1.34	20.7	270°	Durand. York style. Willoughby Gardner (via Mrs Gardner 1963); ex Tetney hoard.
483.	1.07	16.5	180°	Durand. York style. Willoughby Gardner (via Mrs Gardner 1963); ex Tetney hoard.
484.	1.16	17.9	0°	Durand. York style. Willoughby Gardner (via Mrs Gardner 1963); ex Tetney hoard.
485.	1.32	20.3	135°	Durand. York style. Willoughby Gardner (via Mrs Gardner 1963); ex Tetney hoard.
486.	1.19	18.3	180°	Durand. York style. Willoughby Gardner (via Mrs Gardner 1963); ex Tetney hoard.
487.	1.36	21.0	0°	Durand. York style. Willoughby Gardner (via Mrs Gardner 1963); ex Tetney hoard.
488.	0.73 fragment	11.2	90°	Du[ ]nd (*Durand*). York style. Chester (1950) hoard, no. 390.

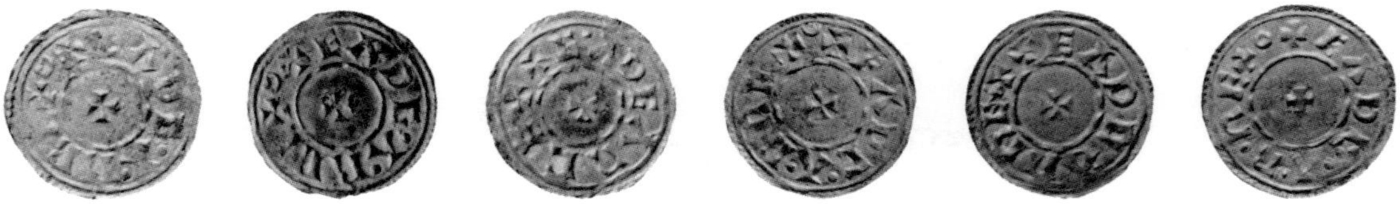

465 466 467 468 469 470

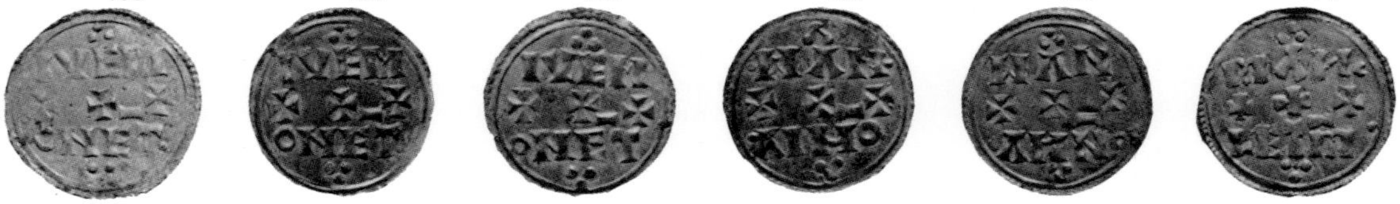

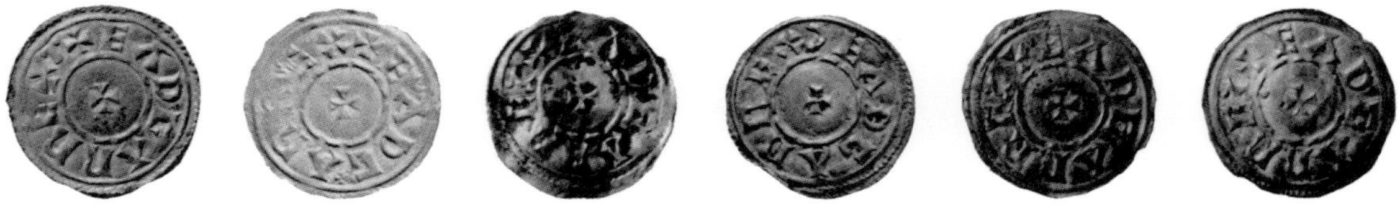

471 472 473 474 475 476

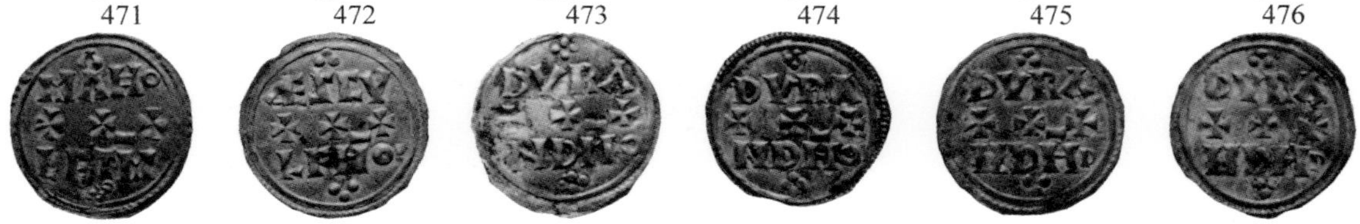

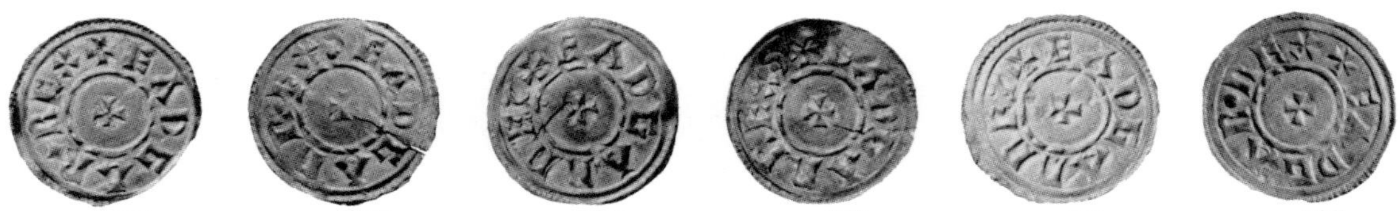

477 478 479 480 481 482

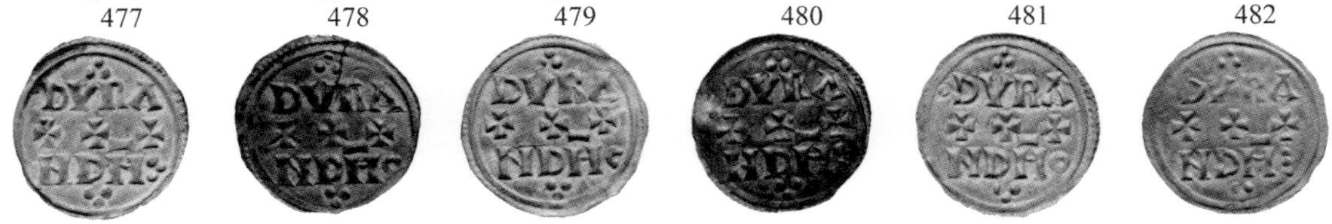

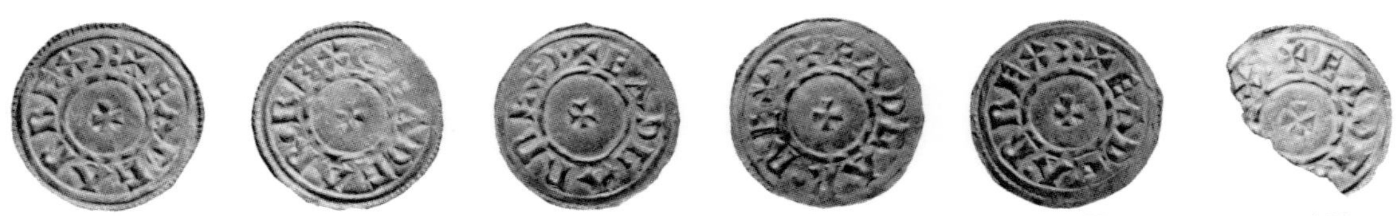

483 484 485 486 487 488

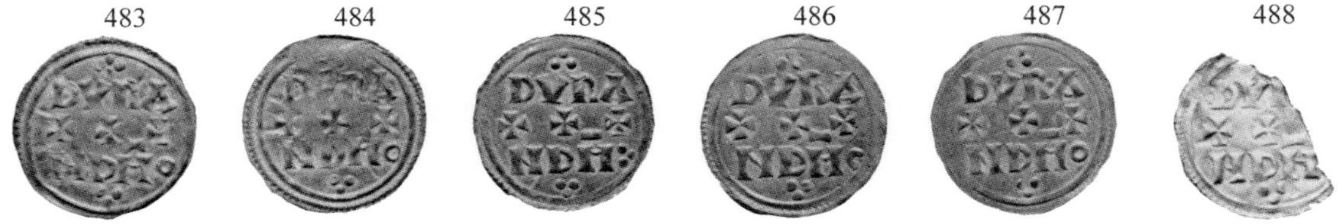

EDGAR (*cont.*)

HT1 type (*cont.*)

	Weight *g*	*gr.*	Die-Axiss	
489.	1.31	20.2	45°	Heriger (*Hereger*). York style. Chester (1950) hoard, no. 406.
490.	1.21	18.6	90°	Heriger (*Hereger*). York style. Chester (1950) hoard, no. 407. Probably die-duplicate of *SCBI 34*, 996.
491.	1.38	21.3	45°	Heriger (*Hereger*). York style. Chester (1950) hoard, no. 408.
492.	1.42	21.9	135°	Heriger (*Hereger*). York style. Chester (1950) hoard, no. 409.
493.	1.15	17.7	0°	Heriger (*Hereger*). York style. Chester (1950) hoard, no. 410.
494.	1.23	19.0	90°	Heriger (*Hereger*). York style. Chester (1950) hoard, no. 411.
495.	1.44	22.2	180°	Heriger (*Hereger*). York style. Chester (1950) hoard, no. 412. Obv. and rev. double-struck.
496.	1.40	21.6	225°	Heriger (*Hereger*). York style. Chester (1950) hoard, no. 413.
497.	1.19	18.3	90°	Heriger (*Hereger*). York style. Chester (1950) hoard, no. 414.
498.	1.39	21.4	135°	Heriger (*Hereger*). York style. Chester (1950) hoard, no. 415.
499	1.25	19.3	0°	Heriger (*Hereger*). York style. Chester (1950) hoard, no. 416.
500.	1.41	21.7	135°	Heriger (*Hereger*). York style. Chester (1950) hoard, no. 418.
501.	1.34	20.7	225°	Heriger (*Hereger*). York style. Chester (1950) hoard, no. 419.
502.	1.14	17.6	270°	Ieriger (*Hereger*). York style. Chester (1950) hoard, no. 417
503.	1.26	19.4	0°	Umbein (*Ubeinn*). Central East Midlands (NE1) style. Chester (1950) hoard, no.420.

HP1 type

504.	1.33	20.5	0°	Ælfstan. York style. Willoughby Gardner; ex P. Carlyon-Britton (1916) 1030; presumably specimen illustrated in Ruding, *Annals of the Coinage of Great Britain*, pl.28, Eadgar 2, then in Rebello collection.

HR1 type

505.	1.40	21.6	90°	Bernard (*Beornheard*). Derby/Unlocated East Midlands style. Willoughby Gardner (via Mrs Gardner 1963). M in obv. field at 10.30 o'clock.
506.	1.00	15.4	315°	Boiga(es) (*Boga*). Derby/Unlocated East Midlands style. Willoughby Gardner; ex Spink (*NCirc* Oct 1911, 92127). M in obv. field at 8 o'clock.
507.	1.26	19.4	180°	Demence. Derby/Unlocated East Midlands style. Chester (1950) hoard, no. 389. M in obv. field at 4 o'clock. Die-duplicate of *SCBI 6*, 504. Same obv. die as *SCBI 34*, 1012.
508.	1.93	29.8	315°	Elfstan (*Ælfstan*). Derby/Unlocated East Midlands style. Willoughby Gardner; perhaps ex P. Carlyon-Britton (1916) 1032 (although the Carlyon-Britton coin may be the specimen now in the Fitzwilliam Museum cited below). M in obv. field at 3 o'clock. Die-duplicate of *SCBI 2*, 692 and of coin in Fitzwilliam Museum, Cambridge CM 1990-1-602, ex Blunt; ex Duke of Argyll. The unusually high weight of this coin might suggest that it is a cast, but the die-duplicate in the Hunterian Museum, Glasgow, is even heavier, weighing 2.19g, and was part of the original collection formed by Dr.William Hunter (died 1783). The coin in the Fitzwilliam Museum, by contrast, weighs 1.27g.
509.	1.13	17.4	270°	Elfstan (*Ælfstan*). Derby/Unlocated East Midlands style. Willoughby Gardner; ex Spink (*NCirc* Jun 1910, 76569) (Sir John Evans collection). M in obv. field at 8.30 o'clock.
510.	1.01 slightly chipped	15.6	0°	Ethelwine (*Æthelwine*). Derby/Unlocated East Midlands style. Willoughby Gardner (via Mrs Gardner 1963); ex Ryan (1952) 786. M in obv. field at 1.30 o'clock.
511.	1.42	21.9	225°	Frethic(es) (*Freothuric/Fredric*). Derby/Unlocated East Midlands style. Chester (1950) hoard, no. 398. M in obv. field at 12.30 o'clock.
512.	1.49	23.0	0°	Frethic(es) (*Freothuric/Fredric*). Derby/Unlocated East Midlands style. Chester (1950) hoard, no. 399. M in obv. field at 3 o'clock.

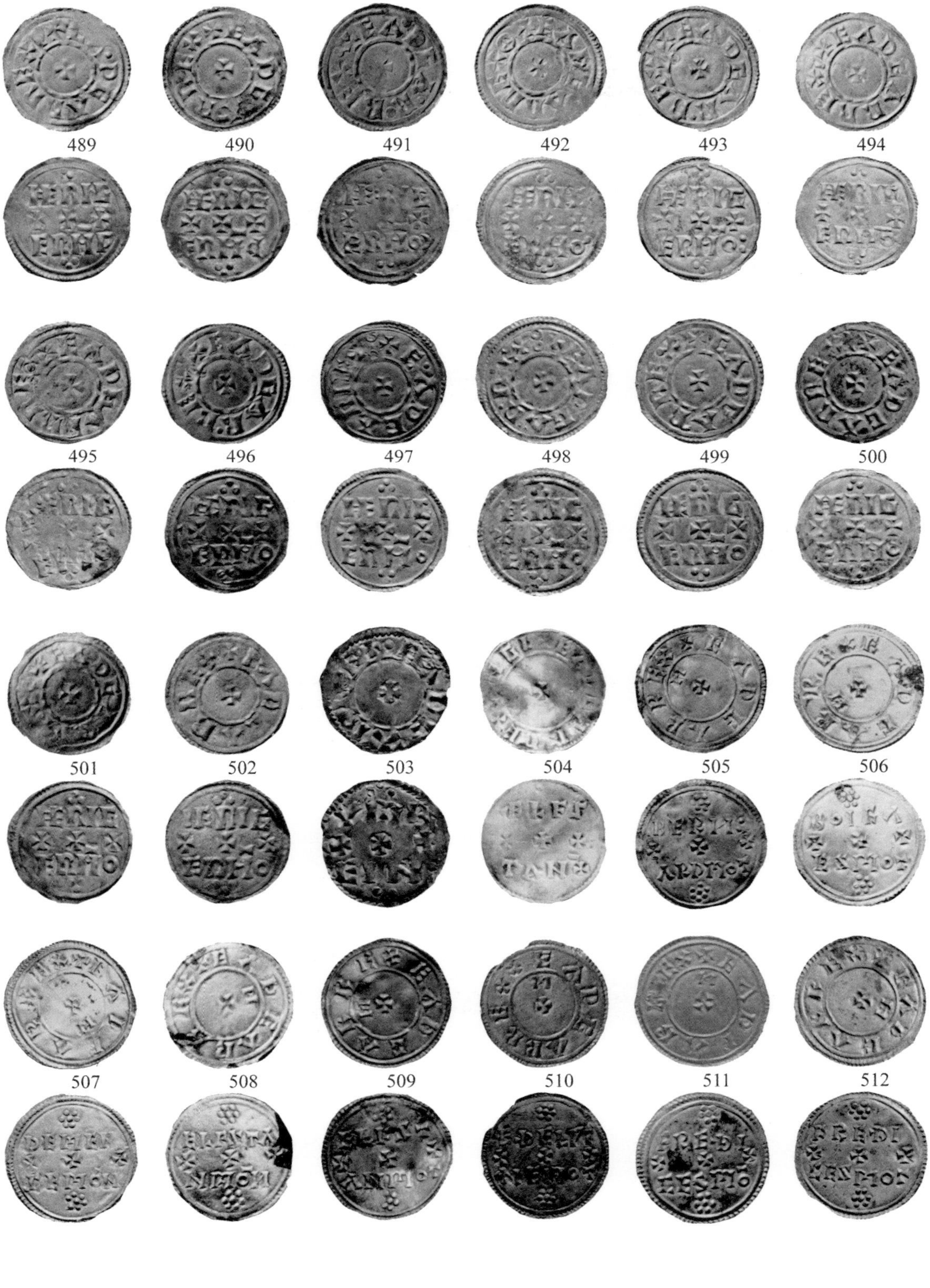

489 490 491 492 493 494

495 496 497 498 499 500

501 502 503 504 505 506

507 508 509 510 511 512

EDGAR (*cont.*)

HR1 type (*cont.*)

	Weight g	*Weight* gr.	*Die-Axis*	
513.	1.14 slightly chipped	17.6	–	Lefman(es) (*Leofman*). Derby/Unlocated East Midlands style. Willoughby Gardner; ex Spink 1941. M in obv. field at 10 o'clock. Die-duplicate of *SCBI 34*, 1021.
514.	1.18 slightly chipped	18.2	0°	Osulf (*Asulfr/Oswulf*). Derby/Unlocated East Midlands style. Willoughby Gardner (via Mrs Gardner 1963); ex Lincoln 21/5/1908 (*sic*).
515.	1.47	22.7	180°	Sigar(es) (*Sigegar*). Derby/Unlocated East Midlands style. Chester (1950) hoard, no. 432. M in obv. field at 8 o'clock.

HR2 type

	g	gr.	Die-Axis	
516.	1.32 chipped	20.3	270°	Ælfred. Chester style. Chester (1857) hoard, Newstead Edgar no. 1. Same rev. die as, and perhaps die-duplicate of, P. Carlyon-Britton (1913) 449.
517.	1.51	23.3	270°	Ælfred. Chester style. Chester (1950) hoard, no. 377. Same obv. die as *SCBI 6*, 581. Perhaps same rev. die as next coin, and as *SCBI 29*, 497.
518.	1.51 chipped	23.3	90°	Ælfred. Chester style. Chester (1950) hoard, no. 378. Same obv. die as *SCBI 29*, 497. Perhaps same rev. die as last coin, and as *SCBI 29*, 497.
519.	1.48	22.8	225°	Ælfsig (*Ælfsige*). Chester style. Willoughby Gardner; ex Spink; ex Reynolds (1914) 63.
520.	1.41	21.7	180°	Ælfsig (*Ælfsige*). Chester style. Willoughby Gardner; perhaps ex Lincoln. Die-duplicate of next and of *SCBI 4*, 788.
521.	1.15 slightly chipped	17.7	90°	Ælfsig (*Ælfsige*). Chester style. Willoughby Gardner (via Mrs Gardner 1963); without a Gardner ticket but Gardner MS cat lists a coin like this ex P. Carlyon-Britton (1916) 1033. Die-duplicate of last and of *SCBI 4*, 788.
522.	0.87 slightly chipped	13.4	180°	Ælfsig (*Ælfsige*). Chester style. Chester (1857) hoard, Newstead Edgar no. 3.
523.	1.50 wt given by Moore	23.1	–	Ælfsig (*Ælfsige*). Chester style. Chester (1950) hoard, 1975 parcel coin 15. (*Not located or illustrated.*)
524.	1.20 chipped	18.5	0°	Ælfsig (*Ælfsige*). Chester style. Willoughby Gardner; ex Lincoln. Same rev. die as Spink sale 6 (10 Oct 1979), lot 272.
525.	1.53	23.6	0°	Ælfsig (*Ælfsige*). Chester style. Chester (1950) hoard, no. 380. Same obv. die as *SCBI 6*, 582.
526.	1.50	23.1	180°	Ælfsige. Chester style. Willoughby Gardner; ex George Day; ex Rashleigh (1909) 277; ex Stretton (1855) 415 (lot purchased by Rashleigh); and therefore presumably from Co. Kilkenny hoard .
527.	1.15 chipped	17.7	270°	Ælfsige. Chester style. Willoughby Gardner; ex Grantley (1944) 1100; ex Cox (1892) 6.
528.	0.85 chipped	13.1	270°	Ealfsige (*Ælfsige*). Chester style. Chester (1857) hoard, Newstead Edgar no. 15.
529.	1.08 chipped	16.6	90°	Aldewin (*Ealdwine*). Chester style. Chester (1857) hoard, Newstead Edgar no. 8.
530.	0.93 chipped	14.3	90°	Aldewine (*Ealdwine*). Chester style. Willoughby Gardner; ex Wheeler.
531.	1.03 broken	15.9	0°	Aldewine (*Ealdwine*). Chester style. Chester (1857) hoard, Newstead Edgar no. 4. Possibly same obv. die as *SCBI 6*, 586.
532.	– broken	–	270°	Aldewine (*Ealdwine*). Chester style. Chester (1857) hoard, Newstead Edgar no. 5.
533.	0.69 chipped	10.6	0°	Ald[ ]wine (*Ealdwine*). Chester style. Chester (1857) hoard, 1981 parcel.
534.	0.55 chipped	8.5	0°	Alhmun[ ] (*Ealhmund*). Chester style. Chester (1857) hoard, 1981 parcel. Perhaps die-duplicate of next two coins.
535.	0.94 chipped	14.5	90°	Alhmund (*Ealhmund*). Chester style. Chester (1857) hoard, Newstead Edgar no. 8. Perhaps die-duplicate of previous coin and next coin.
536.	1.07 chipped	16.5	0°	Alhmund (*Ealhmund*). Chester style. Chester (1857) hoard, 1981 parcel. Perhaps die-duplicate of previous two coins.
537.	0.89 chipped	13.7	180°	Alhmund (*Ealhmund*). Chester style. Chester (1857) hoard, Newstead Edgar no. 7. Die-duplicate of *SCBI 6*, 587 and 588.

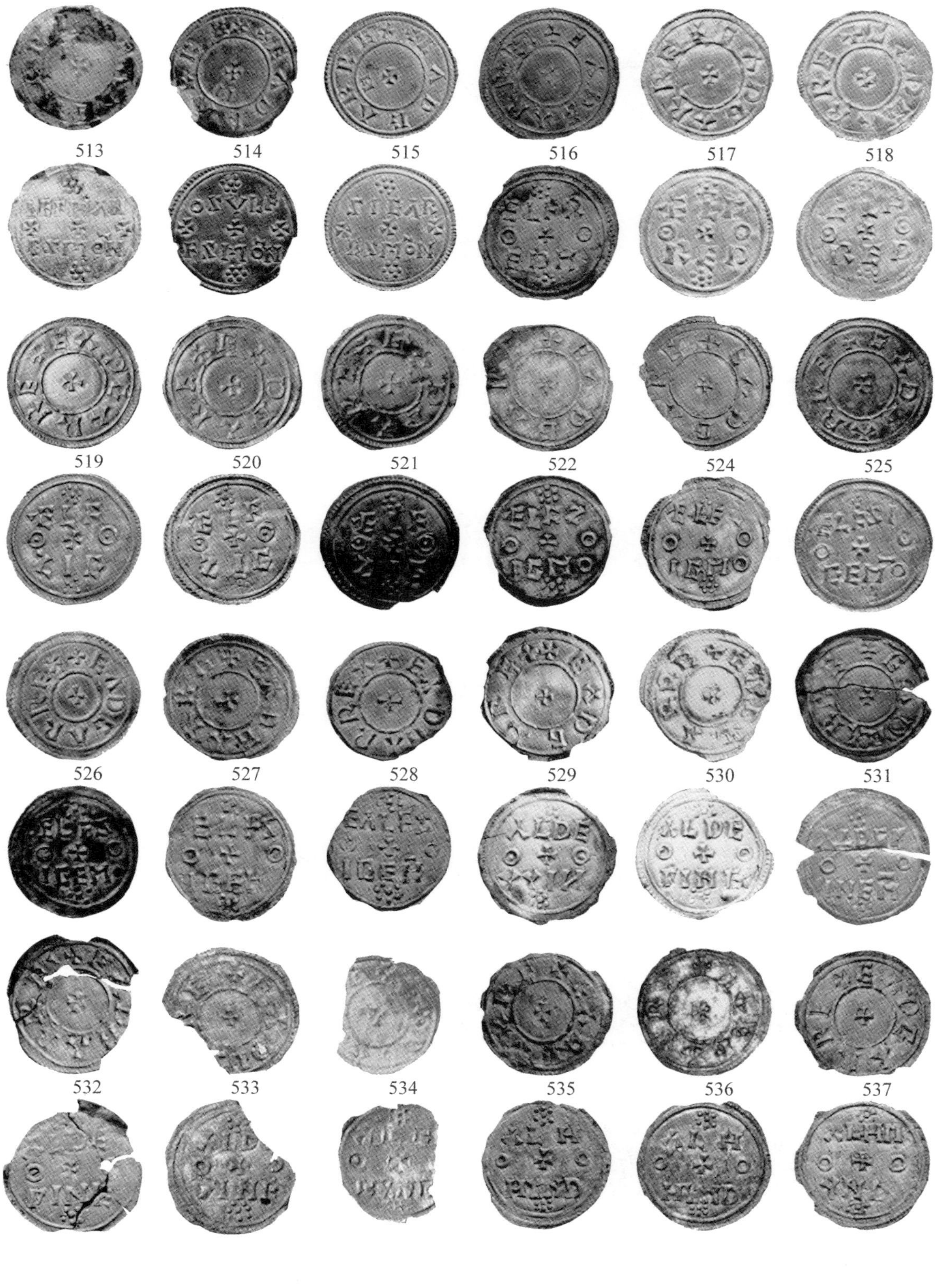

513 514 515 516 517 518

519 520 521 522 524 525

526 527 528 529 530 531

532 533 534 535 536 537

EDGAR (*cont.*)

HR2 type (*cont.*)

	Weight *g*	*gr.*	*Die-Axis*	
538.	1.19 chipped	18.3	135°	Deorulf (*Deorwulf*). Chester style. Willoughby Gardner; perhaps ex Spink (*NCirc* Apr 1906, 26108) (see next coin).
539.	1.08 broken	16.6	270°	Deorulf (*Deorwulf*). Chester style. Willoughby Gardner, provenance uncertain (on ticket with *NCirc* Apr 1906, 26108 provenance, but ticket gives obv. legend as on previous coin, and therefore may belong to previous coin).
540.	0.64 broken	9.8	90°	Deorulf (*Deorwulf*). Chester (1857) hoard, Newstead Edgar no. 19.
541.	1.51 slightly chipped	23.3	180°	Eadmun (*Eadmund*). Chester style. Chester (1950) hoard, no. 392.
542.	1.34	20.7	135°	Eadmund. Chester style. Willoughby Gardner; ex Spink (*NCirc* Oct 1911, 92131); ex O'Hagan (1908) 351; ex Montagu (1895) 743.
543.	0.65 badly chipped	10.1	0°	Ead[ ]und (*Eadmund*). Chester style. Chester (1857) hoard, Newstead Edgar no. 17 (portion of coin lost since recorded by Newstead).
544.	– broken	–	–	Eadmund. Chester style. Chester (1857) hoard, Newstead Edgar no. 16. Same rev. die as next coin.
545.	0.73 badly chipped	11.2	0°	Eadmund. Chester style. Chester (1857) hoard, 1981 parcel. Same rev. die as previous coin.
546.	1.48	22.8	90°	Eoroth (*Iorothr*). Chester style. Chester (1950) hoard, no. 394.
547.	1.53	23.6	45°	Eoroth (*Iorothr*). Chester style. Chester (1950) hoard, no. 396. Same rev. die as *SCBI 9*, 592.
548.	1.24 chipped	19.1	0°	Eoroth (*Iorothr*). Chester style. Willoughby Gardner; ex P. Carlyon-Britton (1916) 1034. Same rev. die as *SCBI 34*, 1197.
549.	1.47	22.7	270°	Eoroth (*Iorothr*). Chester style. Willoughby Gardner; exchanged with Wells; ex Seaby; ex 'A collector' (R. D. Bain), Sotheby 5 May 1928, lot 222.
550	1.21 repaired with sellotape	18.6	90°	Eoroth (*Iorothr*). Chester style. Willoughby Gardner (via Mrs Gardner 1963); apparently ex Seaby 1950.
551.	– broken and mounted on card	–	–	Eoroth (*Iorothr*). Chester style. Chester (1857) hoard, Newstead Edgar no. 9. (*Reverse not illustrated.*)
552.	1.43 chipped	22.1	225°	Freotheric (*Freothuric/Fredric*). Chester style. Willoughby Gardner; ex 'Fran. S. C.' (i.e. ex Grant Francis ?). Probably die-duplicate of *SCBI 29*, 498.
553.	1.42	21.9	90°	Freothric (*Freothuric/Fredric*). Chester style. Chester (1950) hoard, no. 400.
554.	0.94 chipped	14.5	0°	Freothric (*Freothuric/Fredric*). Chester style. Chester (1857) hoard, Newstead Edgar no. 30.
555.	1.14 broken in three pieces	17.6	180°	Freothric (*Freothuric/Fredric*). Chester style. Willoughby Gardner; ex Spink (*NCirc* Apr 1906, 26110). Die-duplicate of *SCBI 34*, 1199 and *SCBI 6*, 599, and perhaps same obv. die as *SCBI 6*, 597.
556.	0.88 slightly chipped	13.6	45°	Frethric (*Freothuric/Fredric*). Chester style. Chester (1857) hoard, Newstead Edgar no. 25.
557.	- broken in four pieces	-	270°	Frothri[c] (*Freothuric/Fredric*). Chester style. Chester (1857) hoard, Newstead Edgar no. 27 or 28.
558.	1.55	23.9	225°	Frothric (*Freothuric/Fredric*). Chester style. Chester (1950) hoard, no. 401.
559.	–	–	–	Frothric (*Freothuric/Fredric*). Chester style. Willoughby Gardner; ex Baldwin; ex Glendining sale 'Aug 1923' (but evidently from Glendining sale 23 July 1923, lot 59, where a coin of 'Frothic' (*sic*) features in a poorly described parcel of coins evidently from a coin hoard deposited in the 960s or early 970s). Perhaps die-duplicate of *SCBI 6*, 595. Same rev. die as coin 562 below.
560.	0.46 badly chipped	7.1	135°	Frothric (*Freothuric/Fredric*). Chester style. Chester (1857) hoard, Newstead Edgar no. 27 or 28.
561.	0.97 broken	14.9	–	Frothric (*Freothuric/Fredric*). Chester style. Chester (1857) hoard, 1981 parcel.

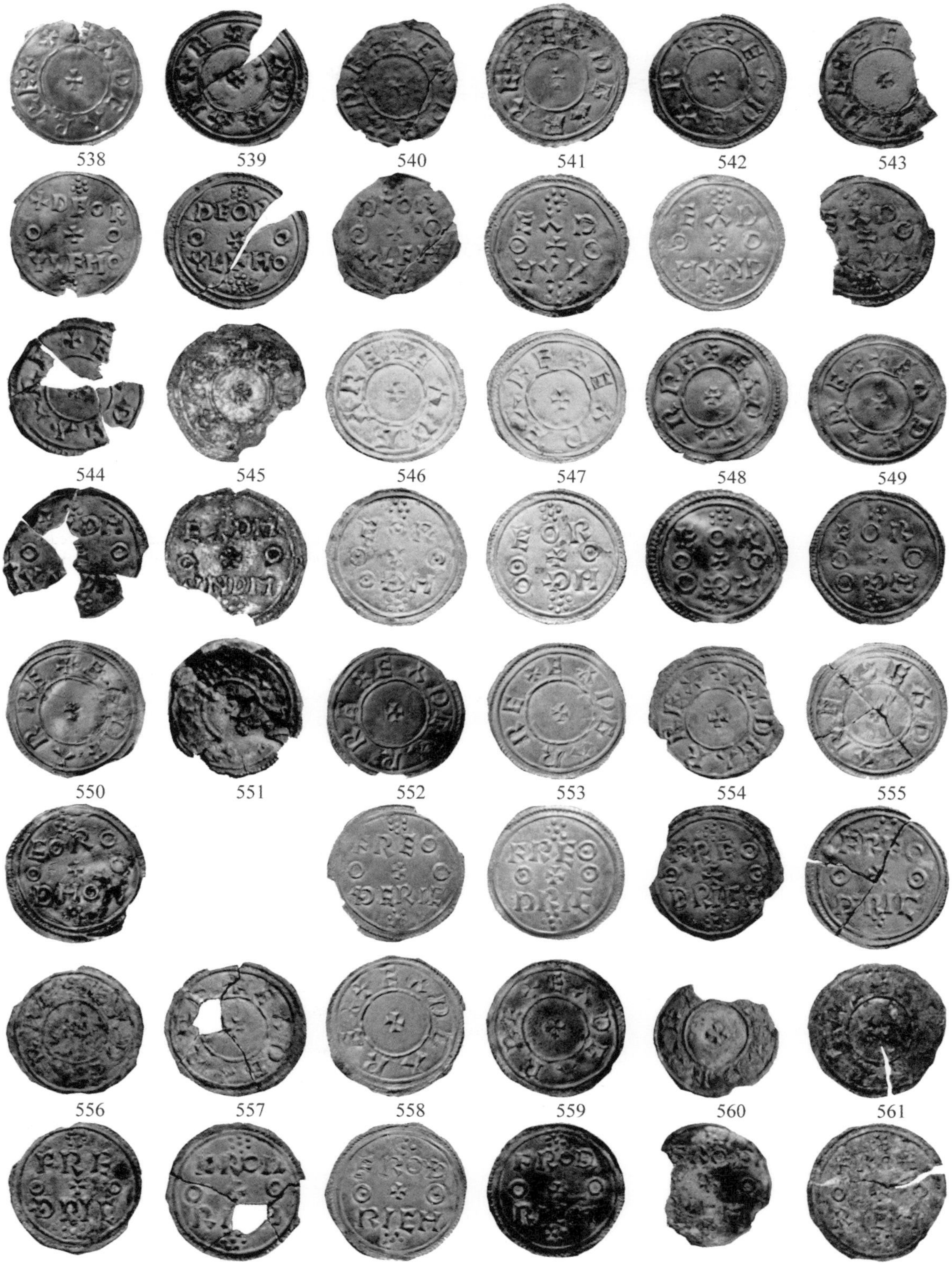

538 539 540 541 542 543

544 545 546 547 548 549

550 551 552 553 554 555

556 557 558 559 560 561

EDGAR (*cont.*)

HR2 type (*cont.*)

	Weight		Die-	
	g	*gr.*	*Axis*	
562.	0.55 badly chipped	8.5	315°	Frothric (*Freothuric/Fredric*). Chester style. Chester (1857) hoard, 1981 parcel. Same rev. die as coin 559 above.
563.	0.50 broken half	7.7	90°	[ ]ric (*Freothuric/Fredric*). Chester style. Chester (1857) hoard, 1981 parcel.
564.	0.45 fragment	6.9	270°	[ ]ric (*Freothuric/Fredric*). Chester style. Chester (1857) hoard, 1981 parcel.
565.	1.29 badly chipped	19.9	180°	Gillis (*Gillys*). Chester style. Willoughby Gardner; ex Wells.
566.	0.80	12.3	135°	Gilyz (*Gillys*). Chester style. Chester (1857) hoard, Newstead Edgar no. 31 or 32. Die-duplicate of *SCBI 34*, 1202.
567.	1.39	21.4	90°	Mertin (*Martin*). Chester style. Willoughby Gardner; ex P. Carlyon-Britton (1916) 1034. Same rev. die as *SCBI 34*, 1204. Probably die-duplicate of next coin.
568.	0.56 chipped	8.6	270°	Mertin (*Martin*). Chester style. Chester (1857) hoard, 1981 parcel. Probably die-duplicate of previous coin.
569.	– chipped	–	–	Mertin (*Martin*). Chester style. Chester (1857) hoard, Newstead Edgar no. 35.
570.	1.04 broken in two pieces	16.1	315°	Mertin (*Martin*). Chester style. Chester (1857) hoard, Newstead Edgar no. 34.
571.	1.51 slightly chipped	23.3	90°	Siferth (*Sigeferth*). Chester style. Willoughby Gardner; ex P. Carlyon-Britton (1916) 1033. Same rev. die as *SCBI 6*, 603.
572.	1.35	20.8	45°	Siferth (*Sigeferth*). Chester style. Willoughby Gardner; ex Spink (*NCirc* Oct 1911, 92132). Probably die-duplicate of *SCBI 34*, 1206, and from same obv. die as *SCBI 6*, 603.
573.	1.01 slightly chipped	15.6	315°	Teothuc. Chester style. Chester (1857) hoard, Newstead Edgar no. 37.
574.	1.19	18.3	270°	Thurmod (*Thormothr*). Chester style. Willoughby Gardner; ex P. Carlyon-Britton (1913) 451. Die-duplicate of next, same rev. die as *SCBI 34*, 1208 and as coin in Fitzwilliam Museum, Cambridge, CM 1990-1-617, ex Blunt.
575.	1.32	20.3	135°	Thurmod (*Thormothr*). Chester style. Willoughby Gardner (via Mrs Gardner 1963). Die-duplicate of last, same rev. die as *SCBI 34*, 1208 and as coin in Fitzwilliam Museum, Cambridge, CM 1990-1-617, ex Blunt.
576.	1.41	21.7	270°	Thurmod (*Thormothr*). Chester style. Chester (1950) hoard, no. 433. Same obv. die as, and perhaps die-duplicate of, *SCBI 6*, 611.
577.	1.45	22.3	180°	Thurmod (*Thormothr*). Chester style. Willoughby Gardner; ex Wheeler (1930) 33.
578.	1.35	20.8	135°	Thurmod (*Thormothr*). Chester style. Willoughby Gardner; ex Spink 1920.
579.	1.31	20.2	0°	Thurmod (*Thormothr*). Chester style. Willoughby Gardner; perhaps ex Gantz (MS cat) (but coin is on *NCirc* Jun 1910, 76572 ticket).
580.	1.35 slightly chipped	20.8	270°	Thurmod (*Thormothr*). Chester style. Willoughby Gardner; apparently ex Wells; ex 'A Collector' (R. D. Bain), Sotheby 5 May 1928, lot 222 (combined evidence of ticket and MS cat).
581.	– broken	–	–	Thurmod (*Thormothr*). Chester style. Chester (1857) hoard, Newstead Edgar 20 (?). Probably from same rev. die as previous coin.
582.	– fragment	–	225°	[ ]od (*Thormothr*). Chester style. Chester (1857) hoard, Newstead Edgar 20 (?). Probably from same rev. die as previous coin.
583.	0.77 chipped	11.8	–	Thurmod (*Thormothr*). Chester style. Chester (1857) hoard, 1981 parcel.
584.	0.74 chipped	11.4	–	Thurmod (*Thormothr*). Chester style. Chester (1857) hoard, 1981 parcel.
585.	0.50 chipped	7.7	180°	Thurmod (*Thormothr*). Chester style. Chester (1857) hoard, 1981 parcel.

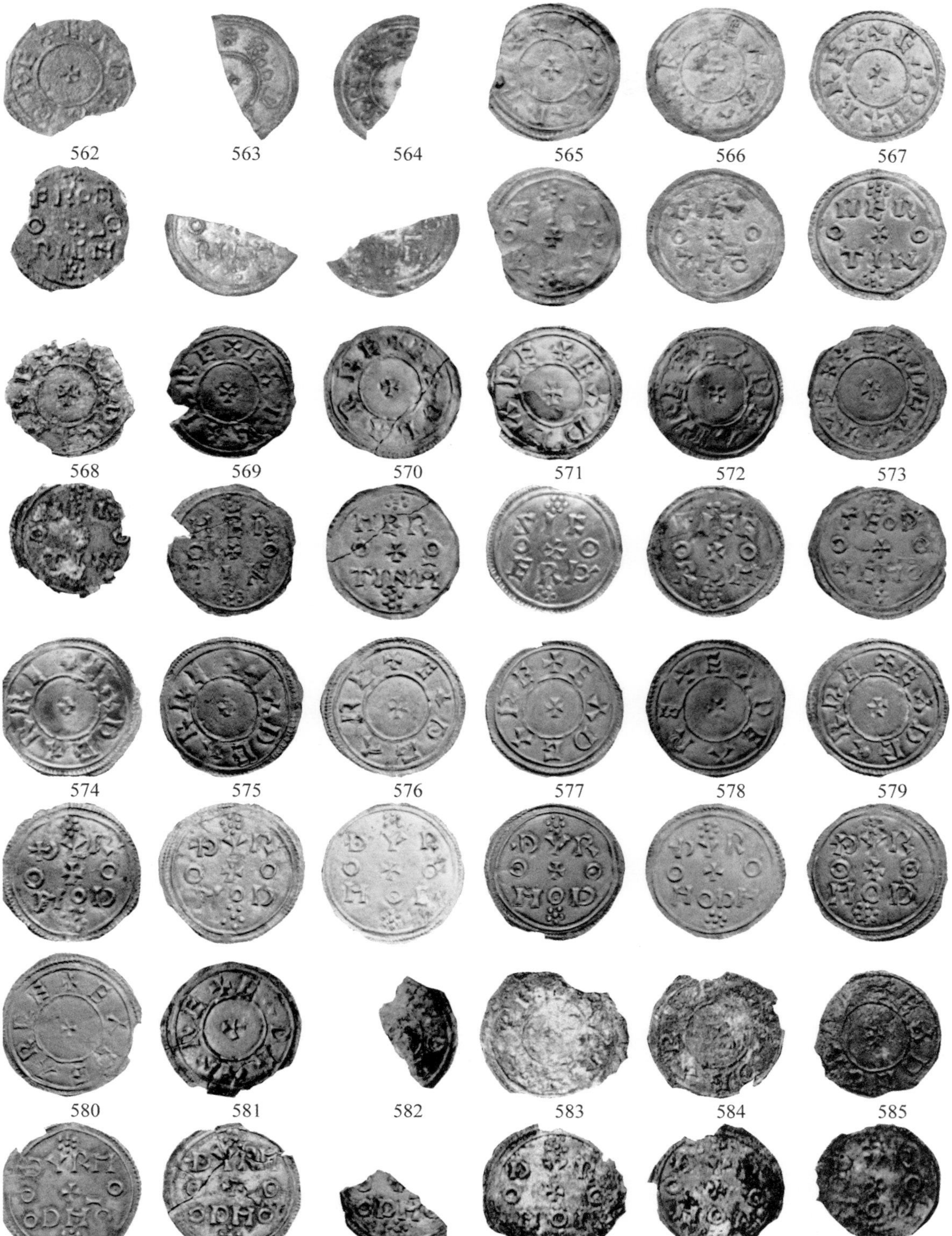

562 563 564 565 566 567

568 569 570 571 572 573

574 575 576 577 578 579

580 581 582 583 584 585

EDGAR (*cont.*)

HR2 type (*cont.*)

	Weight g	*gr.*	*Die-Axis*	
586.	0.71 chipped	10.9	315°	Thurmod (*Thormothr*). Chester style. Chester (1857) hoard, 1981 parcel.
587.	0.69 badly chipped	10.6	0°	Thurmod (*Thormothr*). Chester style. Chester (1857) hoard, 1981 parcel.
588.	1.19	18.3	270°	Werstan (*Wærstan*). Chester style. Chester (1857) hoard, Newstead Edgar no. 36. Same obv. die as *SCBI 6*, 615.
589.	1.19 slightly chipped	18.3	135°	Vverstan (*Wærstan*). Chester style. Chester (1857) hoard, Newstead Edgar no. 38.
590.	1.04	16.1	90°	Blundered inscriptions (+IDGAREREARE ‖ DEA-Ð/O+O/EREO). Chester style. Willoughby Gardner (via Mrs Gardner 1963); ex Baldwin; ex Drabble (1939) 433. Die-duplicate of coin in Fitzwilliam Museum, Cambridge, CM 1990-1-616, ex Blunt. Bottom line of rev. inscription retrograde.

HR2 type/*CC* type *mule*

	g	gr.	Die-Axis	
591.	1.48	22.8	0°	Ælfsig (*Ælfsige*). Chester style. Willoughby Gardner; ex Baldwin; ex Bruun (1925) 115. Die-duplicate of coin in Fitzwilliam Museum, Cambridge, CM 1990-1-668, ex Blunt. Same obv. die as *SCBI 34*, 1186, this moneyer, HR2 type.

HR3 type

	g	gr.	Die-Axis	
592.	1.39	21.4	270°	*Chester* (LE), Deorlaf. Willoughby Gardner (via Mrs Gardner 1963). Same rev. die as *SCBI 6*, 623.
593.	1.14	17.6	200°	*Chester* (LE), Deorlaf. Ford Farm, Hargrave hoard 1997.
594.	0.95 chipped	14.6	300°	*Chester* (LE), Deorlaf. Ford Farm, Hargrave hoard 1997.
595.	0.74 chipped	11.4	270°	*Chester* (LE), Ethelm (*Æthelhelm*). Ford Farm, Hargrave hoard 1997. Same obv. die as *SCBI 5*, 87, same rev. die as *SCBI 5*, 85–6.
596.	1.20	18.5	180°	*Chester* (LE), Flodger. Willoughby Gardner (via Mrs Gardner 1963); exchange with P. Carlyon-Britton; ex Ballaquayle hoard ? (with Carlyon-Britton's ticket, giving provenance as 'M.C. I.O.M.2. 1905'). Die-duplicate of *SCBI 5*, 88.
597.	1.19	18.3	180°	*Chester* (LE), Frothric (*Freothuric/Fredric*). Willoughby Gardner (via Mrs Gardner 1963); apparently ex Dudman (1913) 236. Die-duplicate of *SCBI 5*, 90.
598.	1.34	20.7	0°	*Chester* (LE), Gillus (*Gillys*). Willoughby Gardner (via Mrs Gardner 1963); apparently ex Spink. Die-duplicate of *SCBI 5*, 92.
599.	1.05 chipped	16.2	180°	*Chester* (LE), Thurmod (*Thormothr*). Ford Farm, Hargrave hoard 1997.
600.	0.57 chipped	8.8	180°	*Chester* (LE), Thurmod (*Thormothr*). Chester (1857) hoard, 1981 parcel.
601.	1.40 chipped	21.6	300°	Uncertain mint (NE), Siulf (*Sigewulf?*). Ford Farm, Hargrave hoard 1997.
602.	1.07 chipped	16.5	0°	*Tamworth* (TE), Deorulf (*Deorwulf*). Ford Farm, Hargrave hoard 1997.
603.	1.07 chipped	16.5	350°	*Tamworth* (TE), Monna. Ford Farm, Hargrave hoard 1997.
604.	0.48 badly chipped	7.3	230°	*Tamworth* (TE), Monna. Ford Farm, Hargrave hoard 1997.
605.	– fragment	–	–	Uncertain mint, [ ]ulf. Ford Farm, Hargrave hoard 1997. Perhaps Tamworth mint, moneyer Deorulf (cf. *SCBI 34*, 1229).
606.	– fragment	–	–	Uncertain mint, [ ]e. Ford Farm, Hargrave hoard 1997. Perhaps Chester mint, moneyer Aldewine (cf. *SCBI 34*, 1214). The attribution of this fragment to Edgar's HR3 type is conjectural, but seems plausible.
607.	– fragment	–	–	Uncertain mint, uncertain moneyer. Ford Farm, Hargrave hoard 1997.

CC type

	g	gr.	Die-Axis	
608.	0.88 fragment	13.6	270°	Wulfsta[ ] (*Wulfstan*). Southern style. Chester (1950) hoard, no. 521. The authors of *CTCE* state at p. 174 that 'an Oxford mint name seems likely on the missing portion'.
609.	1.33 chipped	20.5	0°	Eoroth (*Iorothr*). Chester style. Willoughby Gardner; ex Gantz. Same rev. die as *SCBI 34*, 1069, which is struck from a CR obv. die.

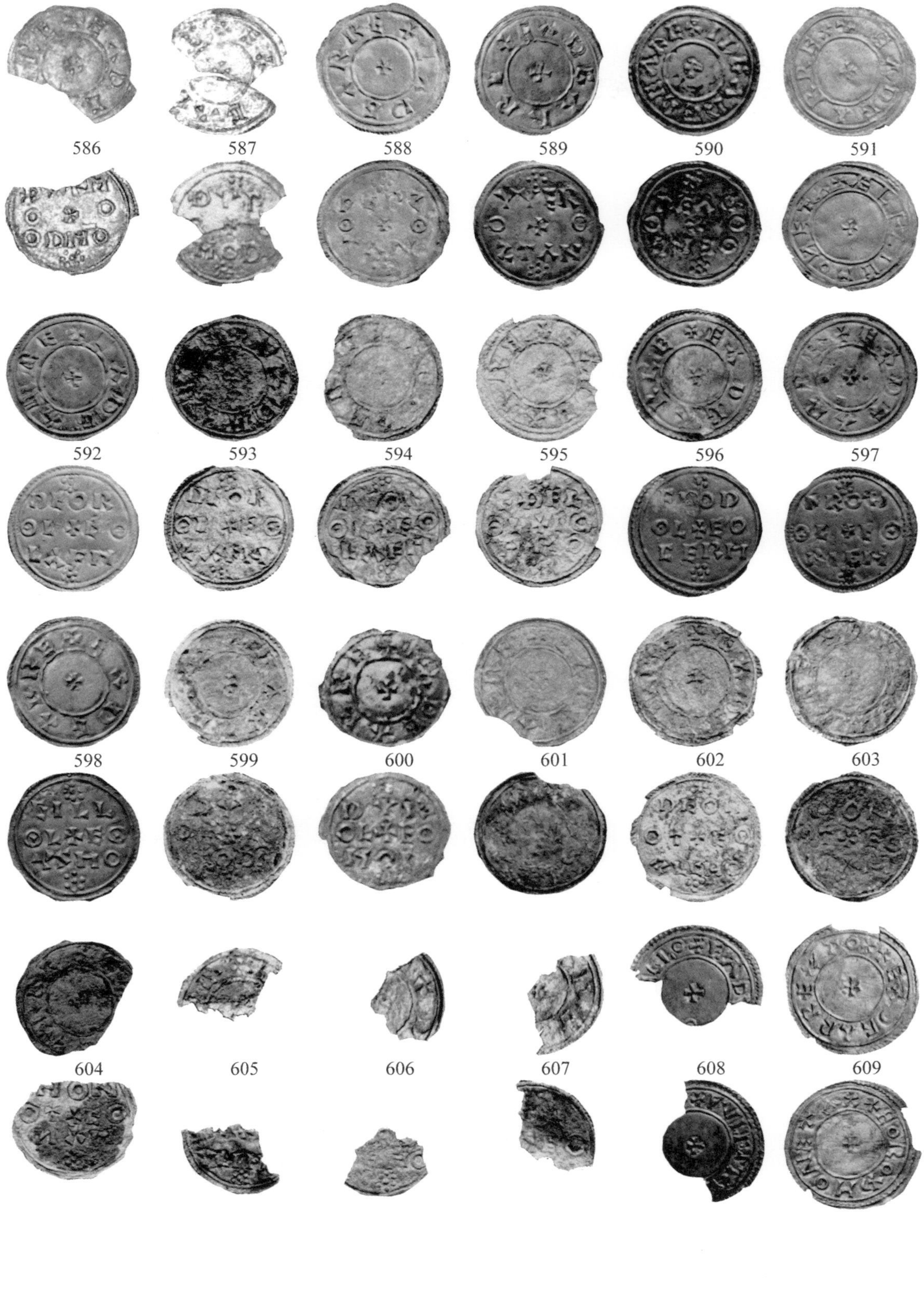

586 587 588 589 590 591

592 593 594 595 596 597

598 599 600 601 602 603

604 605 606 607 608 609

EDGAR (*cont.*)

CC type (*cont.*)

	Weight g	gr.	Die-Axis	
610.	1.24 chipped	19.1	90°	Freotheric (*Freothuric/Fredric*). Chester style. Willoughby Gardner. Same rev. die as *SCBI 6*, 570-1, coin in National Museum of Ireland ex Smarmore hoard and coin in Fitzwilliam Museum, Cambridge, CM 1990-1-658 ex Blunt, all of which have CR obv. die.
611.	1.43 chipped	22.1	225°	Durand. York style. Willoughby Gardner; apparently ex Drabble (1939) 430.
612.	1.03	15.9	180°	Durand. York style. Willoughby Gardner; ex P. Carlyon-Britton (1916) 1043.
613.	1.36	21.0	225°	Durand. York style. Willoughby Gardner; ex P. Carlyon-Britton (1913) 456.
614.	1.30	20.1	180°	Durand(es). York style. Willoughby Gardner; ex P. Carlyon-Britton (1918) 1724. Die-duplicate of *SCBI 34*, 1110. Three pellets in rev. field.
615	1.19	18.3	270°	Durand(es). York style. Willoughby Gardner; ex Walters (1932) 70. Three pellets in rev. field.
616.	1.27 chipped	19.6	0°	Durand(es). York style. Willoughby Gardner. Three pellets in rev. field.
617.	1.30	20.1	135°	Durand(es). York style. Willoughby Gardner.
618.	1.06	16.3	0°	Durand(es). York style. Willoughby Gardner; ex Spink (*NCirc* Apr 1916, 39449). Three pellets in rev. field.
619.	1.17 chipped	18.1	180°	Durand(es). York style. Willoughby Gardner; ex Wheeler (1930) 35. Three pellets in rev. field.
620.	1.28 chipped	19.7	135°	Durand(es). York style. Willoughby Gardner (via Mrs Gardner 1963), apparently ex Baldwin.
621.	1.19	18.3	45°	Fastolf (*Fastulfr*). York style. Willoughby Gardner (via Mrs Gardner 1963).

CR type

	g	gr.	Die-Axis	
622.	1.22 slightly chipped	18.8	315°	*Derby* (DEORBVE), Iole (*Iol/Ioli*). Chester (1950) hoard, no. 445.
623.	1.19	18.3	0°	*Derby* (DEORBVI), Osulf (*Asulfr/Oswulf*). Chester (1950) hoard, no. 448.
624.	1.22	18.8	90°	*Tamworth* (TOMPER), Deorulf (*Deorwulf*). Chester (1950) hoard, no. 457. Die-duplicate of *SCBI 34*, 1046.
625.	1.46	22.5	135°	Ælfsig (*Ælfsige*). Chester style. Chester (1950) hoard, no. 468.
626.	1.60	24.7	45°	Ælfsige. Chester style. Chester (1950) hoard, no. 467. Same rev. die as Eadwig coin 442 above and *SCBI 34*, 858, Eadwig HR3/Edgar CR mules; and same rev. die as *SCBI 17*, 174, CR coin of Edgar.
627.	1.44 wt given by Moore	22.2	–	'Aefsifsige' (*Ælfsige*?). Chester style. Chester (1950) hoard, 1975 parcel coin 11. Legends recorded by Moore as EADGAR REX TO and AEFSIFSIGE MO (*sic*), but reverse reading should no doubt be AELFSIGE MO. (*Not located or illustrated.*)
628.	1.55	23.9	180°	Deorulf (*Deorwulf*). Chester style. Chester (1950) hoard, no. 474.
629.	1.19 badly chipped	18.3	135°	D[ ]ulf (*Deorwulf*). Chester style. Willoughby Gardner; ex Lincoln. Die-duplicate of *SCBI 34*, 1054.
630.	1.21	18.6	0°	Deorulf (*Deorwulf*). Chester style. Willoughby Gardner; ex Seaby; ex 'North of England Collector', Glendining 6 Jun 1934, lot 63.
631.	1.17	18.1	45°	Eadmund. Chester style. Chester (1950) hoard, no. 476.
632.	1.34 slightly chipped	20.7	225°	Eoroth (*Iorothr*). Chester style. Willoughby Gardner; perhaps ex Drabble (1939) 433.
633.	1.56	24.1	45°	Freotherci (*Freothuric/Fredric*). Chester style. Chester (1950) hoard, no. 481.
634.	1.40	21.6	90°	Freotheric (*Freothuric/Fredric*). Chester style. Willoughby Gardner; ex Joseph Young (1919) 32. Perhaps same obv. die as *SCBI 34*, 1060 and *SCBI 6*, 575.

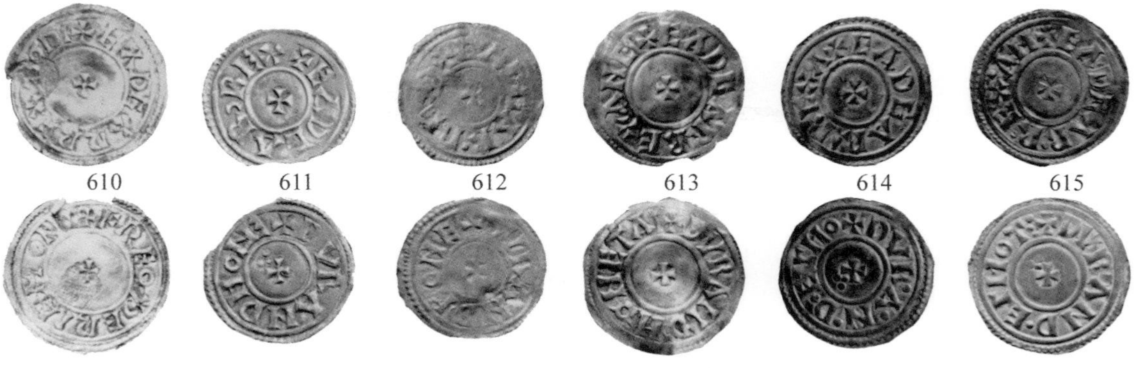

610 611 612 613 614 615

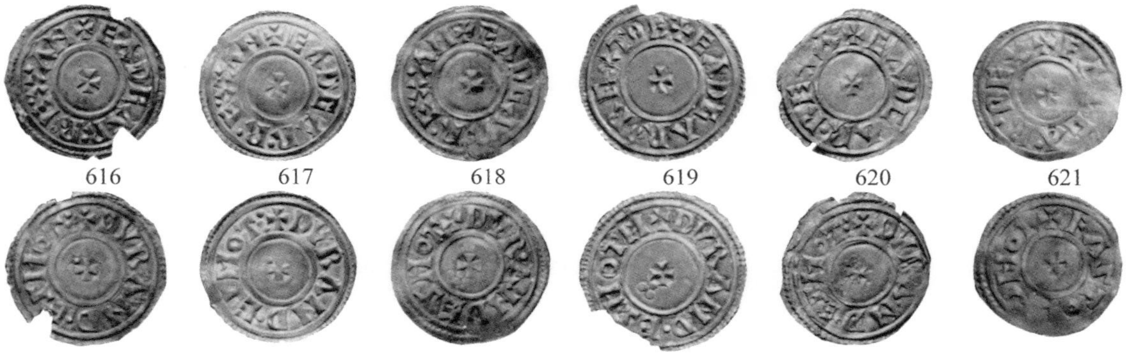

616 617 618 619 620 621

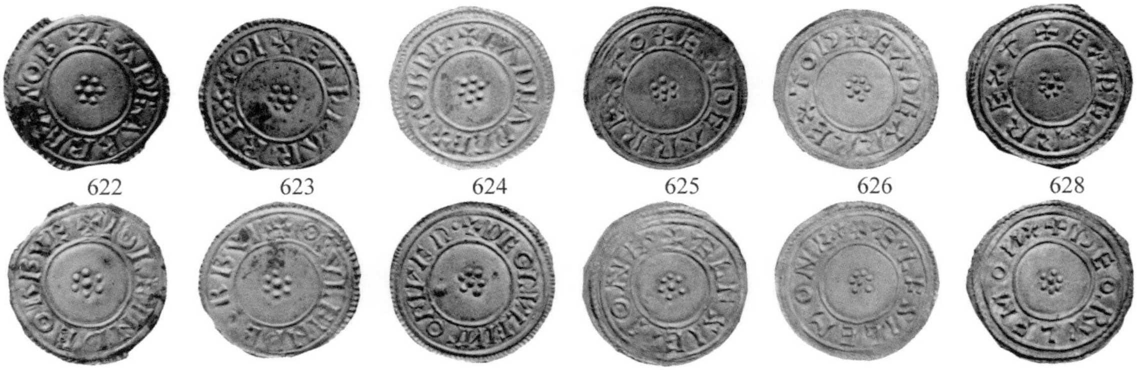

622 623 624 625 626 628

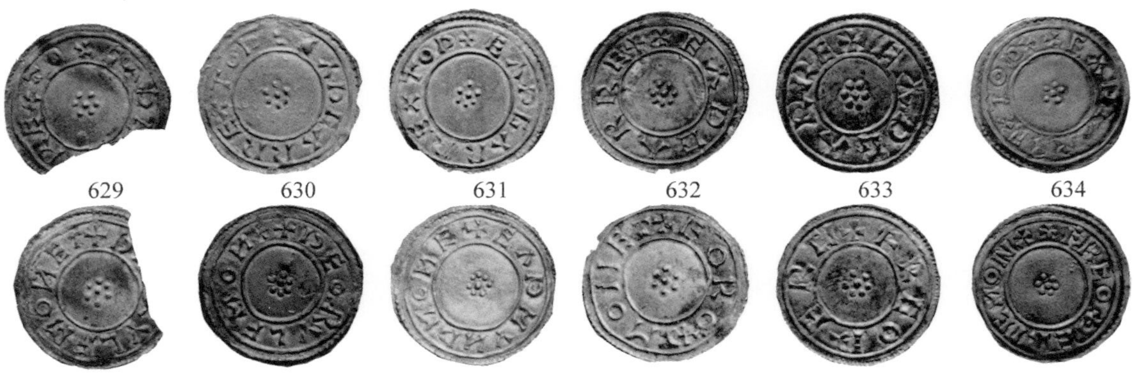

629 630 631 632 633 634

EDGAR (*cont.*)

CR type (*cont.*)

	Weight *g*	*gr.*	Die-Axis	
635.	1.55	23.9	270°	Freotheric (*Freothuric/Fredric*). Chester style. Willoughby Gardner; ex Baldwin; ex Parsons (1929) 112 (c).
636.	1.48	22.8	225°	Siferth (*Sigeferth*). Chester style. Chester (1950) hoard, no. 465. Same obv. die as *SCBI 34*, 1065, perhaps same rev. die as *SCBI 34*, 1064.
637.	1.36	21.0	0°	Siferth (*Sigeferth*). Chester style. Willoughby Gardner; ex Baldwin; ex Grantley (1944) 1101. Same obv. die as previous coin.
638.	1.49	23.0	135°	Siferth (*Sigeferth*). Chester style. Willoughby Gardner; ex L. S. Forrer 1945; ex Virgil Brand; ex P. Carlyon-Britton (1913) 459. Die-duplicate of *SCBI 6*, 577 and of *SCBI 9*, 416.
639.	1.21 slightly chipped	18.6	135°	Thurmod (*Thormothr*). Chester style. Willoughby Gardner; ex P. Carlyon-Britton (1918) 1723; ex Spink (*NCirc* Dec 1899, 58571).
640.	1.36 slightly chipped	21.0	270°	Thurmod (*Thormothr*). Chester style. Willoughby Gardner; ex Wheeler (1930) 39; ex Roth (1918) 76.
641.	1.40 slightly chipped	21.6	180°	Thurmod (*Thormothr*). Chester style. Willoughby Gardner; ex Spink (*NCirc* Sep–Oct 1920, 85636) (C. M. Crompton-Roberts collection); ex Montagu (1895) 748; ex Gibbs. Same rev. die as Christie 16 Jun 1970, lot 115, and perhaps as *SCBI 6*, 578 and next coin.
642.	1.30 slightly chipped	20.1	90°	Thurmod (*Thormothr*). Chester style. Willoughby Gardner; ex Spink Nov 1912 (presumably *NCirc* Nov 1912, 107200, but obv. legend given there as +EADGAR REX T). Perhaps same rev. die as previous coin, and perhaps die-duplicate of *SCBI 6*, 578.
643.	1.38	21.3	90°	Thurmod (*Thormothr*). Chester style. Chester (1950) hoard, no. 488. Same obv. die as *SCBI 34*, 1037–8, and *SCBI 5*, 78, which have rev. die reading ÐVRMOD MO LEX, i.e. incorporating Chester mint-signature LE.
644.	1.51	23.3	225°	Thurmod (*Thormothr*). Chester style. Chester (1950) hoard, no. 489. Die-duplicate of *SCBI 34*, 1067.
645.	1.25 slightly chipped	19.3	180°	Wilsige (*Wilsig*). Chester style. E. J. Harris 1962 (purchase, GM 144 5.62).
646.	1.19	18.3	180°	Deorulf (*Deorwulf*). Unlocated North-West Midlands style. Chester (1950) hoard, no. 473.
647.	1.32	20.3	90°	Deorulf (*Deorwulf*). Unlocated North-West Midlands style. Willoughby Gardner; ex Spink; ex P. Carlyon-Britton (1918) 1723.
648.	1.34	20.7	180°	Elfstan (*Ælfstan*). Unlocated North-West Midlands style. Chester (1950) hoard, no. 469. Die-duplicate of Spink sale 58 (30 Apr 1987), lot 23. Perhaps same obv. die as next and as *SCBI 34*, 1056.
649.	1.30	20.1	0°	Elfstan (*Ælfstan*). Unlocated North-West Midlands style. Chester (1950) hoard, no. 470. Perhaps same obv. die as last.
650.	1.47	22.7	180°	Eofermund (*Eoformund*). Unlocated North-West Midlands style. Chester (1950) hoard, no. 463. Symbol in rev. field. Perhaps die-duplicate of *SCBI 34*, 1059 and of P. Carlyon-Britton (1913) 459.
651.	1.30	20.1	180°	Frothald (*Freothuweald*?). Unlocated North-West Midlands style. Chester (1950) hoard, no. 479.
652.	1.55	23.9	–	Hild[ ] (*Hildulfr*). Unlocated North-West Midlands style. Chester (1950) hoard, no. 484.
653.	0.45 fragment	6.9	270°	Siulfl[ ]. Unlocated North-West Midlands style. Chester (1950) hoard, no. 519. Presumably a coin of the moneyer Siulf, known in the HR3 type with the apparent mint-signature NE (coin 601 above).
BC type				
654.	1.40	21.6	270°	*Bedford* (BE), Ælfsig (*Ælfsige*). Chester (1950) hoard, no. 491. Cross in rev. field. Same rev. die as *SCBI 34*, 1147.
655.	1.32	20.3	180°	*Huntingdon* (HVNTEN), Prim (*Pirim*?). Chester (1950) hoard, no. 494. Eaglen 1999 no. 12.
656.	0.65 chipped	10.1	90°	Ælfs[ ] (*Ælfsige*?). Willoughby Gardner; ex P. Carlyon-Britton (1916) 1017. Cross (?) in rev. field. Coin struck on small flan.
657.	1.58	24.4	270°	Baldvvin (*Baldwin*). Chester (1950) hoard, no. 501. Pellets in rev. field. Die-duplicate of next coin and of *SCBI 34*, 1162.
658.	1.05 chipped	16.2	0°	Baldvvin (*Baldwin*). Chester (1950) hoard, no. 502. Pellets in rev. field. Die-duplicate of previous coin.

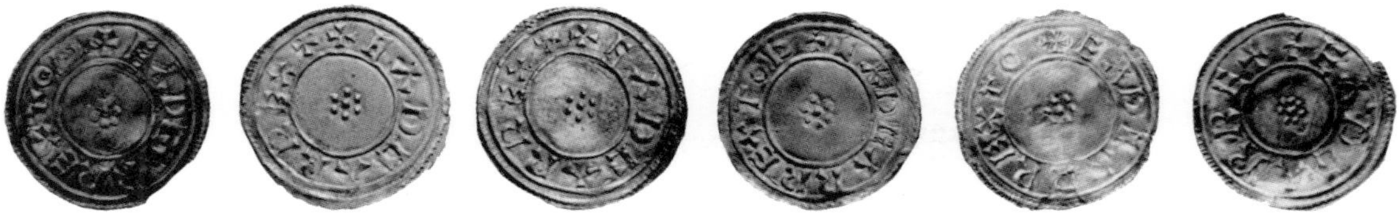

635 636 637 638 639 640

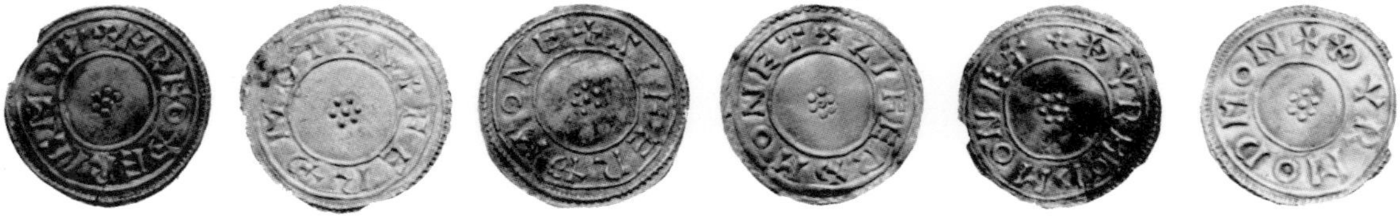

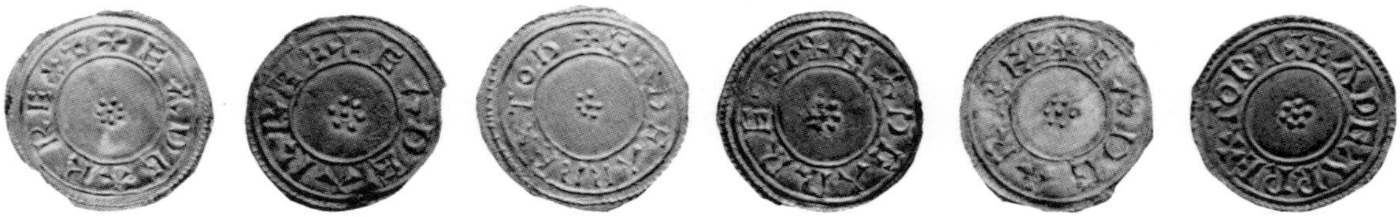

641 642 643 644 645 646

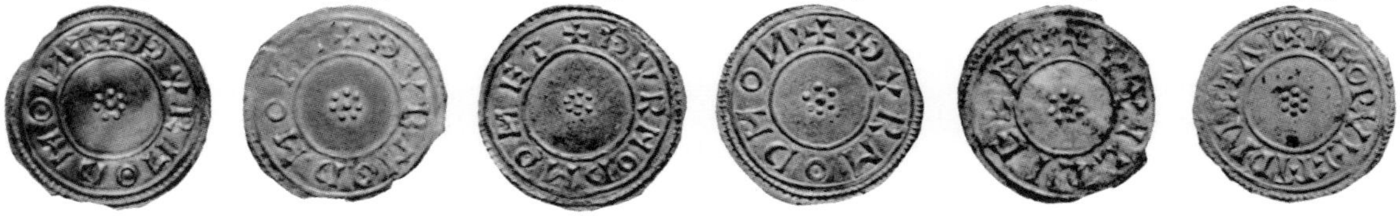

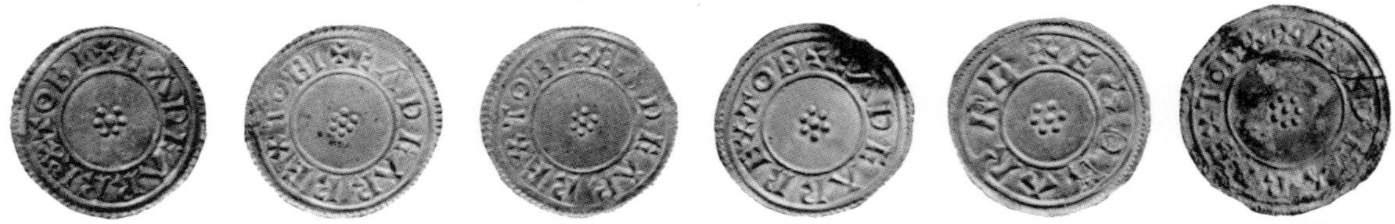

647 648 649 650 651 652

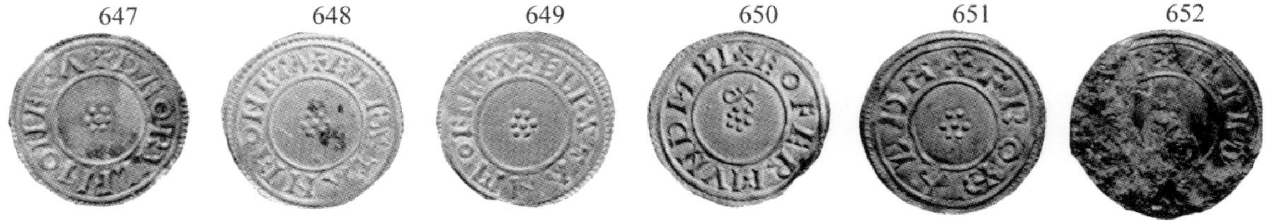

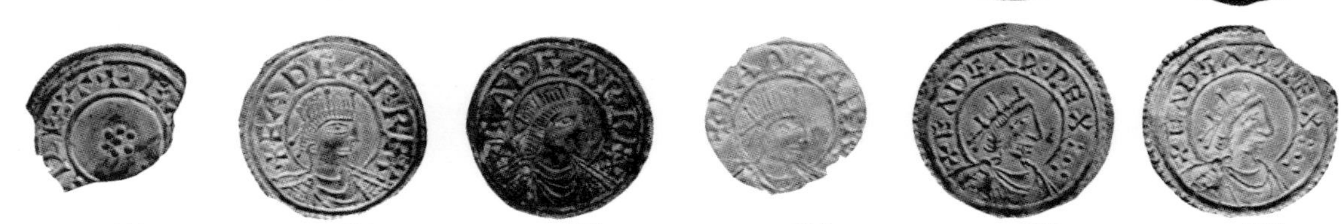

653 654 655 656 657 658

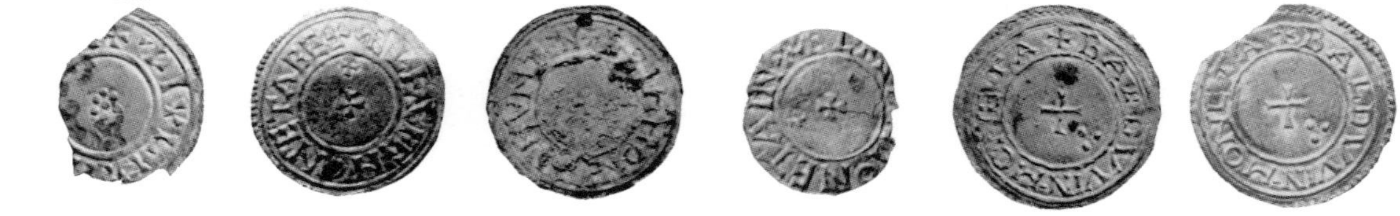

EDGAR (*cont.*)

BC type (*cont.*)

	Weight g	*Weight* gr.	*Die-Axis*	
659.	1.37	21.1	0°	Baldvvin (*Baldwin*). Chester (1950) hoard, no. 499.
660.	1.34	20.7	225°	Liofstan (*Leofstan*). Chester (1950) hoard, no. 504.
661.	1.38	21.3	0°	Liofstan (*Leofstan*). Chester (1950) hoard, no. 505. Pellets in rev. field.
662.	– two fragments	–	225°	Sif[ ] (*Sigeferth*). Chester (1950) hoard, nos. 487 and 513.
663.	1.30	20.1	180°	Wulstan (*Wulfstan*). Chester (1950) hoard, no. 511. Die-duplicate of *SCBI 34*, 1170.

PRE-REFORM PERIOD, UNCERTAIN RULER

HT1 type

664.	– fragment	–	–	+EAD[ ]+, Leofric. Southern/Unlocated Midlands style. Chester (1950) hoard, no. 91. Attributed to Eadmund in publication of Chester (1950) hoard, but the group of three pellets at the end of the obv. legend is a feature more familiar on coins of HT type of Eadwig.

Uncertain type (*HT1?*)

665.	– fragment	–	90°	+E[ ]EX, Thur[ ]. Southern/Unlocated Midlands style. Of possible reign attributions, an attribution to Eadred seems the most likely; as regards moneyer, the coin is not particularly similar to known coins of the Midlands moneyer Thurstan, active at this period, and the identity of its moneyer is uncertain. Chester (1950) hoard, not in published list.

POST-REFORM PERIOD

EDGAR (959–75)

Reform Small Cross type (Hild. C2; *BMC* vi)

666.	0.98 badly chipped	15.1	135°	*Northampton* (HANT), [ ]fsili (*Leofsige*?). Edward Davies (GM 277.55); ex Chester (1914) hoard, Hill no. 14, 15 or 16. Die-duplicate of next two coins.
667.	1.17	18.1	45°	*Northampton* (HANT), Leofsili (*Leofsige*?). Edward Davies (GM 278.55); ex Chester (1914) hoard, Hill no. 14, 15 or 16. Die-duplicate of preceding coin and next coin.
668.	0.92 badly chipped	14.2	315°	*Northampton* ([ ]), Leofsili (*Leofsige*?). Edward Davies (GM 279.55); ex Chester (1914) hoard, Hill no. 14, 15 or 16. Die-duplicate of preceding two coins.
669.	1.19 fragment	18.3	270°	*Rochester* ([ ]), Sidema[ ] (*Sideman*). Edward Davies (GM 281.55); ex Chester (1914) hoard, Hill no. 10.
670.	1.34	20.7	180°	*Stamford* (STANFO), Cnapa. Edward Davies (GM 280.55); ex Chester (1914) hoard, Hill no. 19. Die-duplicate of *SCBI 27*, 1059.

EDGAR *or* EDWARD THE MARTYR (975–8)

Reform Small Cross type (Hild. C2; *BMC* vi)

671.	0.73 fragment	11.2	–	*Stamford* (STANF), moneyer uncertain. Obv. reading uncertain. Edward Davies (GM 282.55); ex Chester (1914) hoard, Hill no. 122. Listed by Hill as a coin of uncertain reign of the Stamford mint by a moneyer]ar, 'probably Wulgar', but the portion of the coin that carried the letters AR is no longer present. Perhaps from same obv. die as *SCBI 27*, 1063-4, coins of Edgar, Stamford mint, with moneyer's name on rev. Wulgar (coin 1063) and Wulfgar (coin 1064). Rev. die is not dissimilar to that of *SCBI 27*, 1095, Edward the Martyr, Stamford mint, moneyer Wulfgar.

EDWARD THE MARTYR (975–8)

Reform Small Cross type (Hild. A; *BMC* i)

672.	1.21 badly chipped	18.6	0°	*Bedford* ([ ]EDA), Ælfstan. Edward Davies (GM 293.55); ex Chester (1914) hoard, Hill no. 25.
673.	1.31	20.2	0°	*Bedford* (BEDA), Ælfstan. Edward Davies (GM 292.55); ex Chester (1914) hoard, Hill no. 26.

[*continued overleaf*]

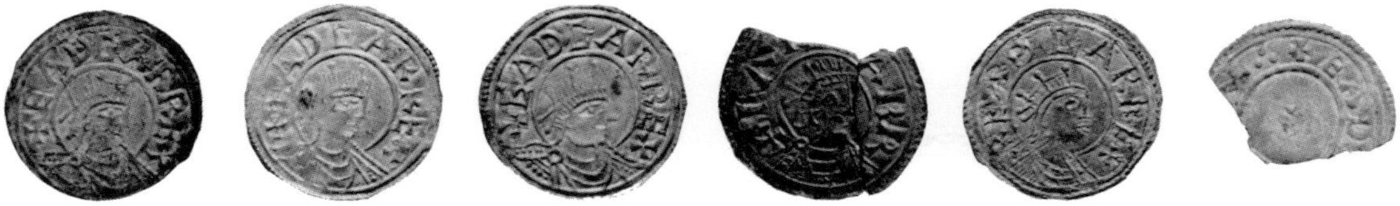

659 660 661 662 663 664

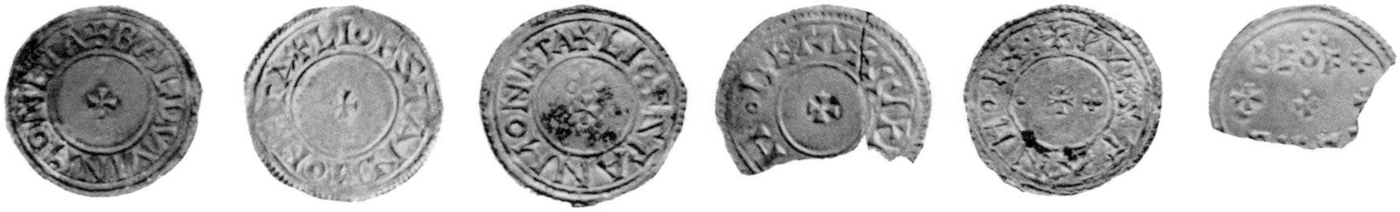

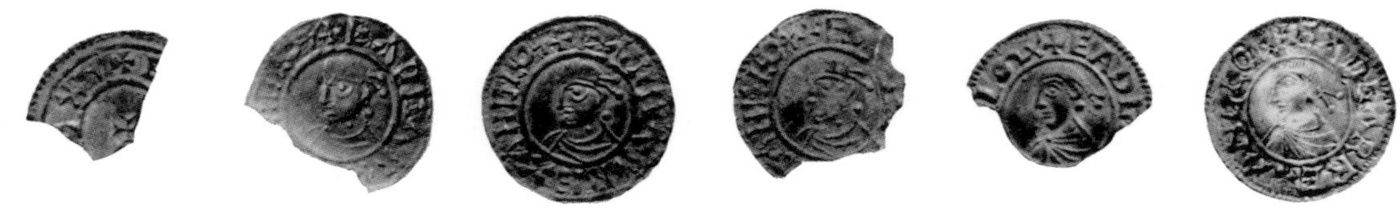

665 666 667 668 669 670

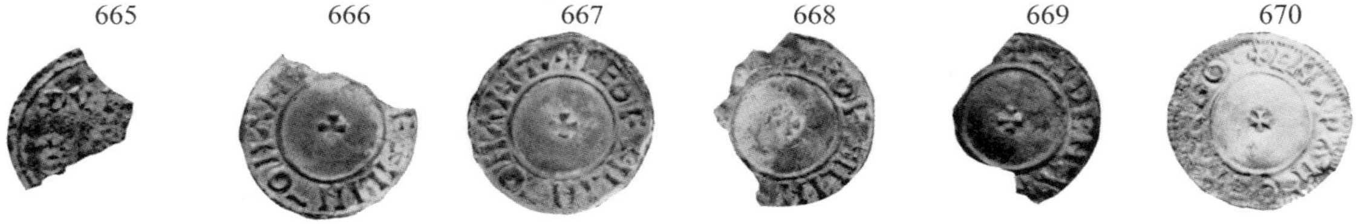

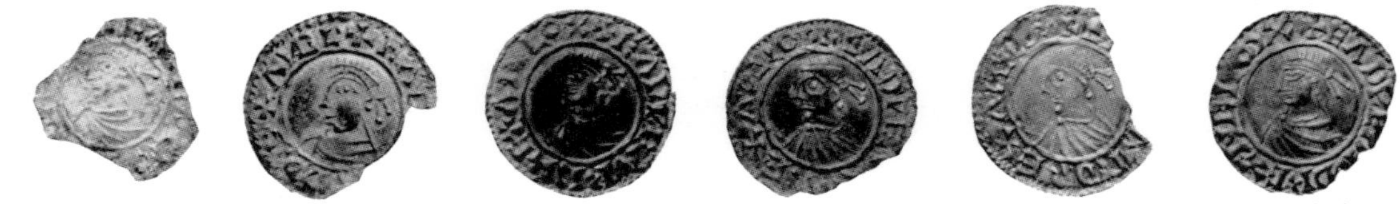

671 672 673 674 675 676

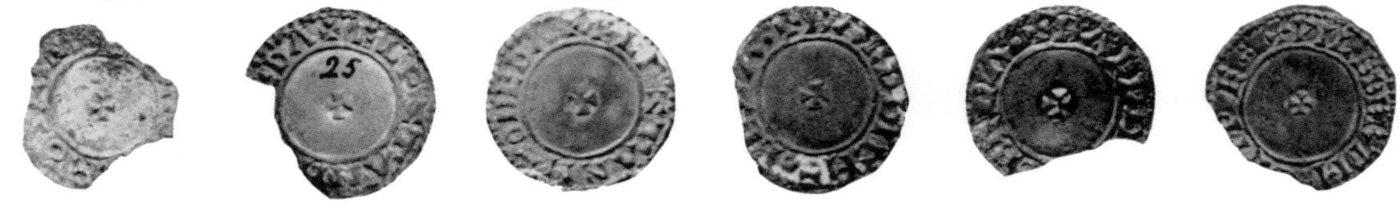

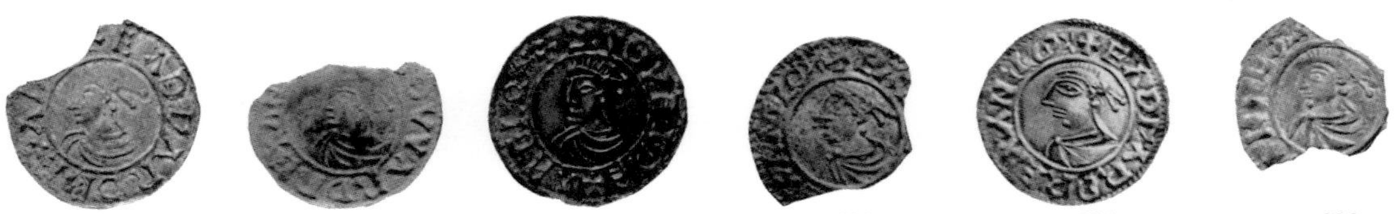

677 678 679 680 681 682

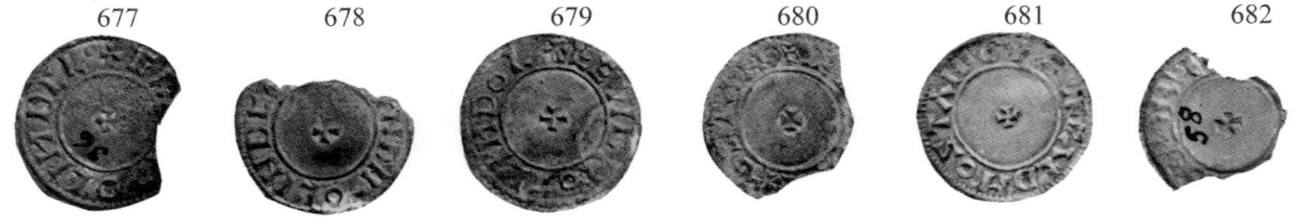

EDWARD THE MARTYR (*cont.*)

Reform Small Cross type (Hild. A; *BMC* i) (*cont.*)

	Weight *g*	*gr.*	*Die-Axis*	
674.	1.28 chipped	19.7	270°	*Bedford* (BEDA), Balddig (*Bealdic*). Edward Davies (GM 290.55); ex Chester (1914) hoard, Hill no. 30. Probably die-duplicate of next coin.
675.	1.12 badly chipped	17.3	90°	*Bedford* (BEDA), Baldd[ ] (*Bealdic*). Edward Davies (GM 291.55); evidently ex Chester (1914) hoard (but not listed by Hill). Probably die-duplicate of previous coin.
676.	1.36 chipped	21.0	0°	*Ipswich* (GIPE), Wilebert (*Wilbeorht*?). Frank Haswell (gift, GM 1949-450); then stated to have been 'found near Chester Cathedral', but perhaps a stray from the Chester (1914) hoard.
677.	1.17 chipped	18.1	315°	*Lincoln* (LINDCL), Gr[ ] (*Grimr*). Edward Davies (GM 294.55); ex Chester (1914) hoard, Hill no. 36. Dies not in Mossop 1970.
678.	1.04 badly chipped	16.1	0°	*Lincoln* (LINDC[ ]), [ ]ind (*Grind*). Edward Davies (GM 295.55); ex Chester (1914) hoard, Hill no. 37. Die-duplicate of *SCBI 2*, 744, Mossop 1970 I/24.
679.	1.43	22.1	135°	*Lincoln* (LINDOL), Levig (*Leofwig*). Edward Davies (GM 296.55); ex Chester (1914) hoard, Hill no. 39. Dies not in Mossop 1970.
680.	1.09 badly chipped	16.8	135°	*Stamford* (STAN), Æ[ ] (*Ælfweald*?). Edward Davies (GM 288.55); ex Chester (1914) hoard, Hill no. 55. Perhaps from same dies as *SCBI 27*, 1067, this moneyer. Same obv. die as *BMC* 21.
681.	1.29	19.9	90°	*Stamford* (STANFO), Ælfwald (*Ælfweald*). Edward Davies (GM 284.55); ex Chester (1914) hoard, Hill no. 56.
682.	0.66 fragment	10.2	–	*Stamford* (ZTAN), [ ] (*Ælfweald* or *Æscmann*). Edward Davies (GM 289.55); ex Chester (1914) hoard, Hill no. 58. Attributed by Hill to a moneyer Æ[ ], but the portion of the coin with the letters AE on is no longer present.

EDWARD THE MARTYR (*cont.*)

Reform Small Cross type (*cont.*)

	Weight *g*	*gr.*	*Die-Axis*	
683.	1.04 badly chipped	16.1	180°	*Stamford* (**STANFOR**), [ ]pa (*Cnapa*). Edward Davies (GM 287.55); ex Chester (1914) hoard, Hill no. 61. Same rev. die as *SCBI 27*, 1080.
684.	– several fragments	–	–	*Stamford* (**STAN**[ ]), [ ]cer (*Wacer*). Edward Davies (GM 286.55); ex Chester (1914) hoard, Hill no. 64 (portions of coin since lost).
685.	0.94 badly chipped	14.5	180°	*Stamford* (**STANF**[ ]), Wul[ ]r (*Wulfgar*). Edward Davies (GM 285.55); ex Chester (1914) hoard, Hill no. 65. Die-duplicate of *SCBI 27*, 1098.
686.	1.07 badly chipped	16.5	–	*York* (**EFORƿI**[ ]), [ ] (*Beolan* or *Isulfr*?). Edward Davies (GM 297.55); ex Chester (1914) hoard, Hill no. 74. From an obv. die used to strike coins of this reign and type by the York moneyers Beolan (*SCBI 4*, 820; *SCBI 29*, 513) and Isulf (*SCBI 9*, 431), although no rev. die-identity has been traced (ex inf. W. Lean).

ÆTHELRÆD II (978–1016)

Reform Small Cross type (Hild. A; *BMC* i)

	g	*gr.*	*Die-Axis*	
687.	1.28	19.7	0°	*Bedford* ([ ]**YDA**), Baldic (*Bealdic*). Edward Davies (GM 312.55); ex Chester (1914) hoard, Hill no. 79.
688.	1.11 slightly chipped	17.1	270°	*Derby* (**DEORABY**), Osolf (*Asulfr*/*Oswulf*). Edward Davies (GM 300.55); ex Chester (1914) hoard, Hill no. 87. Die-duplicate of next.
689.	0.90 chipped	13.9	270°	*Derby* (**DEORABY**), O[ ] (*Asulfr*/*Oswulf*). Edward Davies (GM 301.55); ex Chester (1914) hoard, Hill no. 88. Die-duplicate of last.
690.	1.13 badly chipped	17.4	45°	*Lincoln* (**LINEL**), Ethelre[ ] (*Æthelræd*). Edward Davies (GM 302.55); ex Chester (1914) hoard, Hill no. 95. Three pellets before face on obv. Die-duplicate of *SCBI 27*, 20, Mossop 1970 II/12.
691.	1.15 badly chipped	17.7	45°	*Lincoln* ([ ]**NDOL**), Levig (*Leofwig*). Edward Davies (GM 303.55); ex Chester (1914) hoard, Hill no. 91. Three pellets before face on obv. Die-duplicate of *SCBI 27*, 23, Mossop 1970 II/19.
692.	1.24 chipped	19.1	225°	*Lincoln* (**LI**), Rodbert. Edward Davies (GM 304.55); ex Chester (1914) hoard, Hill no. 97. Three pellets before face on obv. Die-duplicate of next coin and of coin in BM, Mossop 1970 II/23. Same obv. die as next three coins.
693.	1.13 badly chipped	17.4	180°	*Lincoln* (**LI**), Rodb[ ] (*Rodbert*). Edward Davies (GM 306.55); ex Chester (1914) hoard, Hill no. 98. Three pellets before face on obv. Die-duplicate of preceding coin, and same obv. die as next two coins.
694.	1.10 badly chipped	16.9	180°	*Lincoln* (**LINC**), [ ]dbert (*Rodbert*). Edward Davies (GM 305.55); ex Chester (1914) hoard, Hill no. 99. Three pellets before face on obv. Same dies as coin in BM, Mossop 1970 II/21.Same obv. die as previous two coins and next coin.
695.	1.32 chipped	20.3	315°	*Lincoln* (**LIN**), Rodbert. Frank Haswell (gift, GM 1949-449); then stated to have been 'found near Chester Cathedral' but perhaps a stray from the Chester (1914) hoard. Die-duplicate of *SCBI 27*, 24, Mossop 1970 II/22. Three pellets before face on obv. Same obv. die as previous three coins.
696.	1.00 chipped	15.4	315°	*Stamford* (**STAN**), Wul[ ]r (*Wulfgar*). Edward Davies (GM 309.55); ex Chester (1914) hoard, Hill no. 103. Annulet in rev. field.

First Hand type (Hild. B1I; *BMC* iia)

	g	*gr.*	*Die-Axis*	
697.	0.90 fragment	13.9	270°	*Lincoln*(?) ([ ]), S[ ]ting (*Svertingr*). Edward Davies (GM 311.55); ex Chester (1914) hoard, Hill no. 121. So attributed by Mossop 1970 III/21, followed by Jonsson 1986, p.70, but the mint name is absent and only the bottom stroke of the initial letter of the moneyer's name survives.
698.	1.55	23.9	90°	*London* (**LVND**), Alfwold (*Ælfweald*). Edward Davies (GM 308.55); ex Chester (1914) hoard, Hill no. 117.
699.	1.43 badly chipped	22.1	90°	*Winchester* (**ƿINT**), Ae[ ]ige (*Ælfsige*). Edward Davies (GM 310.55); ex Chester (1914) hoard, Hill no. 119. Die-duplicate of *SCBI 2*, 809.

[*continued overleaf*]

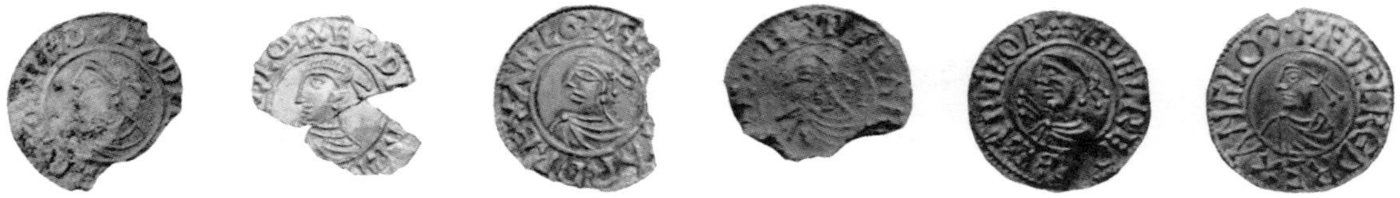

683 684 685 686 687 688

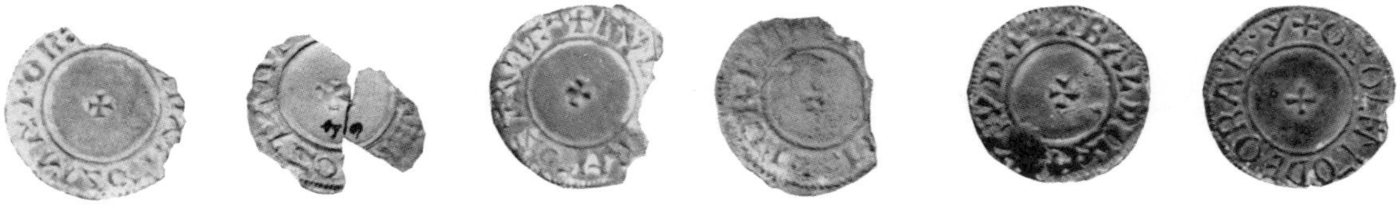

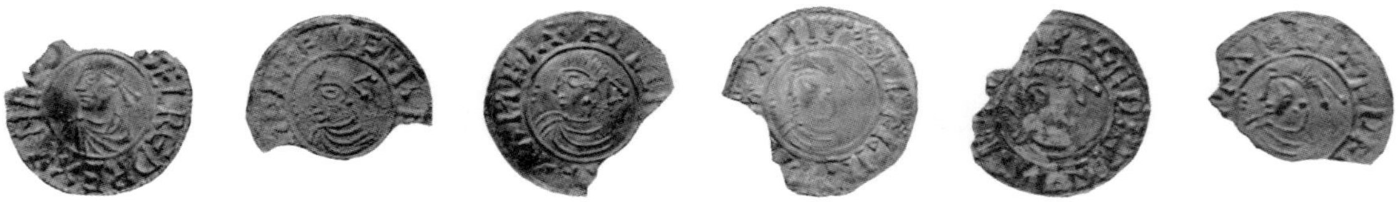

689 690 691 692 693 694

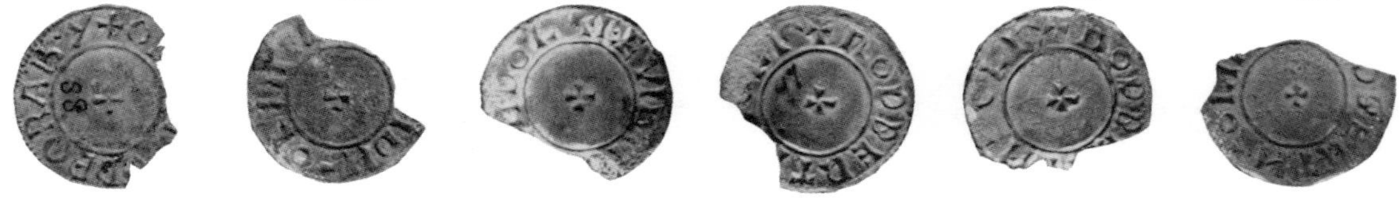

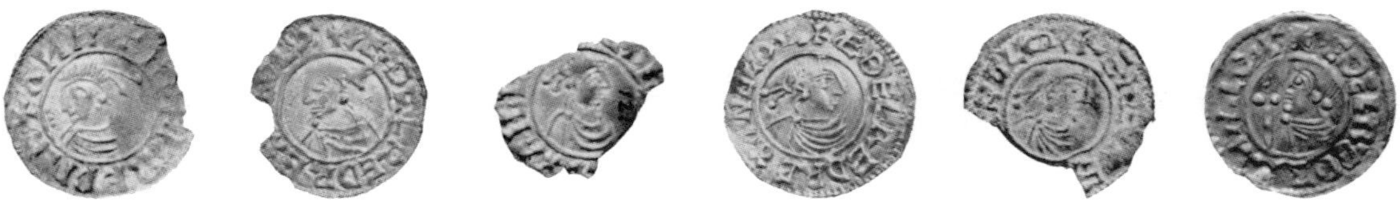

695 696 697 698 699 700

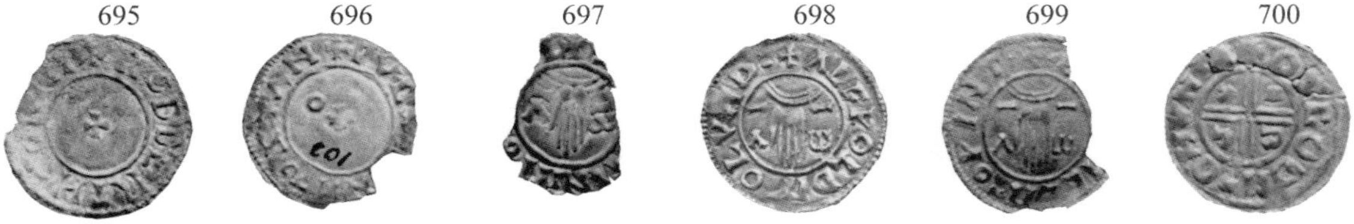

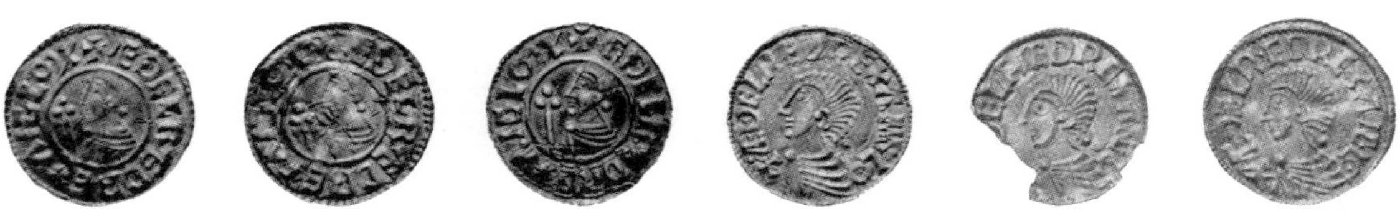

701 702 703 704 705 706

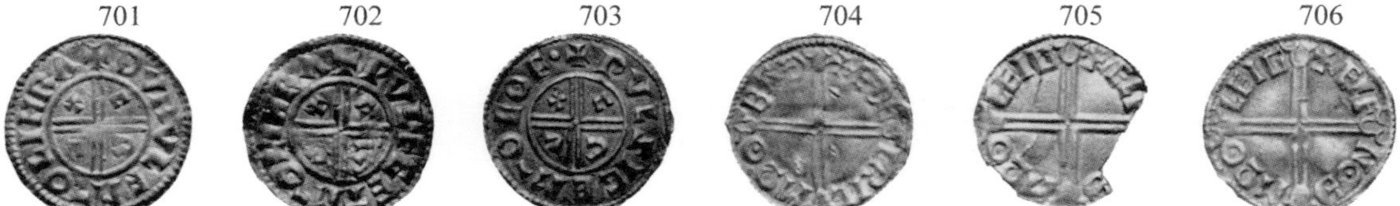

Plate 29 (*cont.*)

ÆTHELRÆD II (*cont.*)

Crux type (Hild. C; *BMC* iiia) (*cont.*)

	Weight g	Weight gr.	Die-Axis	
700.	1.25 cracked	19.3	180°	*Huntingdon* (HVNTA), Osgod (*Asgautr*). W. Pritchard (bequest), 1905 (then identified as being of Winchester mint). Eaglen 1999 no. 39 (only specimen recorded from these dies).
701.	1.54	23.7	90°	*Leicester* (LIHRA), Thurulf (*Thorulfr*). Willoughby Gardner (via Mrs Gardner 1963); ex Baldwin (with Baldwin stock ticket H1592).
702.	1.67	25.7	90°	*Leicester* (LIHRA), Wulfget (*Wulfgeat*). Willoughby Gardner (via Mrs Gardner 1963).
703.	1.24	19.1	90°	*York* (EOF), Wulsige (*Wulfsige*). 'Prob[ably] Meols' (note by Nicholas Moore, with the additional suggestion that the coin might be ex Thomas Hughes), but not listed as a Meols find in Dolley 1961.

Long Cross type (Hild. D; *BMC* iva)

704.	1.72	26.5	270°	*Bath* (BAÐ), Ædelric (*Æthelric*). Willoughby Gardner (via Mrs Gardner 1963); ex Spink. Pecked and presumptively from a Scandinavian hoard.
705.	1.64 chipped	25.3	0°	*Chester* (LEIG), Ælf[ ]th (*Ælfnoth*). Willoughby Gardner (via Mrs Gardner 1963); ex Seaby; ex Grantley (but not in 1944 sale?); ex L. A. Lawrence. Same rev. die as next, and possibly same rev. die as *SCBI 5*, 126.
706.	1.73	26.7	270°	*Chester* (LEIG), Ælfnoth (*Ælfnoth*). Willoughby Gardner (via Mrs Gardner 1963). Same rev. die as last, and possibly same rev. die as *SCBI 5*, 126.

ÆTHELRÆD II (*cont.*)

Long Cross type (*cont.*)

No.	Weight g	Weight gr.	Die-Axis	
707.	1.68	25.9	0°	*Chester* (LEIG), Osulf (*Asulfr/Oswulf*). S. & B. Coins 2001 (purchase). Pecked and presumptively from a Scandinavian hoard.
708.	1.55	23.9	0°	*Exeter* (EAXE), Dunstan. Edward Davies (GM 307.55).
709.	1.57	24.2	0°	*Lincoln* (LNC), Æthelnoth. Willoughby Gardner. Mossop 1970 IX/25. Pecked and presumptively from a Scandinavian hoard.
710.	1.80	27.8	180°	*London* (LVND), Leofric. Lieut.-Col. Alan Williams 1953 (gift, GM 156 M 1953).
711.	1.68	25.9	90°	*Warwick* (ƿÆRI), Osmær. Lieut.-Col. Alan Williams 1955 (gift, GM 1955 28–3).

Helmet type (Hild. E; *BMC* viii)

No.	Weight g	Weight gr.	Die-Axis	
712.	1.45	22.3	270°	*Chester* (LEIG), Leofwine. Purchased 1971; ex Elmore Jones (1971) 175.
713.	1.16	17.9	180°	*Leicester* (LEHRA), Ælfric. Willoughby Gardner (via Mrs Gardner 1963). The mint-signature looks as if it may have been reworked, but Ælfric is a Leicester moneyer in this type.
714.	1.38 pierced	21.3	270°	*York* (EOF), Outhgrim (*Authgrimr*). Willoughby Gardner; ex Baldwin (with Baldwin stock ticket B5159).

Last Small Cross type (Hild. A; *BMC* i)

No.	Weight g	Weight gr.	Die-Axis	
715.	1.28	19.7	0°	*Chester* (LEGC), Ælfnoth. Willoughby Gardner (via Mrs Gardner 1963). Die-duplicate of next.
716.	1.38	21.3	90°	*Chester* (LEGC), Ælfnoth. Willoughby Gardner (via Mrs Gardner 1963). Die-duplicate of last. Pecked and presumptively from a Scandinavian hoard.
717.	1.42	21.9	180°	*Chester* (LEIG), Alcsige (*Ealhsige*). Willoughby Gardner (via Mrs Gardner 1963). Die-duplicate of *SCBI 5*, 161–2. Pecked and presumptively from a Scandinavian hoard.
718.	1.42	21.9	180°	*Chester* (LEIG), Leofnoth. Willoughby Gardner (via Mrs Gardner 1963); ex Lincoln. Die-duplicate of *SCBI 5*, 166–7. Pecked and presumptively from a Scandinavian hoard.
719.	1.72	26.5	180°	*Chester* (LEGC), Leofwine. Willoughby Gardner (via Mrs Gardner 1963). Die-duplicate of *SCBI 5*, 171. Pecked and presumptively from a Scandinavian hoard.

CNUT (1016–35)

Quatrefoil type (Hild. E; *BMC* viii)

No.	Weight g	Weight gr.	Die-Axis	
720.	1.00	15.4	0°	*Chester* (LEG), Ælnoth (*Ælfnoth*). Bryn Maelgwyn hoard (Boon 1986, 4). Same rev. die as *SCBI 5*, 179.
721.	0.95	14.6	270°	*Chester* (LEG), Alcsi (*Ealhsige*). Bryn Maelgwyn hoard (Boon 1986, 16). Same rev. die as *SCBI 5*, 180–1.
722.	1.01	15.6	0°	*Chester* (LEG), Alcsi (*Ealhsige*). Bryn Maelgwyn hoard (Boon 1986, 53). Die-duplicate of *SCBI 5*, 188.
723.	0.89	13.7	270°	*Chester* (LEG), Elewine (*Ælfwine*?). Bryn Maelgwyn hoard (Boon 1986, 27). Same obv. die as *SCBI 5*, 199.
724.	0.97	14.9	90°	*Chester* (LEI), Godwine. Bryn Maelgwyn hoard (Boon 1986, 83). Same obv. die as *SCBI 5*, 203, and same rev. die as *SCBI 5*, 204.
725.	1.00	15.4	0°	*Chester* (LEG), Leofa. Bryn Maelgwyn hoard (Boon 1986, 106).
726.	0.98	15.1	90°	*Chester* (LEGCS), Leowi (*Leofwig*). Bryn Maelgwyn hoard (Boon 1986, 134). Die-duplicate of next and of *SCBI 5*, 220.
727.	1.00 chipped	15.4	0°	*Chester* (LEGCS), Leowi (*Leofwig*). Willoughby Gardner (via Mrs Gardner 1963); ex Spink. Die-duplicate of last and of *SCBI 5*, 220.
728.	1.11	17.1	0°	*Chester* (LE), Leowine (*Leofwine*). Purchased from Seaby July 1970 (GM 97.C.1970), with Seaby stock no. 2859. Same obv. die as next and as *SCBI 5*, 226–7.
729.	1.06	16.3	270°	*Chester* (LEG), Leowine (*Leofwine*). Willoughby Gardner (via Mrs Gardner 1963); ex Bridges (1918) 120. Same obv. die as last, and die-duplicate of *SCBI 5*, 226–7.
730.	1.00	15.4	90°	*Chester* (LEG), Swartic (*Svertingr*). Purchased 1971; ex Elmore Jones (1971) 178.

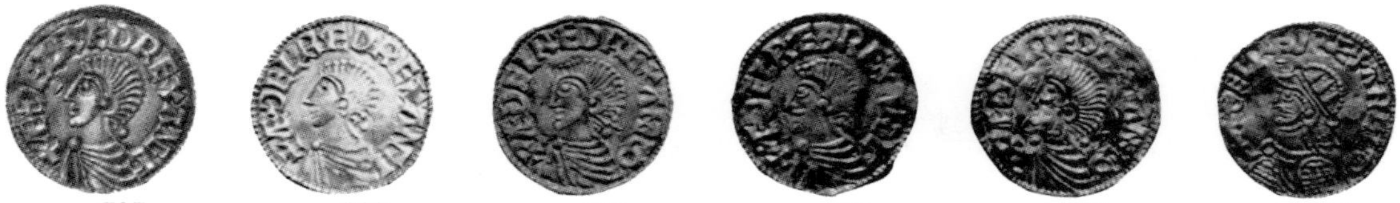

707 708 709 710 711 712

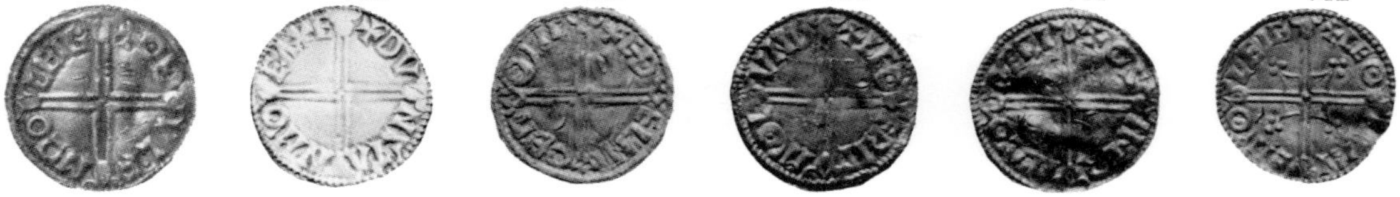

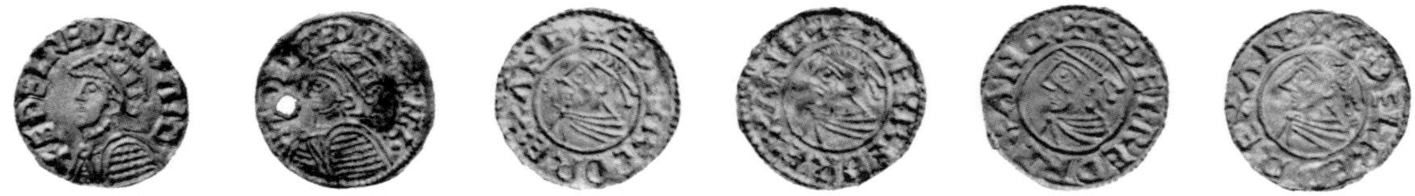

713 714 715 716 717 718

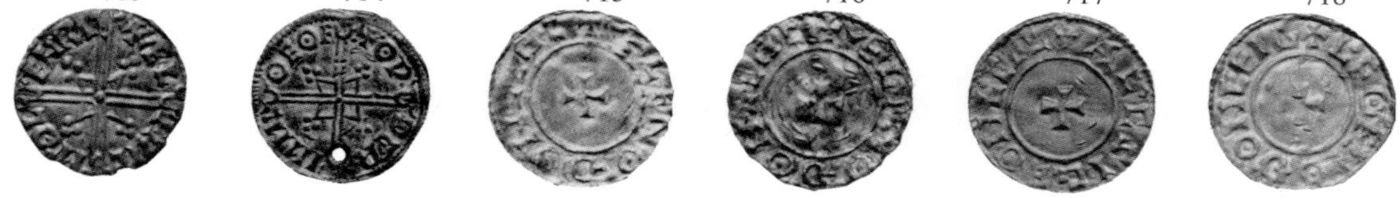

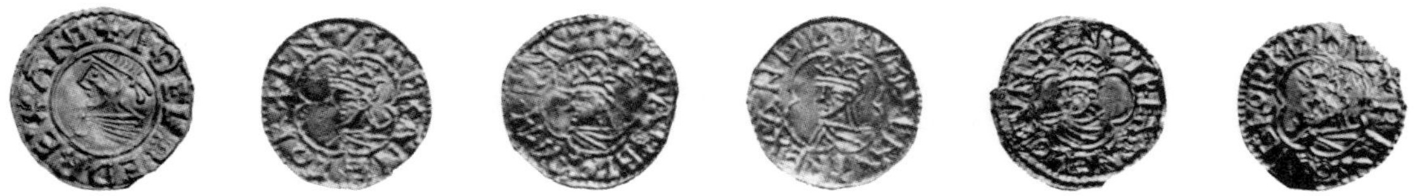

719 720 721 722 723 724

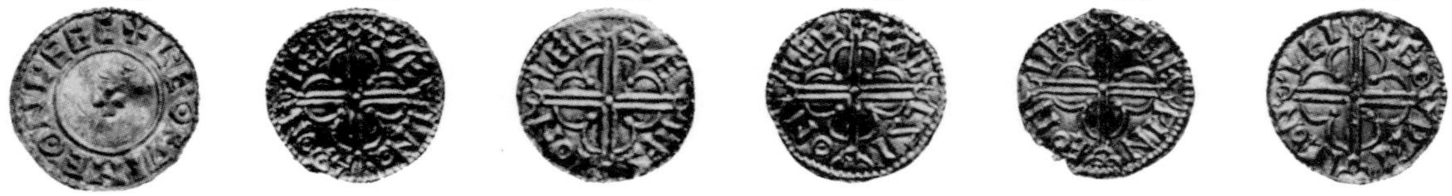

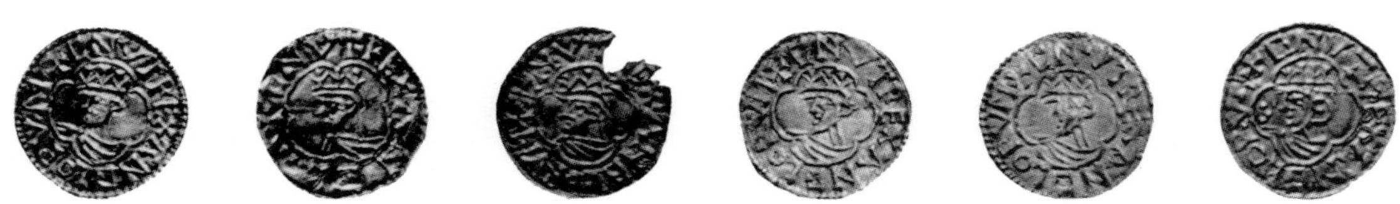

725 726 727 728 729 730

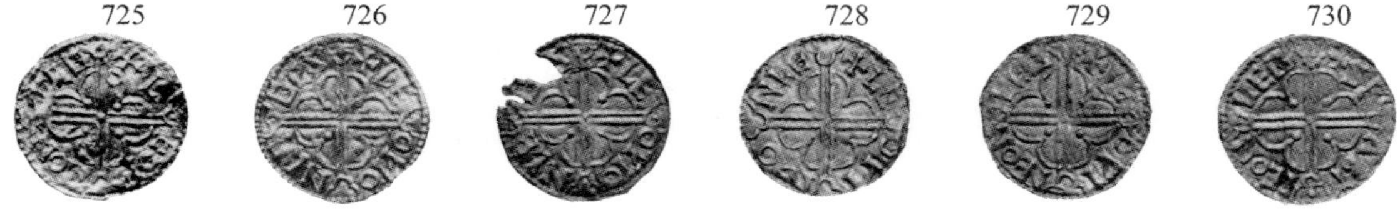

CNUT (*cont.*)

Quatrefoil type (*cont.*)

	Weight *g*	*gr.*	Die-Axis	
731.	0.96	14.8	315	*Chester* (LEG), Trotan. Bryn Maelgwyn hoard (Boon 1986, 169). Perhaps same rev. die as next two coins
732.	1.00	15.4	180°	*Chester* (LEG), Trotan. Willoughby Gardner (via Mrs Gardner 1963); ex 'Seaby no. 61083' (note by Moore, but this seems more likely to be a Spink number from *NCirc*). Perhaps same rev. die as next and previous coin.
733.	0.94	14.5	315°	*Chester* (LEG), Trotan. Willoughby Gardner (via Mrs Gardner 1963). Perhaps same rev. die as last two coins.
734.	0.87	13.4	90°	*Leicester* (LEHR), Wulfnoth. F. W. Longbottom, 1899 gift (GM 118.1899) (attributed to Chester on acquisition).
734A.	1.11	17.1	270°	*Northampton* (HΛ), Leofnath (*Leofnoth*). Obv. +CNVT RE+ ON LEIO. Northampton A style (Blackburn and Lyon 1986, pp. 239-40). Willoughby Gardner; ex Wells; ex Bruun (1925) 166.

Pointed Helmet type (Hild. G; *BMC* xiv)

735.	1.02	15.7	0°	*Chester* (LEICE), Ælfsige. Willoughby Gardner (via Mrs Gardner 1963). Die-duplicate (?) of *SCBI 5*, 241.

HAROLD I (1035–40)

Jewel Cross type (Hild. A; *BMC* I)

736.	1.03 chipped	15.9	90°	*Chester* ([ ]EICEEST), Crocc (*Krokr*). Willoughby Gardner (via Mrs Gardner 1963); ex Seaby (or possibly from Spink, 1947?).

Fleur de Lis type (Hild. B; *BMC* v and vi)

737.	1.16	17.9	180°	*Chester* (LEIC), Leofwine. Purchased 1973 (GM 9 c 73); ex Glendining 14 Mar 1973 ('Polish hoard'), lot 98; ex Stryjewo Wielkie hoard.

EDWARD THE CONFESSOR (1042–66)

Radiate/Small Cross type (Hild. A; *BMC* I)

738.	1.06	16.3	180°	*London* (LVND), Edwine (*Eadwine*). Willoughby Gardner (via Mrs Gardner 1963); ex Baldwin.

Trefoil Quadrilateral type (Hild. C; *BMC* III)

739.	1.10	17.0	–	*Chester* (LEICE), Leofine (*Leofwine*). Purchased 1971 (GM 110 c 1971); ex Elmore Jones (1971) 179.

Short Cross type (Hild. B; *BMC* II)

740.	1.06	16.3	180°	*Chester* (LE), Colbrand (*Kolbrandr*). Willoughby Gardner (via Mrs Gardner 1963); ex Seaby (on Seaby ticket with their acquisition date 1946).
741.	0.81	12.5	180°	*Chester* (?) (LEOIRI), Ælfgar. F. Banks 1965 (purchase, GM 28.C.1965); ex Seaby (mint-signature read as CESTRI by P. Seaby). The attribution of this coin to the Chester mint is possible, for Ælfgar is recorded as a moneyer at Chester in the *Pointed Helmet* type, but the reading LEOIRI would be unusual for Chester and Peter Seaby's reading CESTRI is not credible (the name of Chester does not otherwise appear on coins in this form until the reign of Henry I).

Expanding Cross type (Hild. E; *BMC* V), light issue

742.	1.10	16.9	90°	*Lewes* (LÆƿI), Godwine. No provenance.

Expanding Cross type (Hild. E; *BMC* V), heavy issue

743.	1.57	24.2	–	*Leicester* (LEICESTR), Godwine. Willoughby Gardner (via Mrs Gardner 1963); ex Spink (*NCirc* May–Jun 1921 93242). Numbered 27 on rev. of coin in ink. Die-duplicate of *SCBI 5*, 300.

Pointed Helmet type (Hild. F; *BMC* VII)

744.	1.23	19.0	270°	*Chester* (LEICES), Ælfsiie (*Ælfsige*). Willoughby Gardner (via Mrs Gardner 1963). Die-duplicate of *SCBI 5*, 315–16.

[*continued overleaf*]

PLATE 31

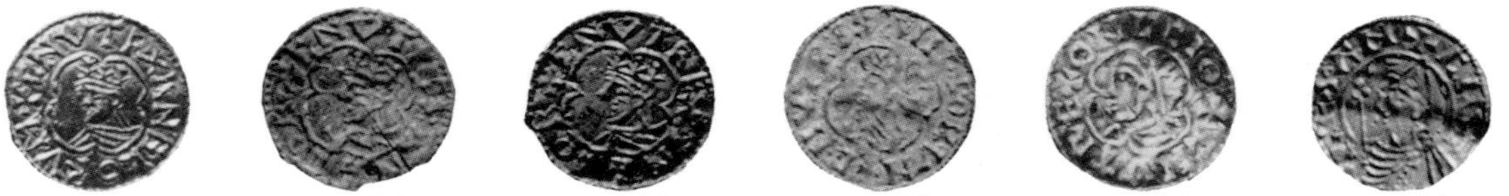

731 732 733 734 734a 735

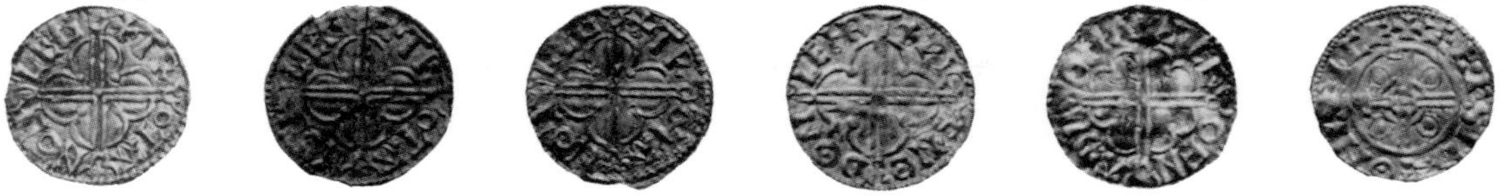

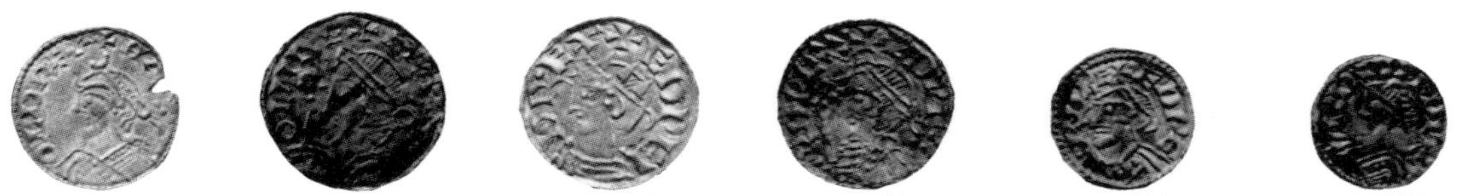

736 737 738 739 740 741

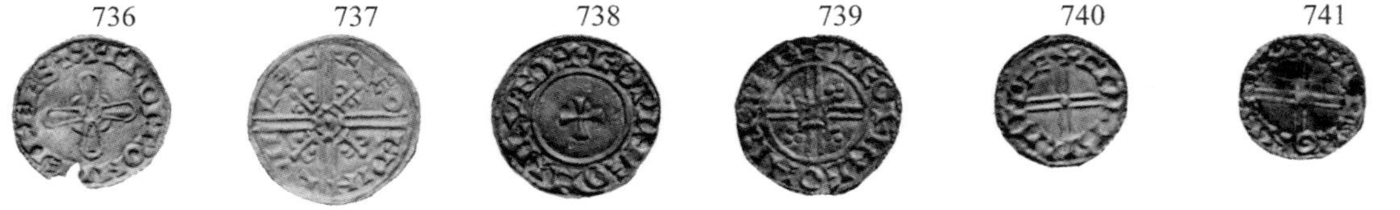

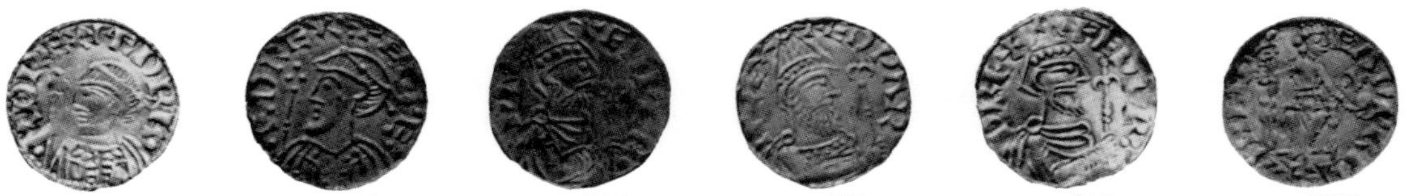

742 743 744 745 746 747

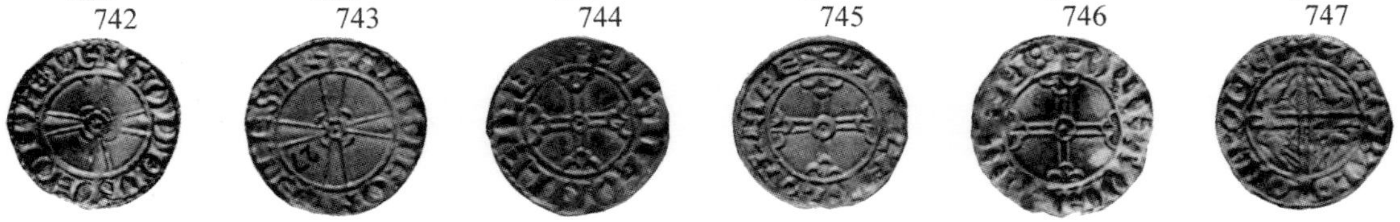

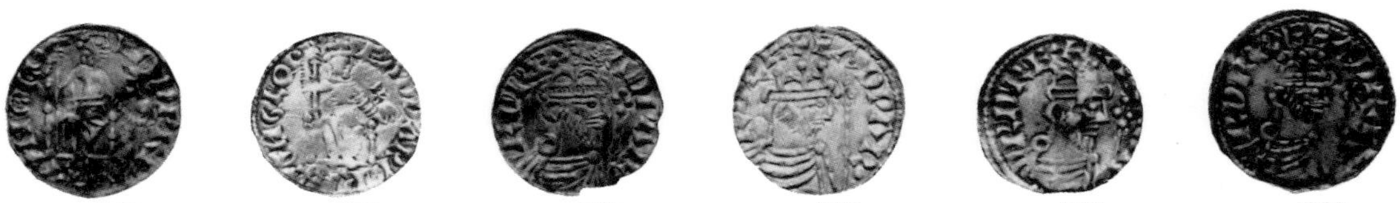

748 749 750 751 752 753

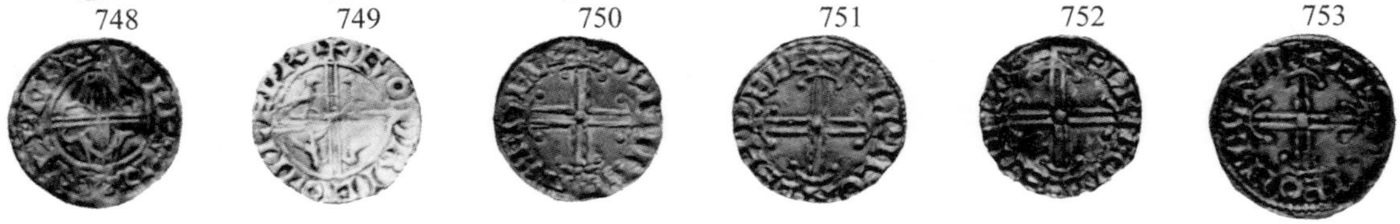

Plate 31 (*cont.*)

EDWARD THE CONFESSOR (*cont.*)

Pointed Helmet type (Hild. F; *BMC* VII) (*cont.*)

	Weight		Die-	
	g	*gr.*	*Axis*	
745.	1.26	19.4	0°	*Chester* (LEICE), Huscarl. Willoughby Gardner (via Mrs Gardner 1963); ex Spink. Die-duplicate of *SCBI 5*, 325.
746.	1.37	21.1	0°	*Wallingford* (ƿALI), Brihtwine (*Beorhtwine*). Willoughby Gardner; ex Joseph Young (but not in 1919 sale).

Sovereign/Eagles type (Hild. H; *BMC* IX)

747.	1.25	19.3	90°	*Chester* (LEGECST), Sweartcol (*Svartkollr*). Willoughby Gardner (via Mrs Gardner 1963); ex Baldwin. Die-duplicate (?) of *SCBI 5*, 34.
748.	1.00	15.4	0°	*Chester* ([ ]), [ ]lfsi. Willoughby Gardner (via Mrs Gardner 1963); ex Seaby (on Seaby ticket with their acquisition date 1946). Rev. inscription given as AELFꞄI ONN LEIGII on Seaby ticket, but this reading seems doubtful.
749.	1.34	20.7	90°	*Leicester* (LEGR), Godric. No provenance.

Hammer Cross type (Hild. G; *BMC* XI)

750.	1.23	19.0	180°	*Chester* (LEGECC), Duninc (*Dun(n)ing*). Willoughby Gardner (via Mrs Gardner 1963); ex Baldwin. Same rev. die as *SCBI 5*, 354.
751.	1.36	21.0	90°	*Leicester* (LEHRECE), Ælric (*Ælfric*). Willoughby Gardner (via Mrs Gardner 1963); ex Baldwin.
752.	1.27	19.6	180°	*Leicester* (LEHECEA[ ]), Ælric (*Ælfric*). Willoughby Gardner (via Mrs Gardner 1963); ex Duart-Smith (1945) 110.
753.	1.25	19.3	90°	*London* (LVND), Æl[ ]ne (*Ælfwine*). Lieut.-Col. Alan Williams 1955 (gift, GM 155 M 53).

EDWARD THE CONFESSOR (*cont.*)

Facing Bust type (Hild. Ac; *BMC* XIII)

	Weight		*Die-*	
	g	*gr.*	*Axis*	
754.	0.96	14.8	90°	*Chester* (LEG), Huscarl. Willoughby Gardner (via Mrs Gardner 1963).
755.	1.06	16.3	0°	*Chester* (LEGECC), Eofnad (*Leofnoth*). Willoughby Gardner (via Mrs Gardner 1963); ex Bridges (1918) 120. Die-duplicate of *SCBI* 5, 366–7. The omission of the letter L before EOFNAD on the rev. is a casual error by the die-cutter. Numbered 14 on rev. of coin in ink.
756.	1.09	16.8	270°	*Leicester* (LEHR), Godric. Willoughby Gardner; ex Gantz; ex Roth (1917) 88.

Pyramids type (Hild. I; *BMC* XV)

757.	1.25	19.3	270°	*Chester* (LEGEEE), Ælfs. This or next Willoughby Gardner (via Mrs Gardner 1963). Die-duplicate of next and of *SCBI* 5, 368–70.
758.	1.28	19.7	90°	*Chester* (LEGEEE), Ælfs. This or last Willoughby Gardner (via Mrs Gardner 1963). Die-duplicate of last and of *SCBI* 5, 368–70.
759.	1.27	19.6	315°	*Chester* (LEG), Bruninc (*Bruning*). Willoughby Gardner (via Mrs Gardner 1963); ex Bridges (1918) 120. Die-duplicate of next two coins and of *SCBI* 5, 374–5.
760.	1.38	21.3	225°	*Chester* (LEG), Bruninc (*Bruning*). Willoughby Gardner (via Mrs Gardner 1963); perhaps ex Lincoln. Die-duplicate of last, next and *SCBI* 5, 374–5.
761.	1.38	21.3	225°	*Chester* (LEG), Bruninc (*Bruning*). Willoughby Gardner (via Mrs Gardner 1963). Die-duplicate of last two coins and of *SCBI* 5, 374–5.
762.	1.31	20.2	180°	*Chester* (LEGE), Duninc (*Dun(n)ing*). Willoughby Gardner (via Mrs Gardner 1963); ex Baldwin Oct 1931. Die-duplicate of *SCBI* 5, 377, same obv. die as *SCBI* 5, 376.
763.	1.25	19.3	90°	*Chester* (LEGE), Huscalr (*Huscarl*). Purchased 1971 (GM 111 c 1971); ex Elmore Jones (1971) 189.

HAROLD II (1066)

Pax type (Hild. A; *BMC* I)

764.	1.32 pierced	20.3	180°	*Winchester* (ƿINCES), Lifinc (*Leofing/Lifing*). W. Pritchard (bequest), 1905 (then identified as coin of Lincoln mint).

NORMAN KINGS OF ENGLAND

WILLIAM I (1066–87)

Two Stars type (*BMC* V)

765.	1.16 slightly chipped	17.9	–	*Canterbury* ([ ]NT), Ielfrd (*Ælfræd*). Tiverton hoard 2000. Ill. *BNJ* 71 (2001), pl. 36, 1. (*Not illustrated.*)
766.	1.26	19.4	–	*London* (LVNDE), Godric. Tiverton hoard 2000. Ill. *BNJ* 71 (2001), pl. 36, 2. (*Not illustrated.*)
767.	1.13 three fragments	17.4	–	*London* (LVND), Godwine. Tiverton hoard 2000. Ill. *BNJ* 71 (2001), pl. 36, 3. (*Not illustrated.*)
768.	– two fragments	–	–	*Shrewsbury* (SI), God[ ]brnd (*Godesbrand?*). Tiverton hoard 2000. Ill. *BNJ* 71 (2001), pl. 36, 4. (*Not illustrated.*)
769.	1.22	18.8	–	*Warwick* (ƿIER), Thiurcil (*Thorketill*). Tiverton hoard 2000. Ill. *BNJ* 71 (2001), pl. 36, 5. (*Not illustrated.*)
770.	1.38	21.3	90°	*Winchester* (CES), Andrbod (*Anderboda*). Willoughby Gardner; ex Parsons. Gardner noted in his manuscript catalogue that this coin was bought by Parsons 'with others from a dealer'.
771.	– broken cut half	–	–	Uncertain mint and moneyer (inscriptions not legible). Tiverton hoard 2000. Ill. *BNJ* 71 (2001), pl. 36, 6.

Paxs type (*BMC* VIII)

772.	1.31	20.2	270°	*Chester* (LECESTRI), Ielfsi (*Ælfsige*). Willoughby Gardner (via Mrs Gardner 1963); perhaps ex Spink (*NCirc* 1939, 81841) (but *SCBI* 5, 399, struck from the same rev. die, is also assigned the *NCirc* 1939, 81841 provenance).

[*continued overleaf*]

PLATE 32

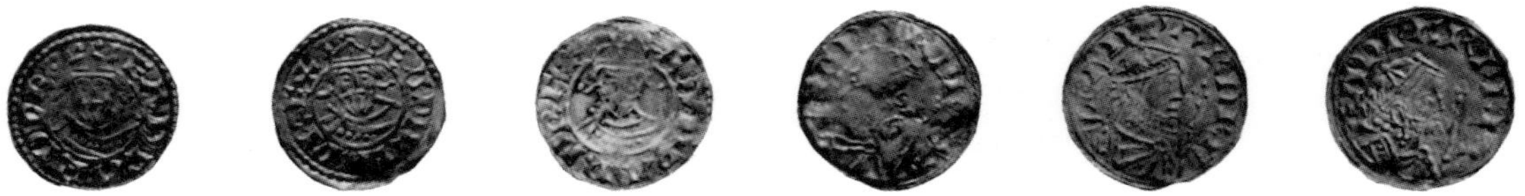

754 755 756 757 758 759

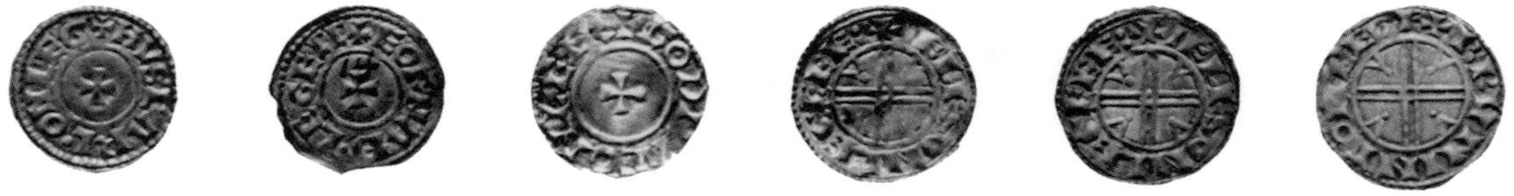

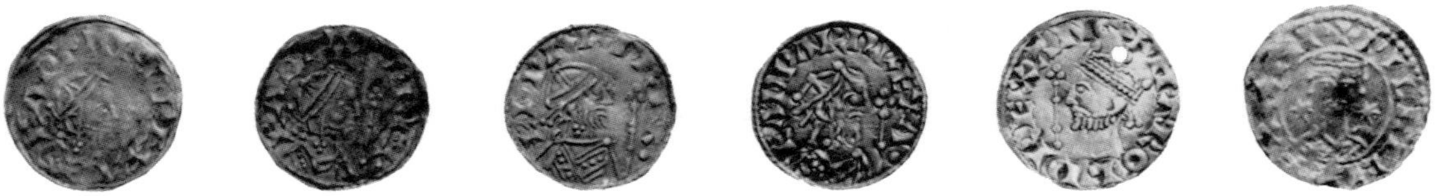

760 761 762 763 764 770

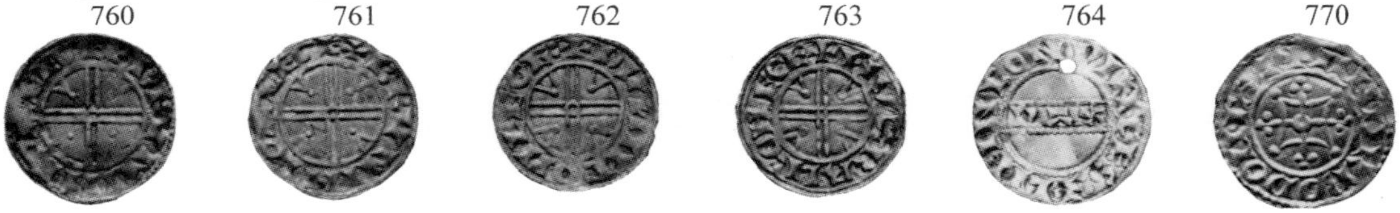

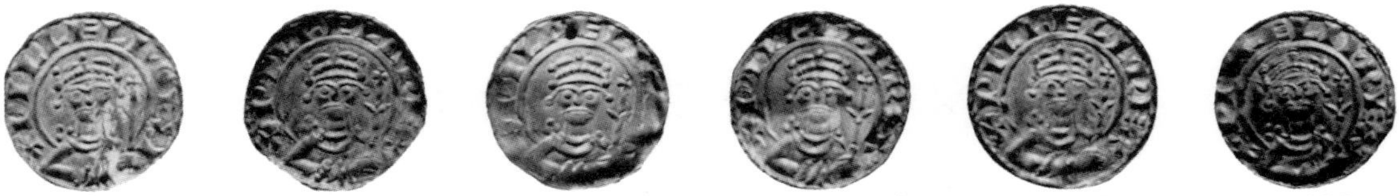

772 773 774 775 776 777

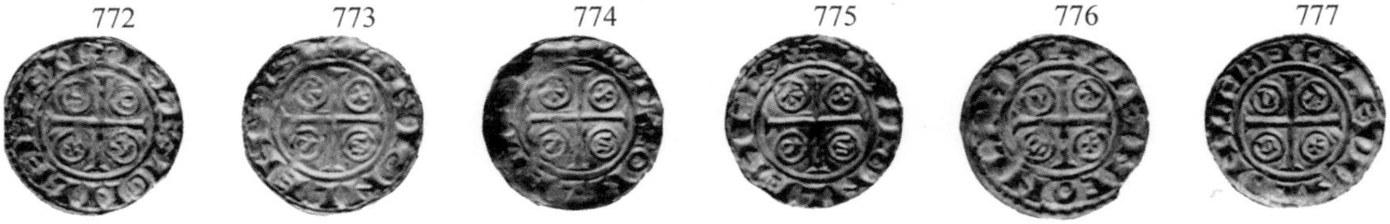

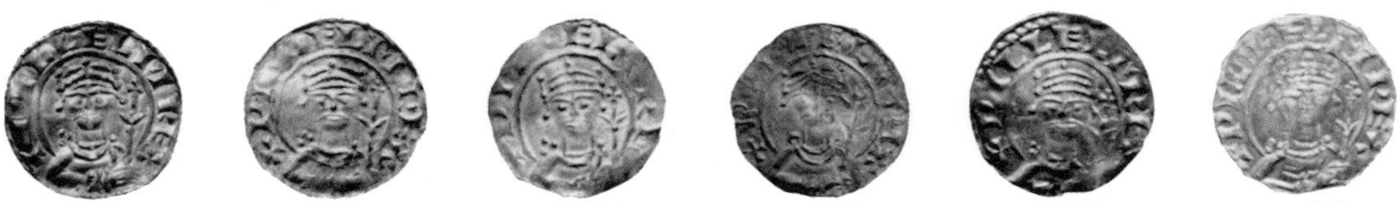

778 779 780 781 782 783

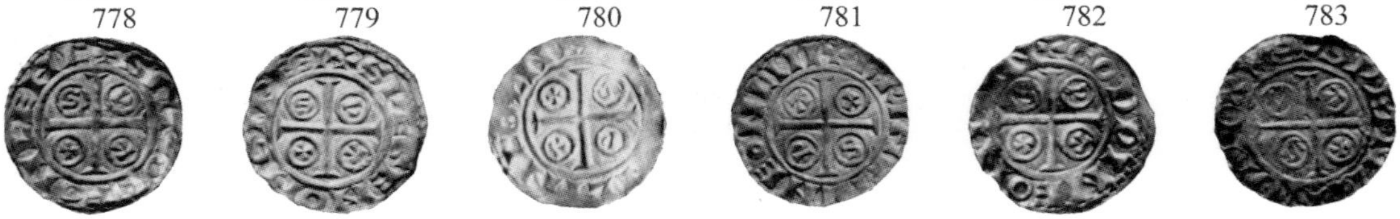

Plate 32 (*cont.*)

WILLIAM I (*cont.*)

Paxs type (*BMC* VIII) (*cont.*)

	Weight		Die-	
	g	*gr.*	*Axis*	
773.	1.33	20.5	270°	*Chester* (LEHECST), Lfnc (*Leofing/Lifing*). Willoughby Gardner (via Mrs Gardner 1963); ex Baldwin. This or next ex Talbot Ready. Die-duplicate of next two and of *SCBI* 5, 402–3.
774.	1.38 pierced	21.3	270°	*Chester* (LEH[ ]), Lfnc (*Leofing/Lifing*). Willoughby Gardner (via Mrs Gardner 1963); ex Baldwin. This or last ex Talbot Ready. Die-duplicate of last, next and *SCBI* 5, 402–3.
775.	1.35	20.8	180°	*Chester* (LEHECST), Lfnc (*Leofing/Lifing*). Willoughby Gardner (via Mrs Gardner 1963); ex Baldwin. Die-duplicate of last two and of *SCBI* 5, 402–3.
776.	1.42	21.9	270°	*Chester* (LEHEC), Lifinc (*Leofing/Lifing*). Willoughby Gardner (via Mrs Gardner 1963); ex Baldwin. Die-duplicate of *SCBI* 5, 401.
777.	1.38	21.3	0°	*Chester* (LECEI), Lifwine (*Leofwine*). Willoughby Gardner (via Mrs Gardner 1963). Die-duplicate of *SCBI* 5, 404–5.
778.	1.38	21.3	0°	*Chester* (LEHC), S[ ]olf (*Sunnulfr*). Willoughby Gardner (via Mrs Gardner 1963); ex Baldwin. Die-duplicate of *SCBI* 5, 410, same obv. die as *SCBI* 5, 409.
779.	1.36	21.0	90°	*Ipswich* (GIPESI), Swegen (*Sveinn*). Willoughby Gardner (via Mrs Gardner 1963); ex 'Spink 66931' (but number not traced in *NCirc*).
780.	1.40	21.6	90°	*Lincoln* (LINCOLNE), [ ] (*Ulfr*). Willoughby Gardner (via Mrs Gardner 1963); ex 'Spink 66791' (but number not traced in *NCirc*). Die-duplicate of Mossop 1970 LXXXIV/3.
781.	1.33	20.5	0°	*London* (LVI), Brihtwine (*Beorhtwine*). Willoughby Gardner (via Mrs Gardner 1963); ex 'Spink 70251' (but number not traced in *NCirc*).
782.	1.40	21.6	270°	*London* (LVN), Godwine. Lieut. Col. Alan Williams 1953 (gift, GM 157 M 1953).
783.	1.38	21.3	180°	*Oxford* (OXFE), Swetman. Edward Davies (GM 314.55).

WILLIAM I (*cont.*)

Paxs type (*cont.*)

	Weight *g*	Weight *gr.*	Die-Axis	
784.	1.39	21.4	0°	*Southwark* (SVÐE), Aldolf (*Ealdwulf*). Purchased 1954 (GM 18 M 54).
785.	1.12 chipped	17.3	–	Uncertain mint and moneyer, Go[ ]. No provenance.

WILLIAM II (1087–1100)

Cross in Quatrefoil type (*BMC* ii)

	g	*gr.*	Die-Axis	
786.	1.21	18.6	270°	*Chester* (LEICC), Lifwine (*Leofwine*). D. H. Hess 1968 (purchase, GM 106 C 68). Probably die-duplicate of Lockett (1958) 2889.

Cross Pattée and Fleury type (*BMC* iv)

	g	*gr.*	Die-Axis	
787.	–	–	–	*Chester* (LEI[ ]), elfwi[ ] (*Ælfwine*) (legends uncertain). Willoughby Gardner; ex P. Carlyon-Britton (1918) 1899.

HENRY I (1100–35)

Pellets on Quatrefoil type (*BMC* xiv)

	g	*gr.*	Die-Axis	
788.	1.41	21.7	–	*Leicester* (LEIC), Chitellus. Willoughby Gardner; ex Baldwin; ex Parsons (1929) 286; ex P.Carlyon-Britton (1918) 1926. Same dies as coin in 'Beauvais' hoard (Glendining 4 Nov 1987, lot 22) (ex inf. Martin Allen). For the mint attribution of this and following coins see note to *SCBI 5*, 425.
789.	1.41	21.7	45°	*Leicester* (LEICES), Chite[ ] (*Chitel*). Willoughby Gardner; ex Carlyon-Britton (1916) 1381; presumably ex Bournemouth (vicinity) hoard (*BNJ* 19 (1927–8), p. 98, where the hoard is incorrectly stated to have been found in Canterbury). Same dies as next. Die-duplicate of *SCBI 17*, 666.
790.	1.30 slightly chipped	20.1	135°	*Leicester* ([ ]ES), Chitel. Willoughby Gardner; ex Baldwin; ex Walters (1932) 116. Same dies as last. Die-duplicate of *SCBI 17*, 666.
791.	1.23	19.0	0°	*Leicester* ([ ]ECE), W[ ] (*Waltere*). Willoughby Gardner; ex Baldwin. Same dies as *BMC* 134 and *SCBI 17*, 667 (ex inf. Martin Allen).
792.	1.44	22.2	315°	*Lewes* (?) (LE[ ]), [ ]dmu[ ] (*Eadmund*). Willoughby Gardner; ex Carlyon-Britton (not in sales ?); presumably ex Bournemouth (vicinity) hoard (*BNJ* 19 (1927–8), p. 98). Previously attributed to a moneyer Warmund, supposed to have worked at Chester or at Leicester (cf. a coin in Leicester Museum, *SCBI* 17, 669), but a die-duplicate in the Lincoln hoard has now demonstrated that the mint of *SCBI* 17, 669 is Winchester. An attribution of the present coin to the Lewes moneyer Eadmund now seems most likely (ex info. Martin Allen).

STEPHEN (1135–54)

'Watford' type (*BMC* I)

	g	*gr.*	Die-Axis	
793.	1.32	20.3	225°	*Chester* ([ ]), Rave[ ] (*Ravensweart*). Willoughby Gardner (via Mrs Gardner 1963); ex Spink (*NCirc* Mar–Apr 1922, 3281) (in a property described as 'chiefly from a very old cabinet and doubtless originally from a hoard').
794.	1.47	22.7	45°	*Chester* ([ ]), Ra[(*Ravensweart*). Willoughby Gardner (via Mrs Gardner 1963); ex Baldwin (with Baldwin stock ticket B10832).
795.	1.13 slightly chipped	17.5	0°	Uncertain mint (*London*?), [ ]ard. Obv. reading uncertain. No provenance (but cf. P. Carlyon-Britton (1918) 1967, rev. reading given as]ARD:ON:[). Perhaps London mint, moneyer Adelard. A note on the ticket that rev. reading may alternatively be EVERARD ON PAR has added comment in Elmore Jones's handwriting 'yes, small probability but might'.
796.	– fragment	–	–	Uncertain mint and moneyer. No provenance (but Pritchard bequest, 1905, included a 'profile penny of Stephen, mintage doubtful').

HENRY II (1154–89)

Cross and Crosslet (*Tealby*) type

	g	*gr.*	Die-Axis	
797.	1.37	21.1	–	*Ipswich* (GIPES), [ ]ole (*Nicholas*). No provenance. Class F1. Die-duplicate of *BMC* 328 (*pers. comm.* Tim Crafter).
798.	1.01 cracked	15.6	–	*Ipswich* (GIPES), [ ] (*Nicholas*). No provenance. Class F1. Die-duplicate of *BMC* 332 (*pers. comm.* Tim Crafter).

[*continued overleaf*]

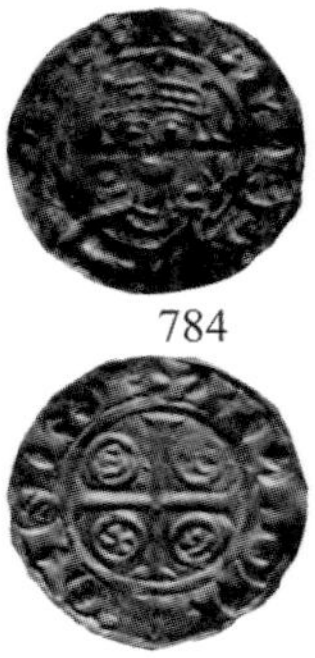
784

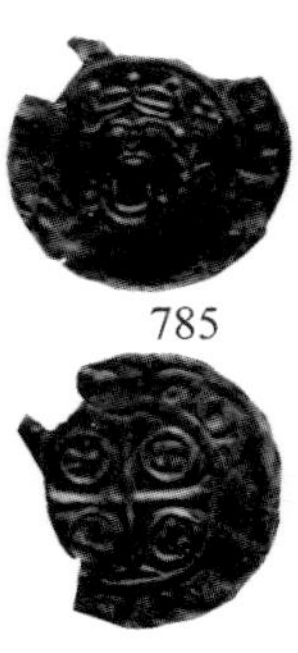
785

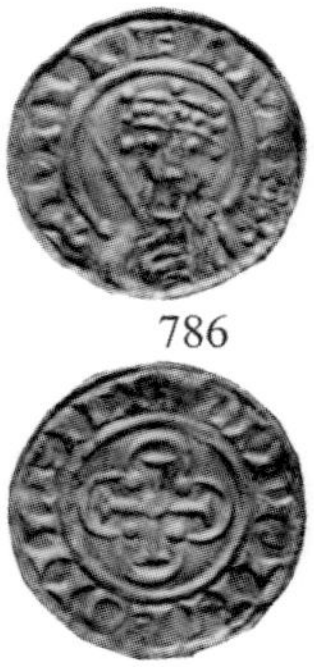
786

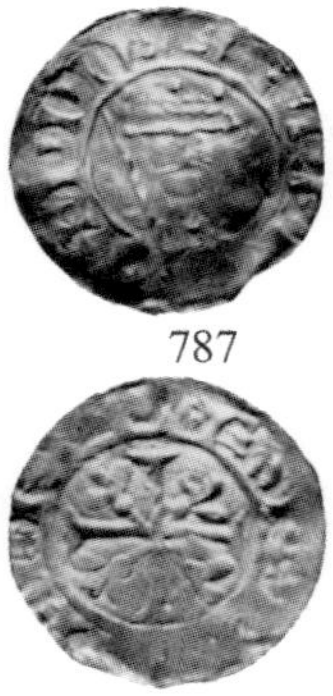
787

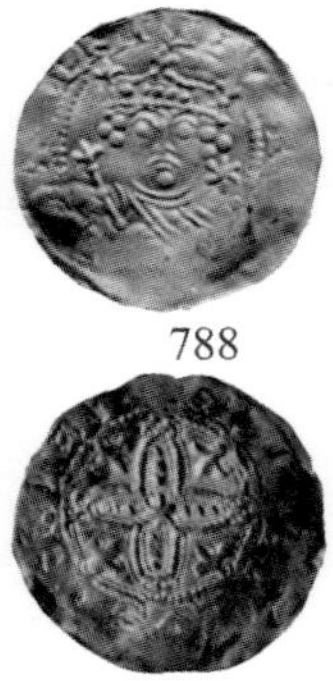
788

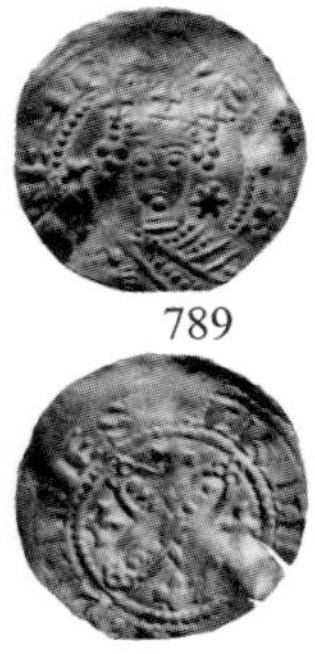
789

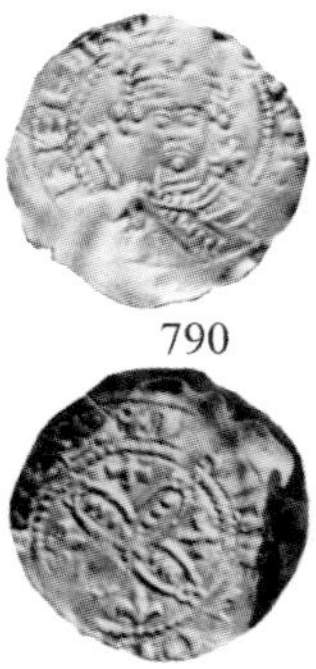
790

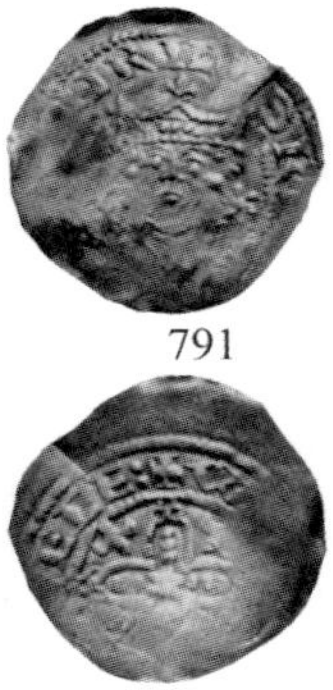
791

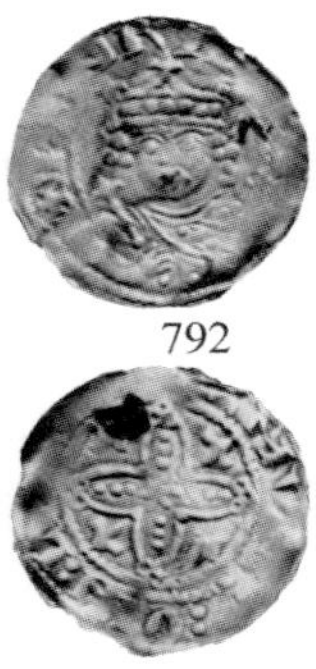
792

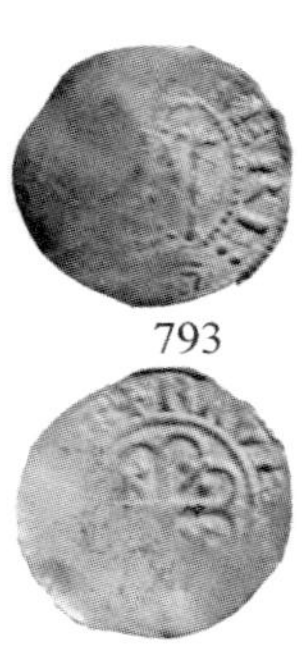
793

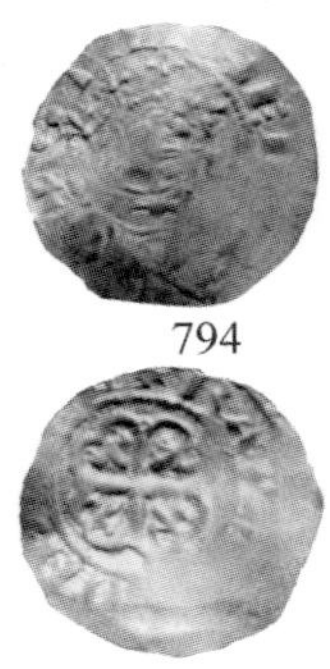
794

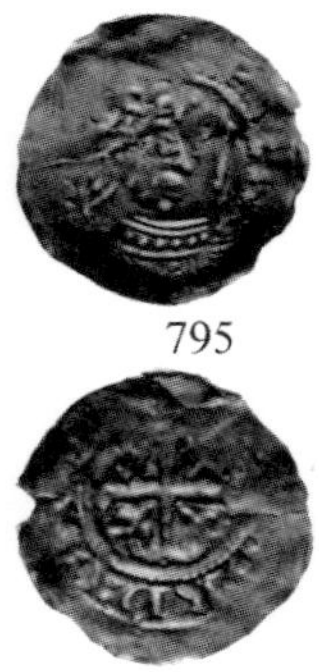
795

796

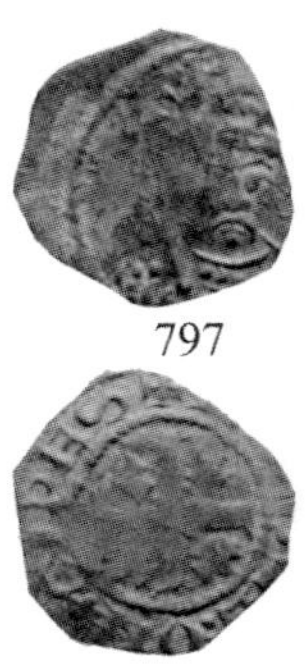
797

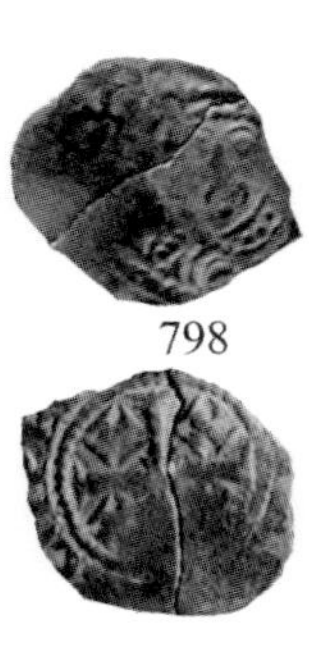
798

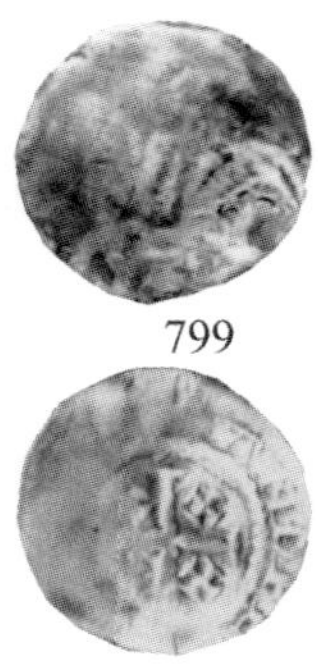
799

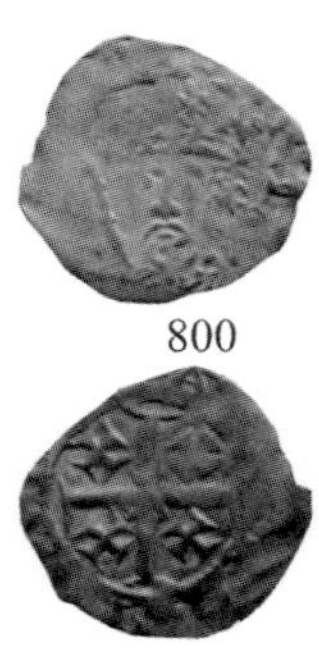
800

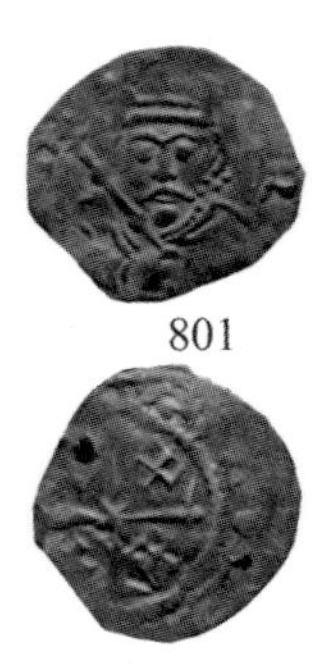
801

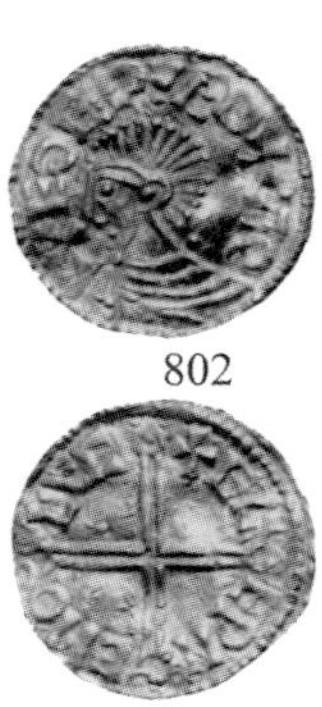
802

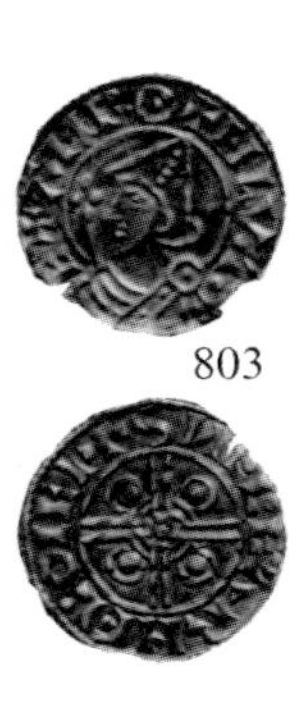
803

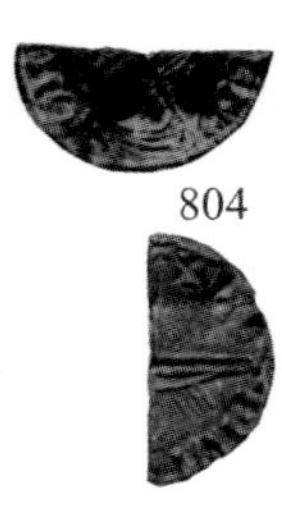
804

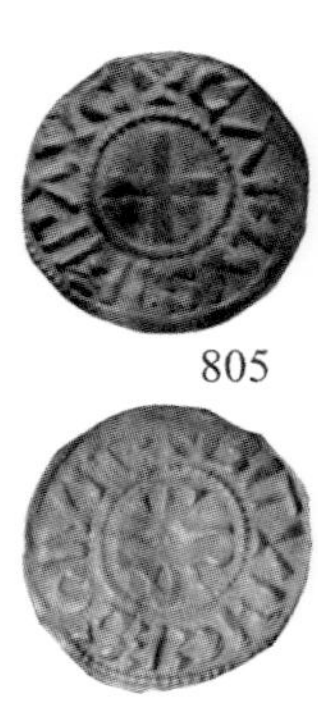
805

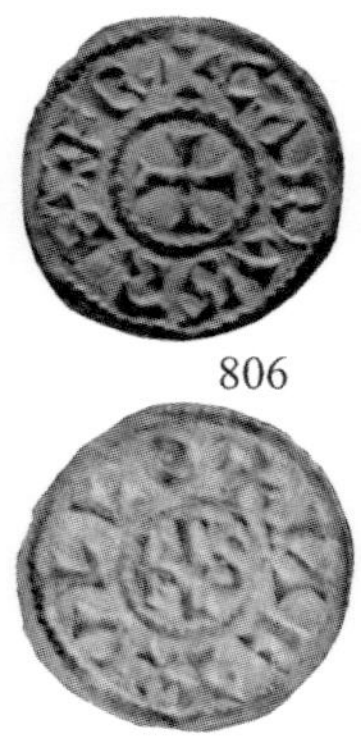
806

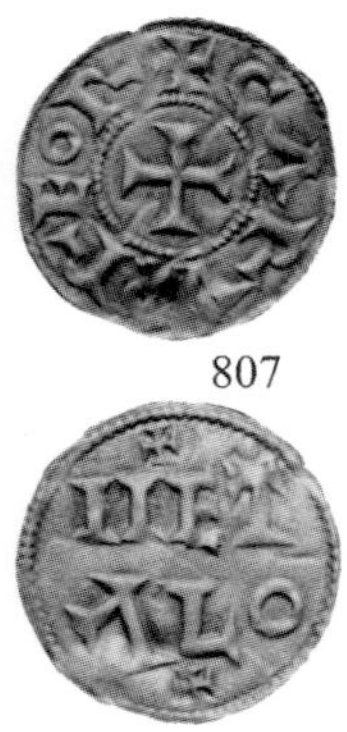
807

Plate 33 (*cont.*)

HENRY II (*cont.*)

Cross and Crosslet (*Tealby*) type (*cont.*)

	Weight *g*	*gr.*	*Die-Axis*	
799.	1.25	19.3	–	*Lincoln* ([ ]), Andreu (*Andreas*). Willoughby Gardner; ex P. Carlyon-Britton (but not in sales ?). Class A. Attribution to Lincoln mint made independently by Elmore Jones and by Crafter; the latter suggests that coin is possibly from same rev. die as *BMC* 378.
800.	1.22	18.8	–	Uncertain mint and moneyer (rev. inscription not visible). Willoughby Gardner (via Mrs Gardner 1963).
801.	1.07	16.5	–	Contemporary forgery (obv. and rev. inscriptions not visible). No provenance. Crafter comments that 'the fabric of these dies is most unusual' that the arrangement of the bust is anomalous, and that 'the cross and crosslets are very thin and badly formed'.

SCANDINAVIAN IMITATIONS

'ÆTHELRED II', 'LONG CROSS' TYPE

802.	1.69	26.1	0°	*'Chester'* (**LEC**), 'Elewne'. Willoughby Gardner (via Mrs Gardner 1963); ex Royal Collection, Copenhagen. Blackburn 1981, no. 101. Die-duplicate of *SCBI 5*, 457–8, same rev. die as *SCBI 5*, 459.

'CNUT', 'POINTED HELMET' TYPE

803.	0.80 chipped	12.3	45°	Blundered inscriptions. Obv, **+ΓIIV.T. / EXΛNΓO**; rev. **+SИEL·EΛRNFL·OIEI**. Purchased per Pirie 1965 (GM 314 C 65); ex 'Yorkshire Numismatic Society lot 173 (Heeley collection)'; ex 'Parsons 60' (but the coin was not lot 60 in either of the Parsons sales held in 1929 and 1954, and no relevant catalogue of the Yorkshire Numismatic Society can be traced).

HIBERNO-NORSE IMITATIONS

PHASE III

804.	– cut halfpenny	–	–	No provenance, but perhaps the 'Hiberno-Danish' coin which reached the Grosvenor Museum in 1899 as part of Charles Potter's collection of coins found on Meols Sands (Longbottom 1908, p. 15; Dolley concludes that the present coin 'might well be' the coin listed by Longbottom (Dolley 1961, p. 201; Bean 2007, pp. 322, 336 (no. 5772) and 349).

CAROLINGIAN KINGDOMS[1]

IMMOBILISED TYPE OF MINT OF BOURGES (LATE NINTH CENTURY)

805.	1.59	24.5	–	'Charles' (**CARLVS IMP AUG**), *Bourges* (**BITVRICES CIVIT**). *MEC* 1, nos. 913–18. Willoughby Gardner; ex Spink (*NCirc* Jan–Feb 1921, 88595); ex Cuerdale hoard.

IMMOBILISED TYPE OF MINT OF MELLE (AFTER 840)

806.	1.61	24.8	–	'Charles' (**CARLVS REX FR**), *Melle* (**METXVLLO**). *MEC* 1, nos 935–61. Willoughby Gardner; ex Spink (*NCirc* Jan–Feb 1921, 88588) (no hoard provenance stated in *NCirc*, but the coin is of a date and appearance which makes it probable that it derives from the Cuerdale hoard).

IMMOBILISED TYPE OF MELLE (MID-TENTH CENTURY)

807.	1.30	20.1	–	'Charles' (**CARVS REOR**), *Melle* (**MET/ALO**). Chester (1950) hoard, no. 522. See *MEC*, pp. 239–40 and Dolley and Morrison 1962, where this and the following coin are illustrated on fig. 1.

[1] Only Carolingian coins from British finds have been included: the Grosvenor Museum's collection contains nine further coins of the Carolingian and Capetian periods, but there is no evidence that any of these derive from finds in the British Isles.

IMMOBILISED TYPE OF MELLE (*cont.*)

	Weight		*Die-*	
	g	*gr.*	*Axis*	
808.	1.58	24.4	–	'Charles' (**CARLVS REOR**), *Melle* (**MET/ALO**). Chester (1950) hoard, no. 523.

BERENGAR II AND ADALBERT, KINGS OF ITALY (950–61)

809.	1.30	20.1	–	*Venice* (cf. Saccocci 2009, p. 144 n. 16). Chester (1950) hoard, no. 524.

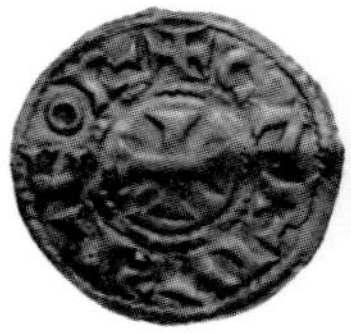

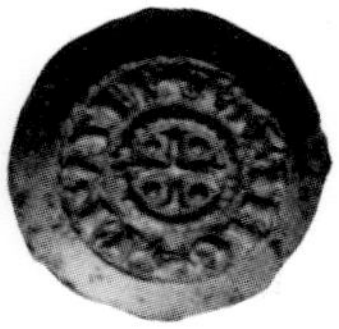

808

809

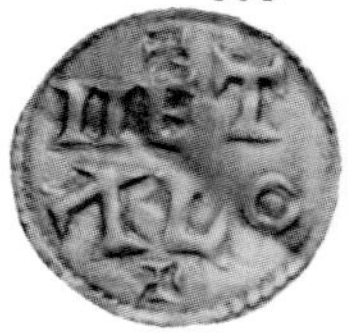

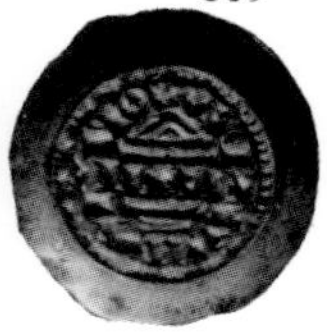

INDEX OF MINTS

INDEX OF MONEYERS

The forms listed are those actually found on the coins, except that the letters *thorn* and *eth* appear as th and the letter *wen* as w. Normalisation has not been attempted, but in cases where names appear in different forms these have been brought together, usually under the fullest form. Cross references are given where a name is found in a markedly different place in the index from its natural alphabetical position.

Period from Edgar's Reform onwards

SYLLOGE OF COINS OF THE BRITISH ISLES

1. FITZWILLIAM MUSEUM, CAMBRIDGE. Ancient British and Anglo-Saxon Coins. By P. GRIERSON. 32 plates, 1958.
2. HUNTERIAN MUSEUM, GLASGOW. Anglo-Saxon Coins. By A. S. ROBERTSON. 42 plates, 1961.
3. COINS OF THE CORITANI. By D. F. ALLEN. 8 plates, 1963.
4. ROYAL COLLECTION, COPENHAGEN. Part I. Ancient British and Anglo-Saxon Coins. By G. GALSTER. 30 plates, 1964.
5. GROSVENOR MUSEUM, CHESTER. Part I. Coins with the Chester Mint-Signature. By E. J. E. PIRIE. 16 plates, 1964.
6. NATIONAL MUSEUM OF ANTIQUITIES OF SCOTLAND, EDINBURGH. Anglo-Saxon Coins. By R. B. K. STEVENSON. 29 plates, 1966.
7. ROYAL COLLECTION, COPENHAGEN. Part II. Anglo-Saxon Coins: Æthelræd II. By G. GALSTER. (Publ. jointly with the Carlsberg Foundation.) 71 plates, 1966.
8. BRITISH MUSEUM. Hiberno-Norse Coins. By R. H. M. DOLLEY. 8 plates, 1966.
9. ASHMOLEAN MUSEUM, OXFORD. Part I. Anglo-Saxon Pennies. By J. D. A. THOMPSON. 42 plates, 1967.
10. ULSTER MUSEUM, BELFAST. Part I. Anglo-Irish Coins, John-Edward III. By M. DOLLEY AND W. SEABY. (Publ. jointly with the Trustees of the Ulster Museum.) 20 plates, 1968.
11. READING UNIVERSITY. Anglo-Saxon and Norman Coins; ROYAL COIN CABINET, STOCKHOLM. [Part VI.] Anglo-Norman Pennies. By C. E. BLUNT AND M. DOLLEY. (Publ. jointly with the Swedish Royal Academy.) 20 plates, 1969.
12. ASHMOLEAN MUSEUM, OXFORD. Part II. English Coins 1066–1279. By D. M. METCALF. 36 plates, 1969.

13–15. ROYAL COLLECTION, COPENHAGEN. Parts IIIA, B and C. Anglo-Saxon Coins: Cnut. By G. GALSTER. (Publ. jointly with the Carlsberg Foundation.) 158 plates, 1970. (3 vols.)

16. NORWEB COLLECTION. Ancient British and English Coins to 1180. By C. E. BLUNT, F. ELMORE JONES and R. P. MACK. 17 plates, 1971.
17. MIDLAND MUSEUMS, Ancient British, Anglo-Saxon, and Norman Coins. By A. J. H. GUNSTONE. 30 plates, 1971.
18. ROYAL COLLECTION, COPENHAGEN. Part IV. Anglo-Saxon Coins from Harold I and Anglo-Norman Coins. By G. GALSTER. (Publ. jointly with the Carlsberg Foundation.) 54 plates, 1972.
19. BRISTOL AND GLOUCESTER MUSEUMS. Ancient British Coins and Coins of the Bristol and Gloucestershire Mints. By L. V. GRINSELL, C. E. BLUNT and M. DOLLEY. 27 plates, 1972.
20. MACK COLLECTION. Ancient British, Anglo-Saxon, and Norman Coins. By R. P. MACK. 56 plates, 1973.
21. YORKSHIRE COLLECTIONS. Coins from Northumbrian Mints *c.* 895–1279; Ancient British and later coins from other mints to 1279. By E. J. E. PIRIE. 54 plates, 1975.
22. ROYAL COLLECTION, COPENHAGEN. Part V. Hiberno-Norse and Anglo-Irish Coins. By G. GALSTER with M. DOLLEY and J. STEEN JENSEN. 22 Plates, 1975.
23. ASHMOLEAN MUSEUM, OXFORD. Part III. Coins of Henry VII. By D. M. METCALF. 53 plates, 1976.
24. WEST COUNTRY MUSEUMS. Ancient British, Anglo-Saxon and Anglo-Norman Coins. By A. J. H. GUNSTONE. 35 plates, 1977.
25. NATIONAL MUSEUM, HELSINKI. Anglo-Saxon and Anglo-Norman Coins. By T. TALVIO. 41 plates, 1978.
26. MUSEUMS IN EAST ANGLIA. Morley St Peter Hoard *and* Anglo-Saxon, Norman, and Angevin Coins, and later coins of the Norwich Mint. By T. H. McK. CLOUGH. 52 plates, 1980.
27. LINCOLNSHIRE COLLECTIONS. Coins from Lincolnshire Mints *and* Ancient British and later coins to 1272. By A. J. H. GUNSTONE. 68 plates, 1981.
28. CUMULATIVE INDEX OF VOLS. 1–20. By V. SMART. 1981.
29. MERSEYSIDE COUNTY MUSEUMS. Ancient British and later coins to 1279. By M. WARHURST. 39 plates, 1982.
30. AMERICAN COLLECTIONS. Ancient British, Anglo-Saxon and Norman Coins. By J. D. BRADY. 30 plates, 1982.

31. NORWEB COLLECTION. Tokens of the British Isles 1575–1750. Part I. Bedfordshire to Devon. By R. H. THOMPSON. 35 plates, 1984.
32. ULSTER MUSEUM, BELFAST. Part II. Hiberno-Norse Coins. By W. SEABY. (Publ. jointly with the Trustees of the Ulster Museum.) 16 plates, 1984.
33. BROOKER COLLECTION. Coins of Charles I. By J. J. NORTH and P. J. PRESTON-MORLEY. 130 plates, 1984.
34. BRITISH MUSEUM. Anglo-Saxon Coins. Part V. Athelstan to Edgar's Reform. By M. M. ARCHIBALD and C. E. BLUNT. 56 plates, 1986.
35. ASHMOLEAN AND HUNTERIAN MUSEUMS. Scottish Coins. By J. D. BATESON and N. J. MAYHEW, 116 plates, 1987.
36. STATE MUSEUM BERLIN. Anglo-Saxon, Anglo-Norman and Hiberno-Norse Coins. By B. KLUGE. (Publ. jointly with the State Museum Berlin.) 41 plates, 1987.
37. POLISH MUSEUMS. Anglo-Saxon and later medieval British coins. By A. MIKOŁAJCZYK. (Publ. jointly with the Archaeological and Ethnographical Museum in Łódź.) 20 plates, 1987.
38. NORWEB COLLECTION. Tokens of the British Isles 1575–1750. Part II. Dorset to Gloucestershire. By R. H. THOMPSON. 41 plates, 1988.
39. NORTH COLLECTION. Edwardian English Silver Coins, 1279–1351. By J. J. NORTH. 46 plates, 1989.
40. ROYAL COIN CABINET, STOCKHOLM. Part IV. Anglo-Saxon Coins: Harold I and Harthacnut. By T. TALVIO. 74 plates, 1991.
41. CUMULATIVE INDEX OF VOLS. 21–40. By V. J. SMART. 1992.
42. SOUTH-EASTERN MUSEUMS. Ancient British, Anglo-Saxon and later coins to 1279. By A. J. H. GUNSTONE with V. SMART and others. 78 plates, 1992.
43. NORWEB COLLECTION. Tokens of the British Isles 1575–1750. Part III. Hampshire to Lincolnshire. By R. H. THOMPSON and M. J. DICKINSON. 51 plates, 1992.
44. NORWEB COLLECTION. Tokens of the British Isles 1575–1750. Part IV. Norfolk to Somerset. By R. H. THOMPSON and M. J. DICKINSON. 50 plates, 1993.
45. LATVIAN COLLECTIONS. Anglo-Saxon and later British Coins. By T. BERGA. 12 plates, 1996.
46. NORWEB COLLECTION. Tokens of the British Isles 1575–1750. Part V. Staffordshire to Westmorland. By R. H. THOMPSON and M. J. DICKINSON. 51 plates, 1996.
47. SCHNEIDER COLLECTION. Part I. English Gold Coins and their Imitations, 1257–1603. By P. WOODHEAD. 83 plates, 1996.
48. NORTHERN MUSEUMS. Ancient British, Anglo-Saxon, Norman and Plantagenet Coins to 1279. By J. BOOTH. 64 plates, 1997.
49. NORWEB COLLECTION. Tokens of the British Isles 1575–1750. Part VI. Wiltshire to Yorkshire, Ireland to Wales. By R. H. THOMPSON and M. J. DICKINSON. 43 plates, 1999.
50. HERMITAGE MUSEUM, ST PETERSBURG. Part I. Anglo-Saxon Coins to 1016. By V. M. POTIN. 54 plates, 1999.
51. ESTONIAN COLLECTIONS. Anglo-Saxon, Anglo-Norman and later British Coins. By I. LEIMUS and A. MOLVÕGIN. 54 plates, 2001.
52. UPPSALA UNIVERSITY COIN CABINET. Anglo-Saxon and Anglo-Norman Coins. By E. LINDBERGER. (Publ. jointly with the University of Uppsala) 37 plates, 2006.
53. SCOTTISH MUSEUMS. English Coins, 1066–1279. By J. D. BATESON. 38 plates, 2001.
54. ROYAL COIN CABINET, STOCKHOLM. Part V. Anglo-Saxon Coins: Edward the Confessor and Harold II, 1042–1066. By F. COLMAN. Part VI supplement. Anglo-Norman Pennies. By M. BLACKBURN and K. JONSSON. 57 plates, 2007.
55. HERMITAGE MUSEUM, ST PETERSBURG. Part IV. English, Irish and Scottish Coins, 1066–1485. By M. MUCHA. 23 plates, 2005.
56. MASS COLLECTION. English Short Cross Coins, 1180–1247. By J. P. MASS. 82 plates, 2001.
57. SCHNEIDER COLLECTION. Part II. English Gold Coins, 1603 to the 20th Century. By P. WOODHEAD. 58 plates, 2001.
58. NATIONAL MUSEUMS OF SCOTLAND, EDINBURGH. Scottish Coins Part I. 1526–1603. By N. M. McQ. HOLMES. 99 plates, 2006.
59. NORWEB COLLECTION. Tokens of the British Isles 1575–1750. Part VII. City of London. By R. H. THOMPSON and M. J. DICKINSON. 61 plates, 2007.
60. HERMITAGE MUSEUM, ST PETERSBURG. Part II. Anglo-Saxon Coins 1016–1066. By V. M. POTIN. 47 plates, 2012.
61. SCHNEIDER COLLECTION. Part III. Anglo-Gallic, Flemish and Brabantine Gold Coins 1330–1794. By P. WOODHEAD. 38 plates, 2011.

62. NORWEB COLLECTION. Tokens of the British Isles 1575–1750. Part VIII. Middlesex, uncertain pieces and forgeries. By R. H. THOMPSON and M. J. DICKINSON. 68 plates, 2011.
63. BRITISH MUSEUM. Anglo-Saxon Coins. Part I. Early Anglo-Saxon Coins. By A. GANNON. 58 plates, forthcoming.
64. GROSVENOR MUSEUM, CHESTER. Part II. Anglo-Saxon Coins and Post-Conquest Coins to 1180. By H. E. PAGAN. 33 plates, 2012.

Published by the British Academy, except Nos. 8, 34 and 63 published by the Trustees of the British Museum, and Nos. 16, 31, 33, 38, 43–4, 46–7, 49, 57, 59 and 61–2 published by Spink & Son Ltd.